John Neale was a successful business person throughout his life whilst also playing sport at a high level, including rugby league and tennis. After managing their family hotel for two years, he entered the IT industry and achieved a competence level which saw him working for the leading companies of the day.

A fork in the road saw he and his wife leave Australia to live overseas on a Greek island, then London and then to live aboard their yacht in various countries in Europe. During this time of residence in many countries and sailing adventures, John became a watercolour artist and sold many of these paintings. After a four-year successful odyssey, he returned home to continue a very full life.

To my children, Steven, Maxine and Carmen.

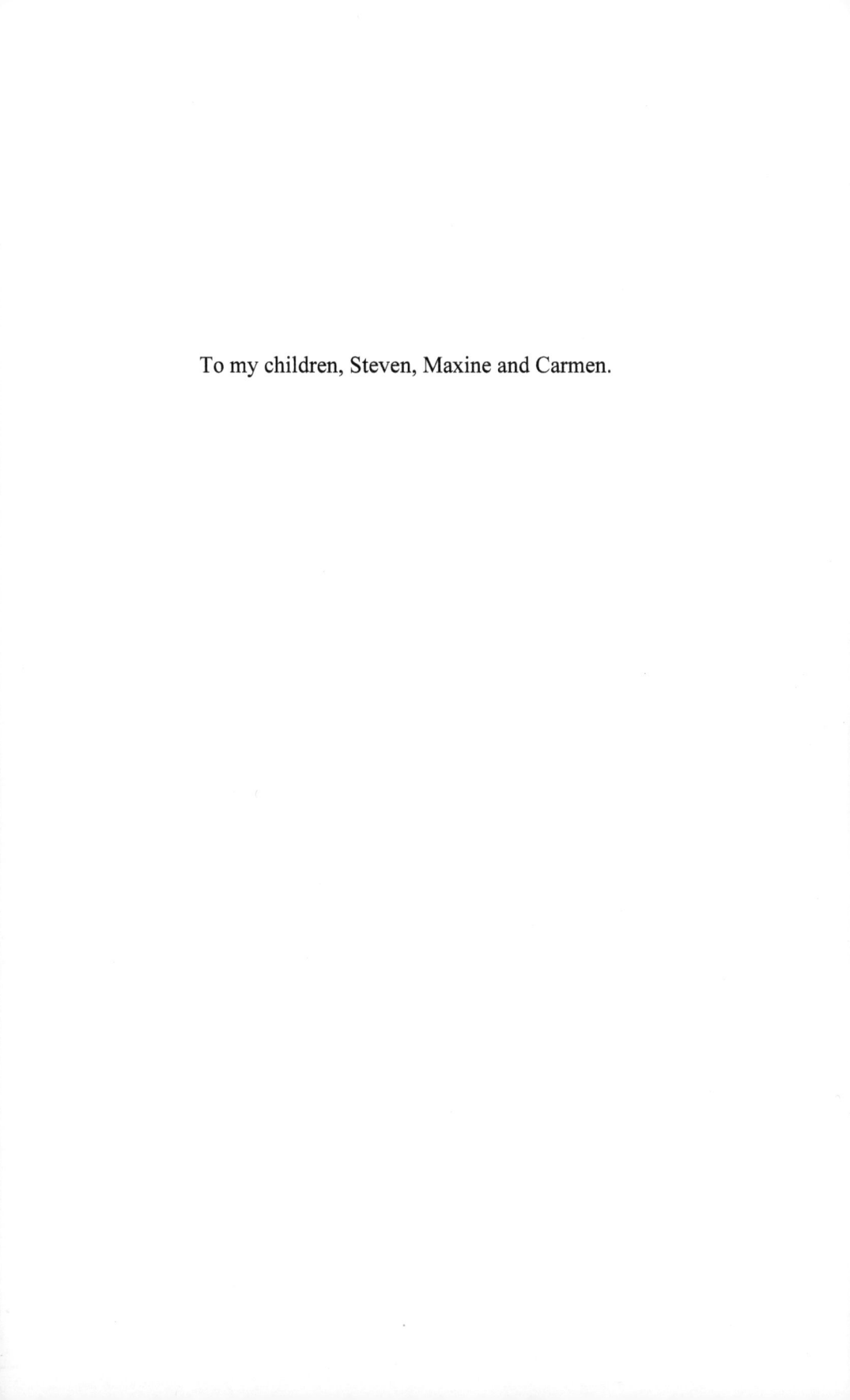

John Neale

JUST GO TO THE AIRPORT

AUSTIN MACAULEY PUBLISHERS™
LONDON * CAMBRIDGE * NEW YORK * SHARJAH

Copyright ©John Neale 2023

The right of John Neale to be identified as author of this work has been asserted by the author in accordance with sections 77 and 78 of the Copyright, Designs and Patents Act 1988.

All rights reserved. No part of this publication may be reproduced, stored in a retrieval system, or transmitted in any form or by any means, electronic, mechanical, photocopying, recording, or otherwise, without the prior permission of the publishers.

Any person who commits any unauthorised act in relation to this publication may be liable to criminal prosecution and civil claims for damages.

A CIP catalogue record for this title is available from the British Library.

ISBN 9781398412774 (Paperback)
ISBN 9781398412781 (ePub e-book)

www.austinmacauley.com

First Published 2023
Austin Macauley Publishers Ltd®
1 Canada Square
Canary Wharf
London
E14 5AA

Table of Contents

Foreword	9
Prologue	10
Introduction	20
Chapter 1: Incubation of a Thought	24
Chapter 2: Samos	27
Chapter 3: House Hunting	39
Chapter 4: The Interlude	67
Chapter 5: The Night in Paris	72
Chapter 6: The Scene is Set	75
Chapter 7: To the United States	80
Chapter 8: England	83
Chapter 9: A Fork in the Road	94
Chapter 10: Preparing for the Departure	99
Chapter 11: France	108
Chapter 12: Into the Mediterranean Sea	146
Chapter 13: The Very Emotional Return	197
Chapter 14: Home	217

Foreword

European Serendipity
Introduction:

This story is told over a three-week period ending on the 30th October 2020. During that time, just passed, quite fantastic occurrences happened at my home on the Sunshine Coast in Queensland, Australia.

It is a story of 3 paintings in watercolour that I painted, and 1 flashback to the period of 2 of the 3 paintings past. Of the paintings there are 2 that I painted during my 4 year / 3 lifestyle changes, Odyssey, that is the subject of my first book, titled, *Just Go to the Airport*. This period ended in 1996. The other painting was completed 5 years ago. The paintings and the flashback are all of scenes in Europe where I lived for some years.

I need to tell the story by returning to the past quite often and then to the present day in this 3-week period. It is necessary to relate to you, the reader, in this fashion because you will need to follow my thoughts as each episode happened.

There are revelations of the past which lead to the stark realisations of the present in a fashion that I still cannot satisfactorily explain. The reader will simply have to try and decide what this story means!

Prologue

To validate the story and qualify my memory I will relate an incidental story which suggests that it is fun to have a good memory. So, back in time we go.

My wife Helen and I left Australia in early January 1992 to live on the Greek island of Samos in the western Aegean Sea. We arrived in Paris to stay a few days and then hired a car to travel through Europe and eventually fly from Athens, Greece, to the island of Samos. After staying with friends in Switzerland we drove to Lake Como in Italy and then to Santa Margherita on the Ligurian Coast of Italy, known as the Italian Riviera. We stayed there for three days and on the second day we travelled to Portofino by bus which is the only way to arrive in this small fishing village as car parking is at a premium.

Portofino is a delightful place and just dripping with wealth. After coffee and cake mid-morning we walked about on dockside along Portofino Bay and up a hill to a church overlooking the bay and the coast to the west. We walked into the church briefly and left after about 10 minutes. I then noticed a road leading along the bay to a dead end. It looked to be a pleasant walk, so off we went. Near the end of the road we came to a large Italian Villa with a sign on the fence saying that visitors were welcome to come inside and view an art exhibition.

It was a two-story villa and the entrance was from the bottom floor and a small fee was paid and we entered the villa. After walking around the rooms at ground level we walked out onto the courtyard which was large. The atmosphere was peaceful with the very well photographed Portofino Bay and coloured buildings in the distance. We then went up the stairs to the first floor and into the dining room. This room had a window overlooking the courtyard and a door leading onto a narrow balcony running along the length of one side of the villa. The sun had emerged and the scene from the dining room through the balcony door was an attraction which took my eye with the hillside in the background.

I asked Helen for one of our cameras and took a quick photo from the dining room to show the door and balcony. At this time I was occasionally sketching scenes of our travels in a small book and I thought that the photo might make for a sketch later. After walking through the other top floor rooms and looking at the art on the walls we left the villa and returned to the village for a fine lunch. Then back to Santa Margherita and eventually to the Greek island of Samos.

Now we fast forward some two- and a-bit years, after we had left Samos and then arrived in England to work for a year. We then purchased a yacht named Tequila Sunrise and started our sailing Odyssey in Europe. We sailed along the French coast to winter in Saint Malo on the Rance River. A perfect spot for a European winter. It was at this time that we had to return to Australia where Helen was to do some marketing contract work for NEC Computers, the company that she worked for when we left Australia. It was a brief stay in Australia and our furnished garden flat at Avalon Beach along the northern beaches of Sydney was perfect.

Before we left Europe for our brief visit home we had purchased some DVD movies to watch in Australia. One of these movies was called Enchanted April. It was an English period piece movie about 4 English girls who decide to rent a castle in Italy for 1 month and holiday there without husbands or male friends.

On about day 3 of our stay in Avalon Beach I decided that I would watch this movie whilst Helen was away with her work.

The movie was about 30 minutes into playing when these girls arrived at San Salvatorie, the small castle, where they were to stay. It was a rainy night when they arrived but the morning broke in sunshine. The scenes then showed the courtyard and some of the bedrooms and then the castle housekeeper called them to lunch with the gong.

The scene then went to the dining room and a ten-seater dining table for lunch. The camera the briefly panned the dining room and then showed a couple of the girls having lunch and discussing what the afternoon's activities would be.

As the movie kept playing I had a feeling that during the scenes in the dining room, I had the distinct awareness that I had recognised one of these scenes. I stopped the movie and then rewound it back to a scene which I thought I recognised. I froze the scene in the movie where the cameraman was filming during the panning of the dining room and this image I thought I knew. It looked like a scene in the Italian Villa in Porofino which we visited.

It was then that I remembered that I had taken a photograph of this scene in Portofino some 2 years before. I also knew that we had packed lots of photos to bring to Australia to show family and friends. They were in 3 bundles in one of the airline carry-on bags. I looked over to one of these bags and pulled out the bundles. The first bundle of photos was the right bundle. I flipped through the photos and there it was! I looked at the TV screen and the freeze frame of the movie and then looked at the photo. It was exactly the same image…gotcha!

The cameraman in the movie must have been standing in the same place that I was to take the photo. San Salvatorie, the castle in the movie, was in fact the large Italian Villa in Portofino…large villa, small castle…what the heck!

I stopped watching the movie and waited for Helen to come home when we could watch it together. After dinner we sat on the lounge to watch Enchanted April.

When the start of dining room scene came with the image of the narrow balcony I said nothing and the movie kept going for about 30 seconds. I then stopped the movie and asked Helen if she had recognised any of the scenes in the last few minutes. She said no. I then rewound the movie and stopped at the balcony image. She still did not recognise it. I then passed her the photo and in an instant she realised what it was all about! Lots of laughter followed and a funny story to tell friends.

All that from what I thought at the time to be a pretty good memory.

Now for the story of the title European Serendipity.

Episode ONE.
Going back in time. We start with the time that we lived and worked in England in 1993 for about a year.

Two of our friends from Australia were visiting Paris and suggested that Helen and I might join them in Paris for a long weekend. We did not need much convincing as I am such a fan of Paris that I have been there over a dozen times.

We arrived from the airport into Paris and had a great night in the Left Bank. After breakfast the next morning I bade goodbye to the others as I was going to walk around Paris and do a couple of sketches and meet the others at a bar in the afternoon and then onto dinner.

After about half an hour of walking I came upon a Place [park] and bought a coffee and walked through a large gate. It was a medium sized park and there are many parks in Paris, some larger and some smaller, all with a layout that allows you to sit down and get the atmosphere without being crowded. The seats are far apart to allow that and I saw one which was at about the middle of the park. Slightly opposite me, where I was sitting, was a girl sitting by herself on these 3 person seats with back rest. I sipped my coffee and put it down on the seat.

Five minutes later I had taken in this scene and decided to sketch it with the girl on the seat sitting opposite. I pulled out the sketch pad and clip board for the pad rest and then surveyed the scene with the girl to be in the centre of the sketch. I needed to go reasonably quickly because I needed to draw her and the seat before she decided to leave. I need not have worried.

As I was drawing her and the seat, I caught a glimpse of her as she was looking at me. It took me about 20 minutes to complete the first part of this sketch and I stopped for a sip of the coffee, which by then was cold. Good job I like cold coffee. It was then that she stood up to leave. She looked at me with a ghost of a smile and I returned a smile with a nod of my head to thank her for staying while I drew her. I was convinced that she knew exactly what I was doing and the enigmatic smile reminded me of the wonderfully subtle expressions that Parisians can display. It reminds me now of the night that I spent in Paris some years later with 7 other Parisians at an outdoor Brasserie and the romantic facial expressions of people in love with their partners and their city.

I finished the sketch taking in the surrounds of the scene. I still have the painting and the second sketch that day was of a window of an Antique Shop and its items in the window. I met my wife and friends later and a good night was had.

Now fast forward to October 2020 and my apartment.

I will watch the TV on most nights for a couple of hours, sometimes longer. On about the 8th or 9th October I was looking at the Netflix offerings and a new series was available called Emily in Paris. It is about a girl, actor Lilly Collins, who is sent to Paris by her employers in the US to join a Public Relations firm which has just been purchased by Emily's US company.

The story centres on Emily's business input to the French way of doing things and Emily's romantic adventures. It is initially a nine-part series.

During episode No 7 or 8 Emily is to meet a friend one morning and the opening scene of this meeting place is a park. There is a wide pan of the park and I immediately sat bolt upright and leaned forward. I knew this park! The scene then zoomed into Emily sitting on a park seat.

It was the same park and the same scene, a single girl sitting on a park seat. I had the painting downstairs in a small area/ studio where I paint.

For my memory at least, when I do a sketch of a scene, where I can be for up to 90 minutes, I never forget that scene. I went downstairs to find the painting and eventually I found it and it was just as I remembered it. It will be framed soon.

As I looked again at the Emily in Paris scene, the seat with Emily sitting on it seemed to me to be in the same position as I remembered of the layout of this park and my painting of the patient girl over 20 years before. Same park, same image of a single girl in about the same spot in the park. What the…?

I could not go to sleep for a while that night just thinking about what had just happened. If you think that is strange then there is:

Episode TWO.

Once again we go back.

During our Odyssey on our yacht we had wintered in Portugal and when the weather became fine Gibralta beckoned and then the Costa Del Sol on the Spanish Coast/ Riviera.

It was in Benalmadena on the coast that we caught up with some of our friends that we met whilst living in Portugal at the marina at Lagos. One of them suggested that we go and stay at a villa in the hinterland of the Costa Del Sol. With that, 7 people in 2 cars set of to stay for 3 days at this villa.

It was about a two-hour travel as we stopped for some great coffee at cafe which also served very good sweets. We arrived at the villa to be greeted by the owner and she showed us to our rooms and introduced us to our chef for the evening meal. The chef was part of this three-day package where he would cook traditional fare…superb.

The villa had a stream running through the living and entertaining room which was large. For all of us, this was unique. The owner bade us goodbye and suggested that we visit the large town in the distance, on a mountainside, in the morning.

The following morning we did exactly that and drove towards a town, painted in white and about 6 kms from our villa. As advised we parked the cars on the road leading up the town and then started to walk.

It felt a little strange for us all to explore a town that had been there for many centuries and like a hundred or more towns on a hillside in Spain it had a unique history.

As we walked up the hill we came to a small building where there was a sign saying Arena de Torres, a bull ring. We all saw this and decided to go and look. The entrance to this bull ring was through a tunnel, where you could drive a car and then onto the arena itself.

We walked onto the arena and I realised that because it was small, it was probably for the young bulls to come and practice as well as the toreadors, picadors and matadors. The ground level barricades were there and the acoustics were fabulous. After realising this, I started to orate some little words of Shakespeare that I knew. I was booed off by the others and one of the girls started an oration that would have done justice to the Globe Theatre in England. After our performances to nobody we moved out of the arena and up to the town for a pre-lunch drink and onto lunch.

Now, fast forward to the very night after the Paris park painting/ *Emily in Paris* episode.

It was a Tuesday night and I normally watch, on the TV, a programme called Rosemary and Thyme. It is a series about 2 English girls who landscape gardens throughout Europe and solve murders as a sideline. In this episode they were in Spain to do a landscape job at a Spanish tennis ranch.

About 15 minutes into this one-hour episode the camera panned a shot of a town, on a mountainside, painted in white. It was the town where the girls, in the episode, were landscaping a garden. The pan shot looked familiar. The episode then revealed that one of the girls was to meet a couple of friends at a place on the edge of this town.

The following scene opened up with 2 people walking through a small tunnel and onto an arena. It was the same arena, in the same hillside town that a few of us had visited, many years before and delivered the orations to a non-existent audience!

I simply laughed at this and with the previous night's experience I thought that this is enough excitement for the week!

These happenings were not over, not by a long shot.

Episode THREE.

Once again we go back in time.

In 2015, my wife Annie was turning 50 and I decided to take her to, where else but Paris, to celebrate the occasion. We stayed in an Air B&B apartment for 10 days and then caught the train to Nice on the Cote D' d' Azur which for me is always the original Riviera.

We stayed in a garden 1 bed flat which was in a very good spot close to the seaside where ferries and day boats would come and go. On about day 3 we hired a car and drove north to Monaco and had a lunch in Monte Carlo and then drove further north to Mentone. On returning to Nice we drove along on of the 2 high roads overlooking the Mediterranean. I looked down at one stage and saw an attractive marina and suggested to Annie that we might visit this marina the following morning.

Going north the next morning, we drove into this marina located in the suburb of Villefranche. Parking was at a premium for any of the dozens of marinas along the Cote d' Azur. We were lucky and walked into the marina where I noticed that the sailing boats in the marina were mostly of the make of Swan yachts. A Swan Yacht Brockerage was there. These yachts are the most expensive production yachts that you can buy. They are the last word in luxury.

We went to the cafe at the marina and had coffee and croissants as of right. I was a little goggle eyed of the scene at this marina and said to Annie that I would like to sketch part of this marina. After the coffee I ordered another coffee to take with me. We walked along the marina key and up to a set of stone stairs to the rampart wall which surrounded the marina. I found a spot on the wall and sat down to do the sketch.

On viewing this scene for the sketch I placed the biggest Swan yacht in the middle. It was about a 70-to-80-footer and its cost would have been many millions of Euros. The sketch was mostly completed and the coffee was of course cold.

We then returned to Nice to visit the old town market.

Now fast forward to late October 2020.

There is a little Sherlock Holmes/deductive reasoning by me in this episode as you will find out.

On scrolling the programmes on the TV, via a streaming service, I noticed a series called Riviera. It starred Juliet Styles.

Now there a many Rivieras in Europe and I tuned into this series and for some reason it started at about episode 5. After the catch up roll I realised that the series was based in Nice. What a slice of luck! I knew it well.

It was about episode 8 when Juliet Styles was to meet a man on the family yacht in a marina. A scene opened where she was walking along a small section of the marina key with some stone stairs in the background leading up to the wall surrounding the marina. I immediately sat bolt upright again and forward. In that brief scene I recognised the marina at Villefranche, where I had done the sketch of the Swan yachts. It was only a brief scene as the story changed locations. I thought to myself…get a grip John! …there are many marinas in this part of the coast and they mostly have walls for protection from the sea.

A scene then showed Juliet Styles stepping onto the family yacht. It showed the deck layout and it looked like the deck of a Swan yacht with the low profile that was inherent for all Swan yachts. It was also a big yacht, probably a 70-to-80-footer. She met the person that she was meant to meet when she went below to the saloon.

I was warming up to this but still not convinced.

They decided to take the yacht out for a sail. During this sail, a shot of the yacht was shown side on and there it was! On all Swan yachts there is a decorative line on the side of the hull about 10 cms down from the toe rail. It has a spear look at the bow end of this line and a dot and dash look at the stern. It was a Swan yacht!

Now you're talking, I thought.

The scene on the yacht turned to a storm that blew up that night and Juliet Styles was washed overboard after killing the other person on the yacht. She was rescued that night at sea by a three-decker power cruiser and brought on board by the crew. The owner's wife put her in a cabin to sleep. In the morning she was okay and appeared on deck for a breakfast. She asked if she could use the radio to report the derelict yacht for rescue. She did this and said to the owner's wife that she needed to get back to shore. The wife said that they would be returning to Villefranche the next morning.

Got it! Nailed it!

I sat in my living room and stopped the Riviera programme on the TV. I then also realised that the Swan yacht in the episode of Riviera was probably the same yacht that I had sketched at this marina in 2015. It was large and there was only one very large Swan yacht in the marina that day.

I thought I should stop watching these TV series as it was becoming absurd. Like something out of the 1960s series, Twilight Zone by Rod Serling, except that this is all oh so true.

And now to cap it all off.

Episode FOUR.

On the last day of October this year I was about to have breakfast when my mobile phone mad a chime indicating that I had a message. After finishing breakfast I found the message. It was from a family friend, Susie Mac who sent a text to say that there had been a tsunami which had hit the Greek island of Samos. She knew that I had lived on this island as she had read my book, *Just Go to the Airport*.

I had caught the news on the TV that morning which reported that an earthquake had hit Turkey. I sent a text message to Susie Mac to thank her for the alert and said that I would watch the Greek News that morning at 9.30 am on the SBS channel.

The Greek news started with a report from the Greek island of Samos, which had also been hit with the earthquake along with the following tsunami. The report showed a map of that part of the Aegean Sea and showed the epicentre to be between Samos and the Turkish mainland.

The TV coverage and the reporters were showing the buildings on the island and the attendant damage. I then thought that the capital of Samos is Samos Town flanking a harbour which has its entrance to the north. It was through that where a tsunami would come. Then the TV coverage showed Samos Town and the buildings along the bay. I recognised it well.

There then appeared a reporter standing at the end of the harbour, on a street covered in water with the town in the background.

I was at this stage standing in my kitchen and I looked across to a painting hanging on a wall. It was a painting that I completed when I was living on this island. It was of Samos Town and as the reporter was shown from afar, standing on this street at the end of the harbour, I looked at the painting and back to the image of the reporter on the TV screen. They were the same image with the reporter standing on the street which was at the bottom right-hand corner of my painting.

The cameraman, filming the tsunami flooding, must have been standing very near to where I sat to do the sketch and then the painting all those years ago.

I give up! In 3 weeks, 3 paintings revisited and 1 flashback and 1 memory.

What is that? Over to you, the reader.

Introduction

During 1988, my wife Helen and I were working in the computer industry. Helen was National Sales Manager of NEC Computers and I was Major Accounts Manager [one of four people] at Canon Australia.

The computer industry then was much the same as it is now…fast-paced with technology and always upgrading existing products where a new feature on a machine, be it computer or peripheral, was released as a new model. It is always the case that you could be out of date with a product in a matter of months.

People who worked in the computer industry were from all parts of life and it was generally accepted that the best people were employed in this industry. One of the main reasons for this was the high salaries and packages offered for the best people, particularly in Marketing. It was very easy to admit that we were financially captured by this industry. Another reason was that technology and the products were relatively new and you had to have a fairly athletic brain to keep up with technology, products and how to present them in a sales situation.

Helen and I were part of this work place and with it came the stresses of targets and budgets in this high-pressure environment. It was also a lot of fun.

Most of our friends were in the same industry. At play, our conversations were about business and the successes and failures of our activities. We were all rather stressed and we each knew this and our inability to relieve the stress. So I suggested to a group of friends that we should get to the other side of the world and investigate a sailing holiday in the Greek Islands. The suggestion came from my visit to the Travel Expo at Darling Harbour, where I met Trevor Joyce who owned three sailing yachts on the Greek Island of Samos. These yachts were of course for charter.

It was 16 people who met at our home to watch a 30-minute video taken by Trevor Joyce of the scenes of the base port of Pythagorio in Samos and other Greek Islands where the charter yachts would sail during a two-week period. It was a fun gathering and most of the people there wanted to go sailing in that beautiful part of the world. As is always the case in this situation, when it came to booking and paying for the trip, there were many reasons why most people did not go. I think that the main reason here was that it would take people out of their comfort zone of destinations and lead to a less than enjoyable holiday.

How unfortunate for those people and what we related to them on our return.

Six people eventually booked one of the sailing yachts and flew to the Island of Samos for the two weeks of sailing.

On arrival in Pythagorio and its beautiful small harbour, we acclimatised for two days then boarded our Beneteau First 405 Yacht. The name of our yacht was "INDIAN" and the other boats in the small flotilla were also named after oceans of the world.

Our skipper for the two weeks was an English lady named Michelle who was a great party goer and sea lady. We sailed to and partied on the islands of Patmos, Arki, Lipsi, Leros, Kalymnos and Amorgos. Every night we were in port or anchored in a beautiful quiet bay.

We went swimming every day either from the yacht or from a beach and there is nothing in the water such as sharks or other beasties to bother. As each day concluded with a wonderful sunset, we were all totally enchanted with the beauty of the Greek Islands. It is a beauty that has not changed in thousands of years.

When we returned to Pythagorio, our base, we stayed one more night as a group and then flew out of the local airport in Pythagorio to a connection at

Athens for home to Australia or in my case to Paris, France. This was a city that I kept returning to over the following years as it is easily as beautiful as the Greek Islands for exhibiting the best that this world can offer.

As Helen and I waited at Athens Airport for our flight to Paris, I remembered what Trevor Joyce had told me at our home when he showed the video of some of the experiences to be enjoyed in the Greek Islands. Trevor said to me that once you visit the sailing in the Greek Islands, you will always return!

Trevor did not realise how true this prophecy turned out to be. When I returned to Australia, the thought was planted. Dare I dream of the life that I was now dreaming; this dream unfolded in the following fashion.

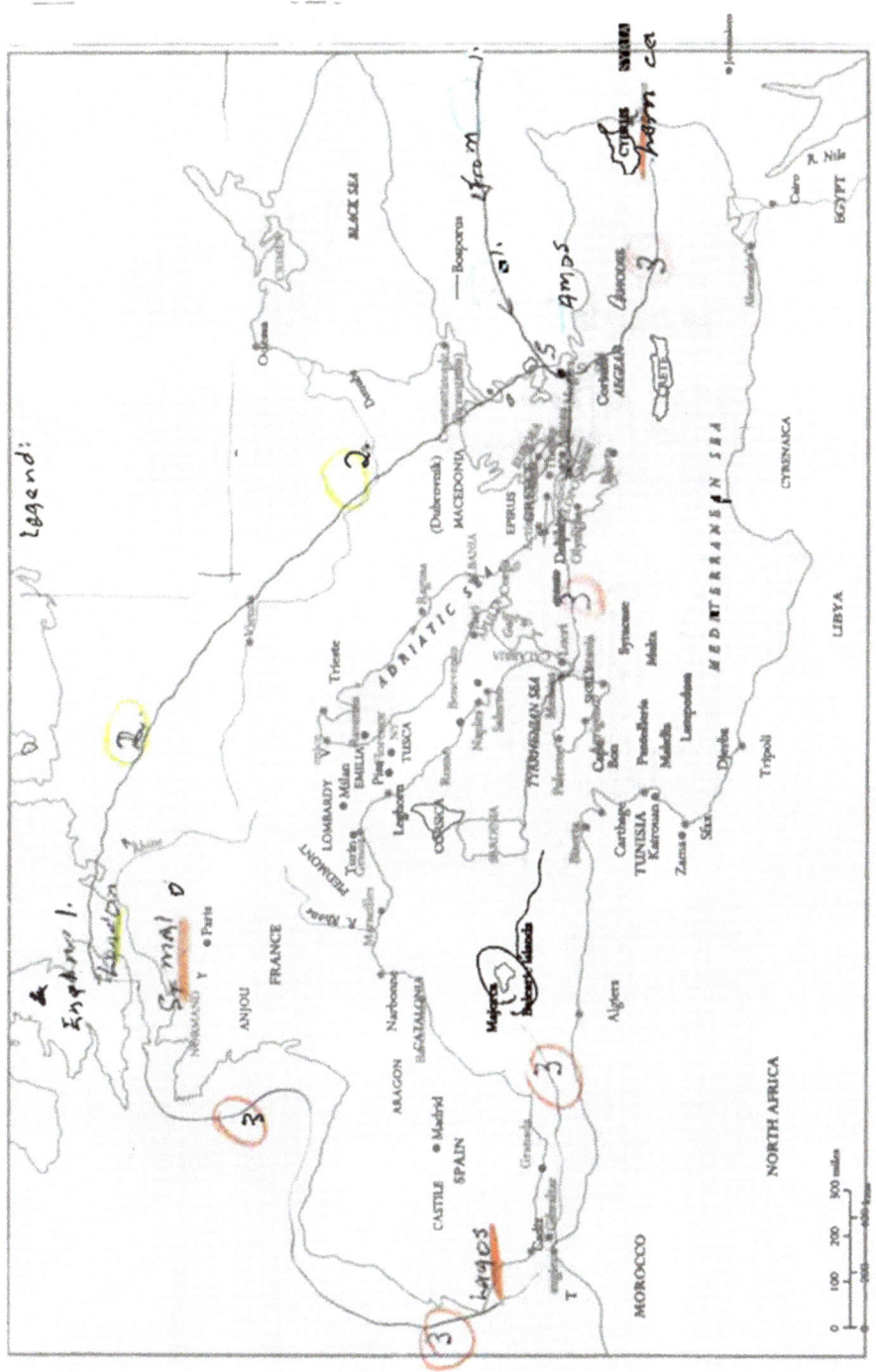

Chapter 1
Incubation of a Thought

After we returned from the Greek Islands and Paris, we were all very chilled out and not particularly ready to step back into that fast lane of the computer industry. The six people who were on the yacht and a few more friends met for dinner one night at the Malay Restaurant in North Sydney.

It was about a week and a half since we were all back at work and we each expected that the others would be back in the groove. Not so!

You see, what had happened is that we had seen Nirvana and the experience was difficult to put aside whilst getting on with life at hand. I compared it to an astronaut after splashing back down to Earth and then having dinner two weeks later with his family. It would still be very hard not to think that you had done something very special two weeks before. The experience had been so wonderful that we all kept drifting back to many scenes in the Greek Islands in our quiet moments.

The trouble was that there was a lot of drifting back scenes and a lot of quiet moments. At the end of the night, we urged each other to go to work and think more of work activities, if for no other reason than to earn some more money to do this all again!

And so, the six of us gradually got back into the groove at work and at play. For me it was enjoyable with the occasional break from routine to work at a Convention and catch up with everybody from around Australia in the computer industry including a young Malcolm Turnbull who was part owner of a computer supply company.

I was also playing cricket each summer weekend with a team made up from people from Canon at work and people who had worked at Canon and were now working in the computer industry at other companies. We were at a sub-district level at A2 Grade which was probably a bit too high as we could not always field our best team due to work commitments by a few of our good players.

The name of our team was Refuge Bay Cricket Club and was named after a bay in the Hawkesbury River system near Cottage Point. The idea came to a few of the players after a weekend of drinking aboard a hire boat and a last stop at Refuge Bay as they could not safely go any further. A good enough reason to name a cricket club!

Life was pretty good as we entered 1991 with a bit of sport at the weekend to separate our work life. My wife, Helen was playing netball of a Monday night and joined me of a weekend when a few of us would play a round of golf or a few sets of tennis.

During the early part of 1991, I started to think again of the Greek Island of Samos and our seaside village of Pythagorio which was our base for our sailing holiday. I wondered what it would be like to actually live there. After all, it was paradise and we had gotten on so well with the Greek people.

I went to see Trevor Joyce who had, of course, arranged our sailing holiday. He knew Samos very well and said that to live there would be his dream and he and his wife Maggie had often discussed this possibility. However, they had children that needed to finish high school and their yacht charter business was better run from Sydney than the island of Samos. When Maggie said this, Trevor just shrugged his shoulders in consignment.

Trevor pointed out that if I or my wife wanted to work there then the best time to arrive on the island was early in the year. Bar work and restaurant work would be available and by his reckoning, would be fun for a couple of Aussies who already had an affinity with the Greeks.

The idea of living in Samos started to sound better.

During this period, Helen and I lived a busy work, and a particularly hectic social life. One Friday night, I invited some of the Japanese people from Marketing at Canon to my home for a BBQ. The evening went very well with the wife of one of our Japanese executives asking me could she cook on our BBQ which was constructed of sandstone with a large metal plate and natural timber for heating. I built the BBQ myself and it had a swivel seat so that you could swing between the BBQ plate and the timber storage area flanking the hot plate.

The Japanese lady, Miroshi, was intrigued and I invited her to cook for the people there, numbering about 16. She completed her task with such relish that she pestered her husband that she be allowed to cook on any BBQ that they attended!

It seemed that life could really not get any better. Yet, I had serious thoughts of leaving Australia to live in Europe and to start with a time in Samos in the beautiful village of Pythagorio.

What accelerated the incubation of this thought was a question that I asked Helen one Sunday night. It concerned the previous week and the fact that I could not remember where we had dinner on each of the nights where we ate at a restaurant. We had dinner on four nights and neither she nor I could remember where we had dinner on most of those nights. There was always a group of us at dinner and a designated driver was appointed to drive each couple to their home at the end of the evening. It was a good system because only the driver could remember where we had dinner as the rest of us were in various states of sobriety when we were delivered home.

A month or so went by and I asked the same question on a Sunday night and the same response from both of us did slightly embarrass us both. It seemed that we were near to the top of our professions and our recollections of some social events were hopeless.

I asked myself, "Is this as good as life gets?"

Admitting to myself that it probably was, I thought that life and one's ability to get the best out of it could be a lot more than what it was delivering at this time. Most people would have been quite satisfied with our situation. I, however thought that we could do better. I thought of the options that we had for our lives at that time. We had no obligations at home with children as my three children were now grown up. Helen had professed her desire to not have children. We owned our home and could lease the two-bedroom semi-detached home in Chatswood, which was a busy business and shopping precinct on a rail line.

I asked Helen on a Sunday night that I would love to travel back and live on the Greek Island of Samos and of course would she come with me?

Helen arrived home on Thursday night and said that she had given her notice to leave NEC and would leave in one month.

We were leaving Australia and going to live in Europe!

Chapter 2
Samos

When Helen delivered the news that she had given notice at NEC it came as a bit of a shock. I suggested that she consider my suggestion as I was committed to going. I also suggested that I could leave and find a place to live and she could come to Samos Island later. I realised that for Helen it was now or never and her buoyancy about the move to the other side of the world was wonderful.

Gee whiz! I thought. Now we need to get cracking…the game is afoot. There were lots of things to do before we could 'just go to the airport'.

The first thing to do was to tell our family and friends of our decision.

Our friends numbered up to 100, as we were very socially mobile and we had many friends that we found in business dealings who we decided needed to be told rather than find out via our replacement.

Our business associates and friends all showed surprise at our decision and then a happiness for us and our courage for doing what we intended. Some people said, "You'll be back soon," hoping they would be right and then console us on our attempt to leave the rat race for some years.

Our very close friends were more pensive with their reactions to this news that two of their friends were leaving their lives behind at a time when we were both successful at our professions and secure at home. I put this down to the fact that the very great majority of people have comfort limits that they live by and would never consider what we were about to do. They put up barriers for their lives and will not step beyond them, for fear of being in a strange place and/ or not having the ability to carry on with success. Both Helen and I very well understood this and we assured our close friends that our move was very well thought out.

What supported our decision was this: we both had very great confidence and a keen intellect. When you couple that with an abundance of courage, then anything is possible. As it transpired, some of these personal attributes were almost used up at some stages during the next four years but when one attribute faded then another would take over until the miscreant attribute caught up with the others.

Telling our family of our departure was a delight for both us and them. They were both excited for us and would miss us until we returned. We had no idea that the families would come visit us during our time away.

My father, in particular, was very happy as it corresponded with the move that both my parents made by leaving Australia in 1970 and arriving in England to work. They left my younger brother Jeff in my care. Another reason for my parents extended leave from Australia was to visit my sister Kerry who had also left Australia a year or two earlier and was now living in Hendon, to the north of London.

My parents were away for about one year and when they returned their stories of life and the adventures whilst travelling in Europe in a Thames Trader Van held me captive. Both my parents worked in England where to be an Australian is to be accepted as a good worker and easily employable. This has been the case for decades as I was to find out when I sought employment in England.

As for Helen, her mother was English and so we had relatives to visit when we arrived in England.

The round of farewells with family and friends started immediately with the ever-probing questions like "What about working locally, how are you going to do that? What about visas? What about speaking Greek? You don't even know where you will live…what about that?"

Most of the questions were answered with a flippancy of mine which was laughed at by most people. It did however give some trepidation to Helen and I needed to assure her some times that all would be fine. I even said to her that we would be living in our new home overlooking the Aegean Sea in Pythagorio soon after our arrival. I said this for myself to hear as well as Helen. Little did I realise that this would come true!

Our home, in Chatswood, was leased to two young women who were working as a sister in a hospital and a clerical job in a government position. They were perfect tenants and a friend of mine looked after the collection of rent and took his earnings as per the Real Estate guides.

The most difficult goodbye of all was to our dog, named Radar. He was a Border Collie. He, like all of his breed, was a very intelligent dog. Radar was given little more intelligence than most and it did not take me long to train him. When I brought him home, he was six weeks old, I took him outside to the back yard and put him down onto the grass. When I went to move off, he moved to baulk me in my direction. I turned to walk in the other direction and the same would happen. Amazing! He was rounding me up!

People would ring our house to invite Radar to a party and Helen and I could come if we were on our best behaviour. I asked my son Steven if he could look after him and of course he said yes. There was one problem in Radar staying with my son and his family. They had no fence on the property and no money to build it after just completing the build of their first home. I paid for the fence and that was settled.

The one regret that I have always had for this time is that I could not stay for my son's wedding to Nicole. I was advised to get to the Island of Samos early in the year to have a good chance of getting a job. I was told by Trevor Joyce of yacht lease fame that a chap named Gary had the long lease of the Sail Inn Bar and that I should look him up for a job at the Bar. Ultimately Gary of the Sail Inn could not offer me a job as it was too early in the year for the bar to open!

The advice to leave early in the year was a little misplaced. I could have stayed a little longer in Australia and attended my son's wedding. To this day I hope that he understands.

Our furniture was collected by a removalist and sent to Melbourne to be stored at Helen's parent's home in their garage.

So we were ready to 'go to the airport'.

We stayed with some friends for a night and they drove us to the Airport in Sydney and after we checked in via luggage and passport control we sat in the departure lounge wondering how we were going to do all the things that we said we could do after going to the other side of the world, living in a strange country, strange customs, strange food, strange laws and no firm prospect of being able to work that was legal. Not a problem I thought! We left Australia to arrive in Switzerland to see some of my family friends on route to the Island of Samos.

The aircraft landed at Zurich Airport where we stayed for two nights. It was January and still a bit cold in northern Europe. Zurich is a very cosmopolitan city and quite well planned. It sits on a lake where I could see the scullers rowing fast in their sleek boats. On our first day, we visited a bar for lunch and the barman guessed that we were visitors and suggested that we sit at a particular table, specially reserved for visitors. The idea was that the visitors could speak to each other and help with some suggestions about places that they had been. We took up our seats and soon were joined by other visitors who chatted with us. Out of our chats, we went to the Jules Verne Bar on top of a very tall building in the centre of Zurich. It was a grand panorama and some photos taken. Not perhaps as grand as Sydney Harbour but just as pretty.

After a busy day, after a long flight, we did not need to much rocking to get some sleep. Day two in Zurich and I wanted to visit the Kunsthaus Museum where there was an exhibition of old European paintings. One of these was the Girl with the Pearl Earring by the Dutch artist Johannes Vermeer, the Dutch painter of the 17th century. Vermeer was known as The Master of Light and each of his paintings is sought after for exhibitions. There were only two of his paintings on display during this exhibition.

After about 20 minutes of looking at the paintings, I walked into a room where there was only one painting to see. It was the Girl with the Pearl Earring, his most famous painting. What astounded me was that I was the only person in that room. The painting stood in the middle of the room enclosed in glass. I looked at it from all angles and of course the girl in the frame followed me around. How does that come to be? Some years ago, a good film was made called the Girl with the Pearl Earring and starred the English actor Colin Firth.

Some years later, a very small exhibition of Vermeer's work came to Australia with that famous painting. You had to line up for hours to see it in the National Gallery in Canberra. There are only about 15 or 16 paintings of Vermeer in existence and I was lucky to see his most famous painting all by myself.

It was time to leave Zurich and start our journey towards the Greek Island of Samos. But first, we had to call and see my family's friends in Zuoz in Switzerland. It is near the town of St Moritz which is very famous for its ski fields and the lake in the valley which freezes over during the winter months. We boarded the train in the morning and were at the station at Zuoz by mid-afternoon.

Danny and Evelyn Badilatti greeted us and we went to their home which is only a short walk from the train station. The hospitality was good so we stayed another day or two. We hired some ski gear and went to the chair lifts to rise take us up the mountain. What a sight and what a day! Zuoz, like many small villages in Switzerland will not be added to in terms of homes to build, as the avalanches in some of the areas make the addition of more homes very dangerous. As it is, the residents need to go out and "shoot the avalanche" which means that they fire exploding bullets into the side of the mountain when the build-up of snow is such that an avalanche can be started which is small and where no danger is prevalent.

The following day, we borrowed Daniel's car and drove into St Moritz. It was here that, by co-incidence, we attended the St Moritz Grand Prix Horse Races.

They were held on the frozen lake on the floor of the valley in front of the village of St Moritz.

The races featured jockeys on the horses, being towed by the horses where the jockeys were on skis, being towed by the horses with two people on a sled and where a clown was riding the horse. Serious betting took place and the international set were present as this event was noted on the calendar for the rich and famous. Gold, diamonds and fur coats were the order of the day and the array of vehicles in the carpark would have cost about $30 million to replace.

We returned to Daniel and Evelyn's home and that night we attended a choir recital at 11 pm in the local Church Hall. Choir singing is a very popular activity in Switzerland. Each Canton [area] in Switzerland has its own choir and the competition is very strong for the ultimate accolade as the Best of Switzerland.

The choir master used a tuning fork to hear each group of the choir attain just the sound he wanted. The recital then commenced with the sound and the acoustics to a level which everyone applauded.

Daniel was a member of the choir for his Canton but was not singing that night as this night's choir was competing for some minor prize. We walked out of the recital into a clear and cold night in the middle of Switzerland and slowly walked back home for the night. How wonderful and how very civilised.

At home we had supper and I had left a bottle of wine to chill in the snow at the side door. A glass each and that was the end of a good day.

We said our goodbyes the following morning and boarded the train for our journey to Lago de Como in Italy. This rail trip was on the highest rail in Europe and the vista through the mountains of Switzerland to the Italian lakes was in every sense spectacular. I noticed on one mountain a solitary skier making a faint track down a mountain and one of the passengers said that a helicopter service had taken that person to the top of the mountain for the adventure of getting to the bottom. It was a very long traverse as I watched this skier for five minutes and he had only travelled about a third of the distance to the bottom of the mountain. I kept thinking about an avalanche and said so to my passenger friend. He assured that the season so far had not left a lot of snow on that part of the mountain, so the avalanche risk was minimal. In any case, he said, if you are a good skier you can outrun an avalanche!

Our arrival in Lago de Como was late in the day and as we left the train station we walked to an information booth and the lady there phoned a three-star pension for a booking for us for two nights. That night, we of course had pizza for dinner and a bold red wine. What else do you do in Italy?

The Italian lakes are beautiful. Let us leave it at that as superlatives are not enough. From the piazza in Lago de Como, I could see a funicular railway going up the side of a mountain. The terminal was near the piazza so we walked to the base terminal and purchased two tickets. After waiting for about 20 minutes, we boarded the rail to the top of the mountain. The rail had been there for a long time with the foundations in place that were original. When the Italians build something, they build it to last. When we disembarked from the carriage, I bought two coffees and we set off to explore.

The area was mainly residential with large villas at every turn with views over the lake from every villa. There was of course a Villa Borghese which was probably the biggest in the area. There was to be a similarly named villa in a lot of Italian areas. A popular name for a villa.

The top of this mountain was a place of enchantment. The mood and atmosphere were surreal as all around us was old style and Italian old style does not date. I was so captivated that my coffee went cold. Nothing wrong with good cold coffee, especially Italian.

We returned to the mountain top terminal and railed down the mountain to return to the main piazza. It was time for lunch.

From the centre of the piazza I noticed a bus terminal and behind this was a bar and tavern. Helen was a bit apprehensive weaving our way through the buses to the bar/tavern. My rationale was that wherever the bus drivers drank and eat must be a bit of an adventure. And so it was!

I approached the bar and ordered due birra [2 beers] of whatever the most popular beer appeared to be. We then stood at a bar rest and looked about to see where we had come to drink and eat. Nearby there were two men dressed in shirt and tie and they could overhear us speaking in English. They invited us to join them at their bar rest table as they spoke English.

We accepted with glee and told them that we were from Australia and were heading to a Greek island to live. A sea change. Mario and Bruno were intrigued with this and the conversation was sparkling as we explained why we had chosen to leave Australia to go to a village from where we had sailed from, as a holiday, some years before. We commented on the beauty of this area and they naturally agreed with a comment that it was becoming very expensive for the locals. Such is the price of beauty.

During our conversation, an Italian local approached us in an agitated frame of mind. He thought that we were Americans and spoke of his dislike of them for the bombs that were dropped during the Second World War that destroyed his parent's home. He spoke in Italian and Mario and Bruno were quick to point out that we were Australian. His mood changed quickly and he excused himself for his attitude. All this conversation was being translated on the go by Mario. Our confused visitor kept on with his story with the simultaneous translation by Mario.

He blamed the Americans for all the damage to Italy during that war and particularly on Lago de Como. I could only nod in agreement and he left the table with a handshake. 'Tis best to go along with these things than try to defend.

Mario tried to apologise for this strange Italian interruption but I said that I understood completely and no offence was taken by myself or Helen.

I bought another drink for the four of us and then said goodbye to move to the dining area where we had a great lunch and returned to our Pension.

The following day, we caught the train to Bari on the east coast of Italy to catch the boat to Corfu, an island in the Adriatic Sea. We had to keep moving east towards the Greek island of Samos, our final destination.

On arrival at the train station in Bari we walked to the Ferry Port. We had no idea of timetables for ferry departures. We got onto a line to purchase two fares to Corfu and on reaching the person in the ticket office we were told that the ferry had left earlier that day for Corfu. Our choices were to wait for the following day's ferry or catch the train to Brindisi and from there board the overnight ferry to Corfu. The person in the ticket office said that if we hurried and caught the bus out front to the station we should make the connection for the overnight ferry. Helen walked off first and made the bus stop with me behind by about 50 metres lugging the heavier bags.

No sooner had she put down the light bags including my aircraft carry-on bag than a motor bike came off the street and motored by Helen with the rear passenger scooping up my carry-on bag. I left the main bags and raced up to the bus stop but it was so quick, the operation, that the bike was out of sight in about 15 seconds. I looked across the road to some pedestrians and they stopped briefly and shrugged their shoulders and kept walking. We were the victims of a small cottage industry. I then shrugged it off as well as I always keep money, passports and travel documents in my pockets for just this occurrence.

We caught the bus soon after and arrived for the train to Brindisi. The train trip was swift and our arrival in Brindisi was followed by a taxi ride to the port to get aboard the ferry to Corfu. After explaining to the taxi driver that we were going to Corfu on the night ferry, he tossed our bags into the boot and beckoned us to get in quickly as we had to hurry.

The taxi moved off at a pace and during the trip, if one could call it that, the driver made a phone call to someone and proceeded down dark alleys whilst driving the taxi as only Italian drivers could do. It crossed my mind that we were being set up for another sting and I was ready to defend whatever was going to happen. I need not have worried! The taxi emerged form an alley right on dockside and a motorised trolley was there with driver. The bags were tossed from taxi to trolley in a moment and the trolley disappeared towards the ferry.

No conversation went on whilst all this was happening and I stood there like a stunned mullet. It seemed that the surreptitious phone call on route was to the baggage manager for the ferry. He had sent one of the trolleys to a nominated pick-up spot after the taxi emerged from the frantic drive. Otherwise we certainly would not have made the ferry on time. I thanked the driver of the taxi and tipped him well. He was grateful for the tip which was due for his forethought.

This little adventure restored my faith for what people could do in a pinch. We boarded the ferry for Corfu.

Helen meantime was a nervous wreck. There was an alleviation to this and it was some alcohol. After finding our room for the overnight trip, we hit the bar. The first two drinks did not touch the sides and I reflected on the day just passed. Helen just could not understand me being nonplussed. I explained that we were on the boat as planned with some aberrations on the side. The fact that the emotional graph for the day was all over the place meant that we were living life and that is why we came here. This did not go down so well but the drinks smoothed the emotional graph and it almost looked like a straight line at the end of the drinking session.

The arrival in Corfu put our little adventure way behind us. It was a beautiful day and we were on our first Greek island. Corfu has been occupied by many different peoples in its history and after we checked into a hotel we walked to the main square overlooking a sports oval. Evidence of it varied past could be seen in the architecture of the buildings from Greek to Italian and English styles. A wonderful mix of design and culture. During lunch on an Italian-made veranda, a group of cars arrived at the sports ground. The people were dressed in white and I ventured to say to Helen that cricket players dressed in this rig.

Sure enough, the players walked to the centre of the oval and started to place the stumps at both ends of a cricket pitch. We had arrived to see a game of cricket which is a game that I played in Australia. The game started well with the opening quick bowlers taking a few wickets for about 40 runs. We left the game to do some sight-seeing and during our wanderings we visited the marina and I looked at the yachts with a bit of envy. Would it not be wonderful to have a yacht? Little did I know.

We returned to a bar for the last half of an hour of the cricket game. It was a two-day game and we would not see the result. Whilst Corfu is now mainly Greek inspired, the game of cricket is the visible remnant of the English occupation. It was a relaxing day but we still had to keep going east and the next day we boarded a ferry to the Piraeus which is the port area of Athens, the capital of Greece.

We had booked a flight from Athens to the island of Samos and after arriving in Athens we booked a hotel and visited the Acropolis which is where the Parthenon is to be seen. The Parthenon can be seen from almost anywhere in Athens and no more so than the balcony of our hotel. The Greeks are very proud of the structures on the Acropolis with the main feature as the Parthenon.

This building is more impressive than its position. Once again the superlatives are inadequate. By day the visitor can roam around it. By night there is a sight and sound show from another high point in Athens. Both should be experienced.

That night, we had dinner in the Plaka area which is where many Tavernas are to be found and the Greek hospitality runs amok.
The next morning, we packed for the last time to go to the airport for our flight to our expected home of Samos.

The flight from the old airport took about an hour and we flew across the Aegean Sea to Pythagorio in Samos. As I looked down from the aircraft's window, I saw the wine dark sea which is how the ancients described the Aegean Sea. I did not realise it then but we were to traverse this part of the Aegean by a very different mode in some years to come.

After collecting our luggage at the airport I hired a car for one week. As we drove to the small village of Pythagorio, we recognised some of the features of the area from our first visit some years before. We were excited as we drove down the street to the bay area ringed with tavernas and shops. It was a typically beautiful Greek scene.

The only surprising thing about the bay area was that not too many tavernas were open for business. I parked the car in the town square. On opening the boot of the car to get a small bag, a lady about three cars away, after hearing a conversation with Helen and myself, said that we were a long way from home. I immediately agreed and we introduced ourselves.

The lady was Sandy Karides who was a New Zealander. She was married to Tony [Adonis] Karides who of course was Greek. They had two children, Marisa and Gregory and were living in the village of Pythagorio. We explained that we had arrived to live on the island of Samos and in the village of Pythagorio where our sailing base was some years before. Sandy and Tony turned out to be great friends.

It was then that the affinity of the New Zealanders and the Australians came rushing to the fore. Sandy was almost as excited as we were! Our immediate need was to find a hotel to stay for a while until we found somewhere to rent as our home. Sandy said that it was early for the season to open, that is the tourist season, and not too many hotels were open as yet. She did however hear that Theo was back from his holidays yesterday and that Hotel Theo was not far away. We thanked her and agreed to meet later at 5 pm at a certain Taverna which was open. Under direction we headed off to Hotel Theo and left the car in the Town Square. It was only a five-minute walk and we approached the Hotel Theo and walked up the marble steps to the two doors as the entrance to the foyer and check in desk.

The hotel looked new and so it turned out to be. There was no one to be seen in the foyer. Helen looked around and saw the bell on the check in desk and rang it. A noise was heard from the passage way leading to some rooms behind the desk and eventually a man appeared. He asked us what he could do for us and I replied that we were from Australia and were looking for some accommodation. He pondered this for a little while and then said that he hated Australians. Almost in the same breath he turned away and started to laugh. I was relieved and he said of course he loved Australians as he had just returned from Melbourne where he had once lived.

First things first, we filled in the register and he showed us our room. The hotel was due to re-open in a few days' time and the housekeeper was not due to start for two days. This was okay as our room was sheeted and the kitchen was nearby although not ready for guest's breakfasts. A trip to the supermarket would fix that.

Theo owned Hotel Theo and like a lot of hotels in the village it was named after the owner. Theo was a lovely man who became a good friend and I would go to him for advice about any business that I needed to do where I might be a little unsure of the Greek protocols. We swapped news of Australia and his brothers who were living in Melbourne where I think that the second largest population of Greeks reside outside mainland Greece. Theo was a meticulous man who looked like a classical Greek man from the bronzes adorning many museums. His hair was designed for him to appear as Alexander the Great and he knew it.

His hotel was about 10 months old and all the floors were marble as were many of the fittings in each room. He was very proud of his hotel and it was adorned in the style of himself. After bringing the car a little closer and fetching our bags, Helen and I had a beer with him in the foyer. It was a nice touch. Helen's name did not go unnoticed. It is Greek. So far so good.

Helen and I then repaired to the Taverna to meet up again with Sandy. On reaching the Taverna, Sandy was having coffee with some friends and she immediately beckoned us to join them. We sat down and after the introductions I ordered two beers for Helen and I and a beer for Nico who was there as well, having his evening drink before going back to work where he owned a bike and car rental business on the main street. He was open until 9 pm every day. I mentioned to Nico that we intended to buy two small motor bikes for ourselves and he gave me his business card.

After the frivolities and greetings around the group and our story was known. Sandy mentioned that two of her friends Constantino and his wife Effy had just built two villas near the airport and they were looking to rent them. Sandy made a phone call to Effy and we agreed to meet them here at the Taverna at 4 pm the following day. It sounds like this was all pre-ordained and so it turned out to be.

Chapter 3
House Hunting

We met with Constantino only, as his wife was busy, and he drove us out to the villas near the airport. During the car ride, Constantino mentioned that they also had a further home in the village of Pythagorio. It had not been lived in for about two years and was in a state where it needed painting inside and out and some of the fixtures needed to be renewed and fixed. We inspected the villas which were two bedrooms and new appliances. Either was suitable and Constantino was unsure about showing us the other house as it was a large contrast to the villas. I said that we would like to see the house as it was in town and a lot closer to the population.

The house was on a street off the main road into the village from Samos town. The street was not for cars as it was a series of long steps up to the house, being the last house on the left of the street. It was about 60 or 70 metres from the main road. It was old and dilapidated from the outside and as I turned around after the walk to the house I could see the Aegean Sea over the roofs of the homes below. We entered one of the two entrance doors to the kitchen and bathroom with the second bedroom down three steps off the kitchen.

To get to the living room and second bedroom you had to go out the door to the street and up a set of external stairs to the second entrance door. The living room had a window looking out to sea with the main bedroom behind and above the second bedroom down two levels. It was quirky but it was beautiful. Helen and I asked Constantino if we could paint the house inside and out and help with the repairs and we would then like to move in!

Constantino offered to buy the paint which was reasonable. We then returned to the Taverna which was not far away. We could have walked there but Constantino gave us a lift and all that there was to do was to agree on the weekly rent and sign a Rental Agreement. Effy was at the Taverna having a coffee. We sat down together and Constantino stated that the rent was $200.00 per month! This was not a lot of money.

This was February 1992 and we were renting our home in Chatswood Sydney for $280.00 per week. I agreed for the rent and Constantino ordered more coffee and a round of classes of Metaxa Brandy as well. There was no such thing as a Rental Agreement. A hand shake was offered and that was that. What a way to do business! We were happy and they were happy. The friendship was started. Incredible. This was the end of day four on Samos.

Before we left Australia I said to Helen that we would be living in Pythagorio in a house overlooking the Aegean Sea and it came true on day four of our odyssey. My statement to Helen was of course wishful thinking but here we were living the dream.

After Constantino and Effy left the Taverna, Helen and I were in a state of euphoria.

There was a lot of work to do. Apart from the painting the house we had to furnish the house and furniture shops were not around. We got into Greek time and put that aside as we ordered a souvlaki and Greek salad for dinner.

Greek food is good and we both loved it. It is basic and the Greeks know this. They also know that they live for a long time and the food is partly responsible for this. When we first arrived in Pythagorio for our sailing holiday some years ago, the menus for all the tavernas on all the islands were the same. The basic dishes were all priced as near the same cost. It was government controlled. Tourism is the main income for the islands and is the best product in the Mediterranean. The control however restricts any flair that a Taverna owner may wish to introduce. To get to fine dining one has to book a restaurant and there you will find food more in line with the people who wish to pay more for a better meal. Meanwhile, the tavernas do a great job.

Helen and I were a little dusty when we awoke the following morning in Theo's hotel. I told him of our fortune in finding a home to live in and he said that he was pleased as he knew the people who owned the house and they were fine people.

We then walked to the house to make a list of items that we would need to make the home liveable. It was quite a list. We then drove into Samos town, the capital of the island. A walking tour of Samos town produced another list of shops where we could fit out the house. We had lunch and returned to Pythagorio. A return to the Taverna which we knew only too well saw Sandy and some of her friends again. Our news of our home to be had reached Sandy and our trip to Samos town was almost not necessary. Sandy had anticipated our needs and had some information where we could buy furniture from some of her friends that was second hand. This was day five on the island.

During this day Helen was discussing the colours that she would like to paint our new home. She was thinking of Mediterranean colours and we were not too sure what that meant. We need not have worried about colours as the following morning when we arrived at the house to start with the preparation for painting I saw Constantino walking up the street with two large plastic containers. They were heavy and he had to stop once before arriving and announcing that the paint was here. Helen enquired about colours and Constantine said that the house had to be painted in white to match the neighbourhood and in fact the whole village. The only coloured buildings in the village were the shops and tavernas. It's the Greek thing you see and it works well.

We started the preparation for painting and finished the day at about 6 pm. It had been a long day and still more to do tomorrow. The second day of preparation finished at lunch time and after lunch I started to paint the external walls on an extension ladder. Helen started to paint inside the house. Painting is not one of my favourite activities and we were both glad to finish with the painting on day 8. In the previous days, some of Sandy's friends called by to deliver some of the second-hand furniture including a double bed frame. On day 9, we drove back into Samos town to buy a new mattress for the bed and other items of necessity.

On day 10 we left Hotel Theo and moved into our new home overlooking the Aegean Sea in beautiful Pythagorio on the island of Samos. We visited our favourite Taverna and saw some friends and of course celebrated our luck in doing what we had planned in 10 days.

Luck as I have always said is when opportunity meets ability, but in this case we had some friends to help us. It was somewhat surreal over the next few days as we tidied the house and realised that we were living in another country on the other side of the world. What joyous thoughts we had and great expectations for whatever we decided to do in the future. It was the first of many times when I thought that courage to do something different had shown me that it can be right and can be successful. We were in paradise and looking to meld in with the Greek community and appreciate their way of life. The Greeks have been around for a while and should teach us a thing or two.

The Greeks have given us Democracy from a period BC for about 150 years before it was shaded by autocracy and then revived some centuries later as the only form of governance. They have also given us theatre as the amphitheatres demonstrate throughout the islands and the Greek mainland. Many practical sciences were also introduced by the Greeks and none more so than by the Greek mathematician Pythagoras. He of the right-angled triangle equation and the town we were living in named after him. They also gave us Philosophy which they espoused from many years BC. They led the world to the formation of society as we know it now. So endeth the lesson.

We still had some more furniture to buy and this we did from the Gypsies from Romania who would travel from island to island selling low quality products. We bought a table and chairs for the street outside the kitchen door which became a very popular spot for our visitors to perch when they came to see us.

Our closest neighbour was across the street, about 10 metres away. It was a one-bedroom flat where the owners arrived about three weeks after we arrived to our new home. They were an older couple, Yann and Kaliope. Yanni [John] was very friendly and we soon would sit at our table and drink Ouzo and ice, sometimes with water. Yanni could speak seven languages and English was not his long suit.

Our discussion became very philosophical sometimes and his experience of living in America was not remembered with joy. His wife Kaliope brought us some Dolemadis one day on a plate for Helen and I to eat. There were about 20 Dolemadis which are made from a savoury rice and wrapped in Greek vine leaves. We sat outside and had them for dinner with some fries. Kaliope was pleased that we enjoyed this basic Greek fare and she became our supplier of this food type.

The hospitality was starting to become almost a daily occurrence and we fell into this way of life and responded in kind. We got into Greek time fairly quickly when I said to Helen that some urgent chore could wait until tomorrow. When tomorrow came, I forgot to do it and when Helen reminded me, I said that it could keep until tomorrow. There are no such things as duodenal or peptic ulcers in Greece!

We had of course left Australia early in the year to arrive in Samos to try to get a job in the hospitality industry. I had run a country hotel some years before and had some experience. Trevor Joyce who had sent us on one of his yachts out of Pythagorio years before told me to look up Gary at the Sail Inn which was a bar on the bay front. I had realised that we had arrived too early in the year for the start of the tourist season. I then regretted that I had not stayed in Australia for the wedding of my son Steven to his bride Nicole. I still have this regret.

I went to see Gary at the Sail Inn and we had coffee. He said that the Sail Inn would not open for a few weeks and that for the first two to three months, he would work it with his two permanent employees. No room for me there, however Gary and I became good friends. Together with his fiancée Mary, Helen and I had many a night out and I visited his family home one day on the other side of the island.

The family home was in the town of Karlovasi where his father Jack held court. Helen and I arrived at the home after a long motor bike journey as we had purchased two Piaggio 50 cc bikes recently second hand from Nico. Gary's mother greeted us as well and we were shown over the four-story home. It was ornately decorated with the explanation that it was the Italian Command Building for half the island during the Second World War. Samos was occupied during the war and with very little to do the Italians decided to practice their trades and build frescoes and implant the interior walls with design additions. The result was a superbly designed home with a classical appearance. Not too bad and it cost nothing. The Italians retired from the building in September 1943 when they decided that they did not like the war.

I visited Gary's family home once more, some months later, when Gary invited us to come with him to an 11th century holy shrine about one and a half hours walk into the rainforest at the western end of the island. We were sworn to secrecy as not too many people were supposed to know of its existence. Gary need not have worried about the secret as after the long trek, we were exhausted and could not have found it again on pain of death. It was a serene and beautiful place near a stream with the canopy of the rainforest shading the whole area. Candles were alight in the small building and Gary had still not been told who keeps the candles going. I still think of this experience as being part of our acceptance by the people of Samos.

We returned to our village of Pythagorio which did not have a rain forest anywhere to be found. Samos is one of the few, in fact it may be the only, islands where there is a rainforest at one end and the normal Greek landscape of dry ground and olive trees at the other end. A beautiful combination of topographies and climates.

About two weeks after we had settled into our new home we decided to explore the island and get to know all the good places to go to spend a day by the sea or go to in the mountains. I had heard of a small town called Manolates on the other side of the island. It was located at the top of a mountain and was not reached by bus as the corners in the road were too tight to allow a bus to go there. Either car or in our case Piaggio Italian motor bikes.

The trip to the turnoff to the mountain road leading to Manolates took about one hour. At the turnoff there was a small tavern and we stopped for a Greek Frappe which is an iced coffee. It was needed after the bike ride. We started up the mountain on our motor bikes and it was a very awkward road to travel. I could see the village of Manolates in the distance after about 10 minutes on the bikes. After that, the road became very steep and our bikes started to overheat with the power becoming less and less until we had to stop and let the bikes cool down. We had stopped on a bend and pushed the bikes to the side of the road. It was only then that we saw the valley below us in all its splendour.

It was called the Valley of the Nightingales, named after a bird species local to the area. Both sides of the valley were tiered many hundreds of years before for the growing of olive trees. The scene was so beautiful that I wished that I had brought my sketch book. The valley was large and we were so high up that a white cruise ship sailing past Samos to the Straights of Samos where Turkey is not far away, looked so small as to be a row boat. Both Helen and I were enchanted and looked at the valley for at least 20 minutes to see the homes located on the mountain sides and on the valley floor. I have not seen a more beautiful valley since.

Our bikes got us to the top of the mountain to the village of Manolates. We walked around this small village and into some of the shops where some tourist items were found but mainly pictures by artists and some small sculptures. It was time for lunch and we had seen a small cafe at the entrance to the village and decided that we would go there. An unusual menu for Greece was found and we ordered two omelettes and salad each.

They came out one meal at a time as the old lady in the kitchen could only cook one meal of this type at a time because her favourite small pan could only cook one omelette. This was told to us by her daughter. The wait was worth the experience. I do not know if it was the height above sea level or the different herbs, but that simple lunch remains in memory. We returned to our village and remonstrated with our friends at our favourite taverna.

Both Helen and I enjoyed swimming and there were beaches flanking the harbour and also near the resort of Hotel Dorissa near the airport. We headed there one day and dived into the Aegean Sea, perfect for Helen as the water temperature was just right with only small waves rolling in. The Greek teenage and older boys are always keen to show off their bodies and will play ball games for hours in front of girls to attract them. It was also good entertainment for us as we realised that the human form in Greek mythology is paramount and these young people were perpetuating their forebears.

The bar at the hotel beckoned at we repaired for lunch. We met a Dutch couple at the bar who were there on their honeymoon for two weeks. Anika and Rolf kept us entertained with their stories of their romance which was forbidden to them, as both being employed by the Police Department. The Police forbid any relationships between staff members. We saw them both two or three times before they left for home and we found the Dutch sense of humour as wonderful except for the time when Anika pushed one of the waiters into the pool as I looked on. The waiter was not impressed as he had to change of course to carry on with work. Anika told me later that she and Rolf shouted the waiter many drinks after his shift had finished.

With the prospect of work looking bleak, I decided that I may be able to get a job as one of the managers at the Hotel Dorissa Resort. I made an appointment with the General Manager and arrived to the appointment at 9 am one sunny morning. The General Manager was Georgo and he invited me to sit. He had my CV and it contained some Hospitality Industry experience when I had a hotel for two years and experience in managing city hotels. Whilst he could appreciate my credentials, the places where I would suit were filled. I then asked him if I could fill his roll when he went on leave and he smiled and said that if I could speak German he might consider this. The point being that the Hotel Dorissa was filled with guests from Germany. We bade farewell to each other. You do not know if you do not ask.

It was at this time that I took up again my sketching and watercolour painting. There are many scenes on any Greek island which would make a great watercolour painting. I picked up an old discarded wicker chair from the side of the road and tied it to my motor bike and then went to explore some sights to make sketches of them. It was great fun sitting in the middle of nowhere on my little wicker chair and returning home later to put the sketch in a folder to return later and produce the watercolour painting.

Seascapes were my favourite and I painted some fishing boats and a couple of the owners gave me some money for the paintings. After I had painted a scene of the harbourside and a particular taverna, I showed it to the owner of the taverna and he took it for the cost of about a dozen drinks. I had bought some books and magazines on watercolour painting and had learned a lot. The art of watercolour is the most difficult of all the mediums. I did however have the best materials with Windsor and Newton watercolour paint and three sable brushes.

There were other materials which I used but these were the basic ones needed. There were dozens of scenes to draw and my most unusual sketch at this time was of an old door. It was located by a long line of steps leading down from our home directly to the harbour port. I sat down one morning on a step adjacent to the door at about 9.30 am. After about 30 minutes, some of the young children in the area started to ask why I was drawing a silly door which had not been opened for many years. I said that it was because it was so old and worn out that it would make a good painting. It took me about another hour and I had finished the sketch. I added the watercolour and later on while showing my portfolio, I sold it for US $100.

I soon found out that the life of an artist, even a part time artist like myself, can be frustrating. One night, I went for a long walk to work out what colours I was going to use for a sketch depicting a lone soldier walking back from the front line in the First World War. This was after I sat looking at the sketch for about twenty minutes. When I finished the painting, it was kept by myself after many offers to buy it. It is still in my possession.

Time went by very quickly with painting activity and before long it was Easter approaching. A few days before Easter there was a parade of school children along the harbourside. They were dressed in the style of clothing worn by children hundreds of years before. They lined up in their age groups and walked along the harbour front as Helen and myself watched with delight. It was truly wonderful to see children dressed in very traditional clothing that were made by their parents or grandparents. Such occasions are common in the Mediterranean basin and are not seen in Australia as we are too young a country to have any real tradition.

It was at about this time that the weather was warming and I realised that I needed some summer shirts as I only had packed three or four. Our village had no menswear shop so I ventured to Samos town where I found one shop only. They sold workwear and a small selection of drab shirts. I did not buy anything and thought that I would write to my good friends Bob and Sue back in Australia and ask them to please send me a couple of shirts. They did this and I think that I almost wore them out by the end of year.

Easter in Greece is a more important event than Christmas. The celebrations in our village were very colourful and "He rose again from the dead three days later" was shortened to one day to fit with the schedule of events. It was in my view the only thing in Greece that happens quickly.

The traditional Yourty breakfast was taken on Easter Sunday and Helen and I were invited to a small Chapel a lot further up the mountain near our village. Here were prayers and the traditional breakfast eaten by all of us present. It was then time to descend to our village for more celebrations.

Tony [Adoni] Karides, Sandy's husband, had organised a party at a local Taverna and all the people that we knew were there and a few more beside. If there is one thing that the Greeks know how to do, it is to party and celebrate. We went on into the night and some of us carried on to the Sail Inn until 1 pm, when we were thrown out by Gary, the licensee.

Needless to say, Easter Monday was very subdued with another new friend named Karen coming by to offer a hair of the dog. It took the form of Canadian whisky and I tried a small amount but decided not to pursue the same course as yesterday.

Karen was a native North American with an Irish father and some European blood in her family history. She had left America with her husband Richard mainly because of the treatment of her fellow people. They were working in the village, Karen as a part time cleaner and Richard working for Budget Rent a Car. They were very happy together living in our small village and planned to eventually live in American Samoa. They eventually did this as I received a letter some seven or eight years later after I had returned to Australia. Karen would often visit us in the afternoon and bring some snacks for afternoon tea and I would supply the Ouzo or Retsina wine. Both of these drinks are an acquired taste with the Retsina wine a little bitter for most people. We all enjoyed it and the cost was not great as we were now purchasing as locals and not tourists.

After Easter Tony Karides received some good news. His uncle allowed the lease of a Taverna along the seafront to be given to Tony. As Tony was an excitable fellow anyway, it was an occasion for celebration. His wife Sandy was also very happy as they could both work in the taverna as the hours were long and the season very busy if you could present a good profile to the tourists. The

Taverna name was changed to The Iliad, the Homeric novel. Tony then needed to furnish the Taverna and decide on the colour and pattern for the large awning cover under which most of the customers would sit.

I thought I would like to help Tony with his choices and we went for a walk along the seafront to look at all the other Tavernas and their choice of colours and patterns for chair coverings and awning covers. Straight out I suggested a green theme as a colour as it conjured up a coolness for the hot days to come. The pattern should be floral to appeal to the ladies. To my surprise Tony let me pick the colour and pattern and he then ordered the chairs and awnings to suit my selection with a little help from Sandy. They arrived some weeks later and when set to the Taverna they were indeed very good to look at by anyone passing.

Throughout that season the Iliad Bar/Taverna was the most successful in the village. I noticed one morning when a bus arrived very early on the seafront that most of the tourists headed to the Iliad Taverna in preference to all the others. I still reckon that it was the colour green that did the trick!

It was now time to go to Turkey as part of our Visa requirement where we could not stay longer than three months before we had to leave Greece and visit another country before we could return and carry on as before. We boarded the ferry to Kuşadasi in Turkey and booked accommodation at a B & B operated by an Australian couple. Kuşadasi is not far from Ephesus where there is a Roman amphitheatre and a place of interest for tourists. We decided to go the market in Kuşadasi as we had heard that it is unique. The market was quite an experience as you could buy genuine antiquities with a Turkish Government guarantee to any kind of spice that had ever been made. In area, the market was advertised as the biggest in the Mediterranean and I have no doubt.

We got to the market at about 10 am and stopped for lunch at about 1 pm. Then we traversed the rest of the market and returned to the B&B to go to a local bar and rest. Talking to some acquaintances from the ferry we learned that they had gone to Efusis very early by bus and had walked a long way that day. They were exhausted and the four of us had quite a few drinks before dinner that night.

A one-night stay was all that was needed for the Visa bit and we went to bed that night for what I thought would be a sound night's sleep. How wrong I was. At about 2 am in the morning, the Turkish religious chanting started throughout the city and was amplified by speakers on telegraph poles everywhere. Charming! I walked onto the little balcony from the room and at about the same time another chap appeared on his small balcony. We both agreed that a pair of wire cutters was needed to cut the power to this whining noise. The chanting stopped after about 15 minutes only to start up again at about 5 am. Marvellous.

We were all a little tired when we got onto the ferry to return to Samos and our little village of Pythagorio. We did this trip again for those of us on this Visa status. It was however another experience of so many to come.

We had gathered at this time quite a few friends and a lady named Carol had an uncle who made the best Bazouki music instruments in Greece. His workshop was located in one of the main streets of the village, I had noticed it in my wanderings around the village. Carol introduced me to Stavros in his workshop. He stopped his work and prepared a cup of Greek coffee for himself and me. Now, Greek coffee is another acquired taste as the bottom third of the cup is like sand which is to be avoided unless you can rinse your mouth at the end of the cup.

The workshop was a bit of a mess. Not so the finished product. Stavros showed me all the machinery needed to make a Bazouki which is similar to a guitar. Most of the Bazoukis that he was currently making were for the tourist trade and Greeks who wanted to learn how to play this quintessentially Greek instrument. He earned a good income from this but what gave him the status of the best Bazouki maker in Greece was the three or four Bazoukis that he made each year for sale in Athens on the world market. They were made with a red wood which he shaped and then glued with a secret formula for the glue. He showed me one of the near finished special Bazoukis and it felt like I was holding a Stradivarius violin. A beautiful product.

Later that week Helen and I attended a Taverna where Stavros played his fine instrument for all those attending. The sound was superb and the dancing followed. We thought we were very lucky to be there.

It was April 1992 and the tourist season was just starting in big numbers. With our local Iliad Bar/ Taverna and all the others in full swing, it was a joy to go to the Harbourside every night. German tourists were the main nationality as they filled the Dourissa Hotel where I had enquired about some work. It was to be some time before I met one or two of the German tourists as they tended to keep company with each other.

The weather continued to be fine with the Meltemi wind there each day from the north west. Many of the prevailing winds in the Mediterranean are named and apart from the Meltemi in our area, some of the other areas named the winds as the Mistral, the Tramontana, the Sirocco and the Levante which blows through the Straits of Gibraltar. The cloudless skies lasted for almost five months and one morning in late July we all noticed a cloud in the sky. An odd-looking thing after so long and a good reason to have another party.

During this time Sandy Karides mentioned that the local swimming coach could not teach the children this year as he had obligations at home with his uncle who was ill and needed attention. When he finished work each day he would normally meet the children and do the swimming lessons. I volunteered to do the lessons as I had been taught by Don Talbot in Australia who was at one time the Australian Coach for our Olympic team.

Instead of the Aegean Sea as the place for the lessons, the owner of his recently completed hotel said that we could use the pool at his hotel. It was only a couple of kilometres out of town situated on a hill overlooking the Straits of Samos, looking across to Turkey. It was a beautiful hotel and the pool was perfect. The initial rollup of kids numbered eight or nine. Within a couple of weeks, I had 14 kids which was plenty. One of the little girls was named Elenie who became one of my favourites. She learned freestyle quickly as did a few others. The Samos Championships were coming up in a couple of months and I had some good freestyle kids and a few who wanted to do breaststroke.

We continued on once a week, sometimes twice a week on request, and Elenie just got better. I always had two or three parents to do the translation and the father of Elenie came a couple of times to watch his daughter and translate for all the kids. He was a doctor and the head surgeon on the island. He gave up more of his time as we were nearing the Championships. I spoke to him about Elenie's habit of starting a race with a deep dive from the edge of the pool instead of a shallow dive. You see Elenie liked diving but she was always behind when she emerged on top of the water in a race of one or two laps. Her father explained what I was trying to say and occasionally she would start a race with a shallow dive and of course beat all the others.

The Samos Swimming Championships arrived one morning at the school pool. My kids were all primed and one of the first races was a breaststroke swim which was won by one of my kids. One gold medal for us. Time came for Elenie's final of the freestyle. Small blocks were at the start of each race. Elenie had not started from blocks before. When the gun went off for the start Elenie of course dived in and went deeper that her competitors. When she emerged she was second last and she then started to swim as I had taught her. She finished second and got silver. When she was handed the silver medal her father and I shed a tear. She was also the youngest swimmer in that race. The look in her eyes when she ran to her parents was gold.

We only got those two medals at that meeting. I was so glad that I was able to do the coaching and the coach who I replaced came up to me with a big hug! How do you buy that! Another celebration that night at the Iliad.

Just after this our first visitors arrived from Australia. We must have started something as Karl and Ros arrived and I picked them up from the airport when they informed me that they were on their way to England to work hopefully in the computer industry. They stayed for about two weeks. We took them everywhere as Karl hired a car from Nico. We went to Manolates and the Valley of the Nightingales and had to wait for a while as lunch was omelettes and salad from the taverna on our first visit to Manolates. The lady remembered us from our first visit and we returned with other visitors from Australia.

One morning as Karl and I were walking to the harbour, with the fruit trees showing plenty of fruit, Karl was playing his Game Boy game on the palm sized item of electronics. It then dawned on me that even adults can be captured by this despite being in this place.

Late one afternoon, Karl, Ros, Helen and myself boarded a Greek fishing boat to go to a taverna for dinner and the show. The taverna was located by a bay further along the coast and by the time that we arrived, having drinks on the way, we prepared ourselves for the show. The dinner show was performed by three brothers who danced and did acrobatics for over an hour. The highlight of the show was when one of the brothers, who was also the skipper of the fishing boat which took us there, kneeled down and took one of the small dining tables between his teeth and started to dance across the floor with the table resting on his body. The table still had a bottle and two or three glasses on it. What an effort! He could have gone to the Moulin Rouge in Paris with that trick! False teeth? No.

We returned to our village at about 1 am and immediately went for a swim in the Aegean Sea. Some night! Three days later, Karl and Ros left for England where we would catch up with them later in the year.

***

It was time for Helen and myself to get some sort of a job to help with the expenses. It had to be part time and necessarily in the hospitality industry. It had to be "off the books" as work for us was not allowed. We both got jobs as the English-speaking people in a taverna in my case and a cash register operator at a restaurant in Helen's case.

I was a waiter at a taverna in Posidonio on the shores of the island and about a 25-minute bike ride from the village. It was great fun and the other waiter was Greek whose name was Thermos. It was busy and we shared the workload equally. Our pay was to split the total lunch or dinner bill from the customers as our share of 11% of the total. The pay was good by comparison as I was to find out.

After about a week, I had an accident on my motor bike and sprained my ankle. I arrived at the taverna but it was clear that I could not get around quickly enough to do the job properly. I had to say goodbye and Thermos gave me a big squeeze as I left. I returned home and put my feet up as I was advised to do.

Helen's job was at a Chinese restaurant at the cash register. The reason that she got the job was that nobody at the restaurant could understand the new cash register and its functions as it was new technology. Helen looked over the machine and soon understood its workings even though the numbers were spelt in Greek…ena, dio, tessara, etc. For her, it was a happy time as this Chinese restaurant was the only restaurant in the village that was not serving Greek food. The cook was Dutch and an alcoholic. He started work at 9 in the morning for the lunch preparation and drank all day until 8 pm when he would leave the restaurant almost legless and stager to a bar. The rest of the kitchen staff were fine for the menu orders as the Dutch cook had left all the foods in large containers already cooked.

I filled in for Helen on some nights when she wanted to do something social and the combination a Chinese restaurant on a Greek island with a drunk Dutch cook was at times hilarious.

The local newspaper advertised a position vacant for an assistant to a short order cook at a local hotel. I arrived for the interview at the Hotel Athos and was told that the hours were from 7 am until 11 pm at night with breaks between breakfast and lunch and lunch and dinner. That was a 14-hour day with very poor pay compared with the taverna work which was double the pay. I politely declined the job offer and returned home to find Yannis and Kaliope having a drink at our outside table with Helen.

Yannis told us that they were expecting two people from the United States who were going to rent their small one-bedroom house opposite our house. He asked that I show them into the house and explain a few of the household fittings, being stove, washing machine etc. It was my pleasure and a few days later, husband and wife arrived from New York city for a two-week holiday in paradise. They were both stock brokers and I knew that profession from my experiences when working at 3M in Australia where a number of my customers were stock brokers who would age in appearance a lot in the years that I knew them.

I did not see them until day three of their stay when they were playing checkers on their small table on the street in front of their house. They told me that they hired a car and went to Samos town and a beach. They were not best happy that the roads were very bumpy and they were glad when they could leave the car when back at their home for the holiday. Another complaint came when they told me that it was very noisy on the harbourside at night.

At the end of the first week they returned the keys to me and left for a return to New York. They must have been extremely stressed to not be at ease in Pythagorio, our beautiful village. Perhaps they should have booked in to a New York hotel and drew the blinds and ordered videos delivered each day. To each his own.

Greek People and the Economy.

Both Helen and myself loved the Greek people when we first visited to sail for two weeks a few years before. This time around nothing changed and we made fast friends with about a dozen Greek people who we would continue to correspond with for many years after we eventually returned to Australia.

A good percentage of the Greek people, who we met, would often enquire if we knew their brother Georgo or sister Maria in Melbourne which has the largest population of Greek people outside mainland Greece. The Greek people have a sense of enjoyment of life which would tend to line up with our own Australian joy of life. Tomorrow can look after itself for today we will be happy. They are welcoming and gregarious which is wonderful to experience and to be around.

They are very family orientated and often the old parents of a family would welcome their children who got married to come and live with them. It is an obligation of the Greek family to look after their older members of their family. It is a closeness that would not suit some peoples, but it works for the Greeks. When a family member has to go to hospital the family needs to supply some of the bed linen and most of the meals. In this respect, it could be close to a third world experience but it works.

Sometimes the family obligations can work in a not so favourable way. I noticed a rather attractive lady over a period of months and she was always alone until she reached a taverna. After some time, she would leave on her own. A friend told me that it is a shame that she would probably never be married as she was looking after her aged mother and would be doing this until her mother passed away. Hence she was not a prospect for a man to marry unless he wanted to live with his mother-in-law. This situation was repeated in the village many times and I would feel a little sorry for some of the ladies in this situation as some of them were very presentable.

After some months my painting activities were know as I would head out some days with my little wicker chair strapped to my Piaggio 50cc motor bike to sketch some scene, usually a seascape. Although one day I sketched a small house on a hillside with a mountain in the background. In front of the house was a small wall and this featured in the eventual watercolour painting. I showed Yannis and Kaliope the painting and asked how old the wall may have been.

Yannis told me that it would be about 2500 years old as it was part of a boundary line and fortification when the island was divided into areas of control by the inhabitants. The village of Pythagorio was one of the larger areas and was originally the capital commerce area and the first capital of the island. Some wall! I named the painting "The Wall" and it was eventually sold.

During this time, Dianne, the wife of an artisan on the island asked if I would like to meet one of the most famous artists in Greece. I of course said yes and with the proper protocols an appointment was made for me to visit his studio at 10 am in a few days' time.

His name was Aristateli, although his artist name was Soulenase. I arrived on time at his villa which was located a couple of kilometres out of the village on the coast. His studio was downstairs in the two-level villa. As I entered, I was introduced by Dianne. He was busy arranging some of the paintings to be worked on that day. His painting theme for this particular year was the images of waves. Sea and ocean waves with some coastlines present for some paintings in oil colour. The previous year's paintings were of the human form. Rather a contrast from year to year.

Aristateli allowed me to look around the studio whilst he started work. He had about seven or eight paintings to work on that day. I remarked that it may be unusual for any artist to work on this number of paintings at the one time. He agreed but said that if you choose one theme for the year then the brush strokes and lines are similar to paint even though the finished images were totally different for each painting. In this way, he could paint more images and earn more money. This was a great rationale.

About two months later, I attended his first exhibition for the year in our village. It was held in the ground floor of one of the large hotels and visitors from Athens were present. These were gallery owners and collectors. The exhibition was a success and most of the paintings were marked as sold as we left to repair to a taverna at harbour side.

After drinks were served to about a dozen of us at a table, I found myself sitting next to Ari who was the National Marketing Manager, in Greece, for BMW cars. What a jovial fellow he was and his expense account copped a pounding that night as he insisted on buying drinks out of turn! Sales of BMW cars were going well that year except for the seven Series BMW which was the top of the line. His budget for the seven Series was only eight for the year and they had only sold three so far.

Ari was not concerned as he was to attend Aristateli's major exhibition in Athens in a few months where he knew that there would be plenty of well healed Greeks to buy a seven Series BMW. Ari was switched on in marketing activities.

The season was rolling on and during this time I noticed a lot of hotels, pensions and tavernas being built around the island. I mentioned this to Tony Karides one day and he explained why this was happening. The Greek government had offered to go 50/50 with the cost of building for the tourist industry which was and still is a substantial part of the Greek Gross Domestic Product. I have always thought that the Greek islands to be the best product in the Mediterranean and obviously the Greek Government thought so as well. I t was a bold step.

What the Government did not figure in the forecast was the nature of their own people to abuse this financial help. According to Tony many invoices were written by the owners of the buildings for work which was not in fact done. The budget blew out in Treasury and all financial help ceased some months later. There were plenty of owners who went broke over this. But of course, they had only themselves to blame. Tony blamed the government for their stupidity and one would have to agree.

Almost the opposite behaviour by the Greek community in our village happened to me at this time. My Piaggio bike was stolen from where I would leave it each night. I went to the Police Station to report the theft and I knew the policeman who wrote down the report. He was surprised and embarrassed by this theft. He promised to put the report out there. At the taverna that night, many people were embarrassed as well by the theft.

In Greece, you can do anything in business but to steal is a no no! After a day or so, there must have been a dozen people looking for my bike. After four days, the policeman who I had reported to, came and said that the bike had been found by an old sheep herder near the Army Post about 20 kilometres out of town. It was put down to a soldier serving the mandatory two years' service who stole the bike. It was nobody in the village. Sighs went round and the integrity of the village was restored. Go figure.

Some of the tourists to the island were Danish and Swedish girls. For the Greek teenagers and men, this was very nice as they were mostly beautiful women on holidays. Relationships were started and when the girls left there were tears on both sides. Promises were made and a love was meant to endure as each said that they would visit the other soon. One of the Greek chaps at the beach bar however told me that most of the romances were doomed as it is incumbent that Greek boys/men are obliged to marry Greek girls. This is traditional as their fathers will withhold any financial help if they do not. I saw this realisation on the faces of a lot of chaps. Moreover, the Greek men are rather chauvinistic and this does not sit well with most women. It is not so much an unattractive trait as Greek men think it is their life's duty to look after their women to an extent not seen in most societies.

Tony Karides, the owner of the Iliad Bar, and I would have a heart to heart about once a week. The Iliad was going well and it needed to because he was paying about 33% interest on his loan to set up the bar. I found this hard to believe and he showed me the papers and sure enough it was true. He also said that a saving account would pay 27% interest. This was outrageous interest, but true. The only catch was that you could only withdraw 10% of your savings in any one-year period. It was a great deal if you planned to stay and live in Greece…what a bargain!

So the Greek economy staggered on. Eventually of course the economy and the Treasury imploded. Many reasons were put forward including the retirement age of 60. Things had to change and the pain suffered by many was unfair due to poor government.

More visitors.

Karl and Ros who had stayed with us earlier had put out the word back in Australia that friends of ours should come visit and stay and abuse our hospitality…just joking of course.

John and Louisa came and arrived one day soon after we saw our first cloud, after four and a half months of cloudless skies. It was in August and the weather was hot. We took them on a boat to the island of Chios to watch our Samos island team of soccer players play. The team was on the boat with us and we arrived to take up accommodation in a pension near the boat wharf. That evening, we watched the promenade of people along the waterfront. What a marvellous Greek tradition this is for those of us looking on.

People of all ages were simply walking and socialising with each other and dressed in their finest. Their clothing was mostly Italian and the Italians do for clothing what the French do for cooking. There was music at the waterfront and we all got up to dance to Zorba.

Chios is not a big tourist island and I suspect this suits the locals. It was an island used in ancient times as a hunting ground for the Kings and Queens of the Ottoman, Roman, Phoenician and Greek empires. Hunting lodges were built and some still exist although nobody would tell us where they were.

The following day was the Soccer game which was the final of the competition played at 1 pm in the heat. Samos lost a close game and we boarded the boat to return to Samos. Most of the players were upset at the loss and took it out on alcohol. They abused each other and the coach as well. I had a talk with the coach at the deck railing when he escaped from the fracas. He said that all would be well with the team when we reached our village. He was exactly correct as all players were all over each other with bonhomie. An interesting trip.

Arriving home at about 1 am in the morning, we all went to bed and slept well. John, Louisa, Helen and I went to the beach the next day to chill out. A taverna near the beach was chosen for lunch. We sat near six people from France who were discussing the menu. The first French people that we had come across. We ordered some drinks and about 20 minutes the French people were still discussing the menu. In my limited understanding of their language, I discerned that they would like one meal cooked this way and another that way. This was okay for the French but does not work in Greece. I thought that I would assist and walked over to their table and introduced myself. The gist of my message was that no matter what they ordered it would come to them in the Greek style of cooking. It was good food and when in Rome etc. They laughed well and one of the ladies who could speak English thanked me and winked much to her husband's surprise. They enjoyed their meal and as we left they were ordering more wine and liquors. I had told them to avoid the Greek coffee like the plague.

A strange day.

A couple of days later, we took our visitors to the beach near the Airport. The water temperature was good and the water shallow for about 50 metres. We hired the beach lounges and umbrellas and settled. I pointed that behind us was a stream coming out of the mountain. People would come from all over Europe to sit in this muddy stream and cover themselves with the mud. This mud had an apparent magical quality with its effect on your skin.

We walked over to the stream and there were four or five people covered in mud and sitting on the bottom of the stream, about 30 cms deep. When they arose to move to the rocks to dry the mud, they all fell over as the mud caused a slippery exit from the stream. One chap tried three or four times to get out and gave up. He called to his wife that he would probably be here for the rest of his life and to say hello to the kids when she got home. Exiting this stream was very undignified and as these people were English, it was more so.

The four of us laughed with the fellow who had given up and he asked his wife if could she go and get a can of beer for him as he may as well try to enjoy himself with his present position—untenable. All present were laughing when one of the wives sitting on one of the drying rocks slipped off and landed on her bottom. Modesty went out the window as she tried to regain her spot on the rock. She succeeded after a few minutes as the chap in the stream called for another beer. We returned to our sun lounges and as far as I know the chap in the stream may still be there.

Lunch was back in town at the edge of the harbour in a taverna called Costas Taverna. We took up a table on the beach side in front of the taverna in the sun. The four of us had a pretty good sense of humour and what we had just seen primed it. Drinks were served as we were not in a hurry for lunch. We were in Greek time. After about an hour and a half, I looked at the salt shaker on the table and started to laugh. John asked why and I said the salt shaker had a funny shape. He then started to laugh and our wives joined in.

Our laughter then became uncontrollable, to the extent that John and I fell off our chairs onto the ground which we pounded with our hands. During all this laughter, Costas's son came over to see what was happening and why. I tried to explain but it made no sense. The point being, we were still laughing and pointing to the salt shaker. The father came out to see what was going on and his son just shrugged his shoulders. We then learned that the father's son was also named Costas and his grandfather was the cook who was also named Costas.

There were far too many Costas people here and we kept laughing but for a different reason. When the father asked his son about the wine and did he mix it up with the wine with a bit of fandango in it, we just fell off our chairs again. When one of us could speak about five minutes later, the words were, "You're kidding, but I'm coming back here again! I think it was Louisa."

We were eventually served lunch about 2.30 pm and we all had sore tummies from the merriment. Soon, the afternoon drinkers started to arrive and I pointed out to John and Louisa that the mountain far of would produce a phenomenon which looked like a fire gaining the heights of the mountain on its far side. The glow started and with the afternoon heat mist the impression of a fire was there.

At this point another group of English tourists sat down at a table next to us on the shore. The immediately pointed to the apparent fire on the mountain. John, who was English born, commented that the fire fighters would soon have it out. Sure enough about 15 minutes later the phenomenon or fire stopped and the English tourists remarked that the fire fighters were excellent in their job. We could not stop our laughter any longer.

John eventually explained the particular phenomenon and invited them to try it on some other tourists another day.

Nobody would ever know why the laughter started that day and why it went on for so long about nothing. Whenever I see an odd shaped salt shaker I smile.

An Offer. One day I walked down the outside stairs of our house to the kitchen and Yannis was across the way doing a little exterior painting to the one bed flat. He turned and invited Helen and myself to lunch at his home on the mountainside the following day. I accepted after checking with Helen.

The following day, Yannis was at his flat early to finish the painting and we left home with Yannis to walk to his home. It took us about 20 minutes as we walked around the mountainside rather than straight up the climb. Yannis and Kaliope's home was near new and styled as a rustic place with a large veranda flanking the length of the home and looking over the Samos Straight. This separates Samos from Turkey which lies from three to five miles from Samos. We were elevated about 600 feet from sea level and the view was truly of great beauty as the coast of Turkey was mountainous in that area and surrounded by the "wine dark sea" as the Greeks refer to the Aegean Sea.

After lunch the four of us sat on the veranda and watched the ships making passage in an east and west direction through the Samos Straight. Helen and I thanked our hosts and left at about 4 pm to go to the Iliad Bar to join our friends for the afternoon goss.

A few days later, Yannis asked me if I would help him move some furniture in his home and of course I agreed and we went there about a week after the lunch at Yannis' home. We went in a more direct way this time and stepped over a waist height wall that was about 2500 years old. It was a boundary line for the land owned by Yannis. He picked a fresh fig from a tree and cut and peeled it to offer it to me. It tasted great and I sat on the very old wall and wondered if someone else may have done the same thing when building the wall so long ago.

After moving a couple of pieces of furniture which I thought Yannis could have moved by himself, we went outside for a walk down the hillside and the reason for my visit to the home of Yannis became clear. As we walked, Yannis explained that this large piece of land that he owned, overlooking the Samos Straight, would one day see another home built on it. It would be his son's home as he would be returning from his job in the United States to settle in Samos and in particular on this land in Pythagorio. There was plenty of room on this hillside and after Yannis showed me the other boundaries we stopped walking and Yannis turned and said that he would like to offer me to buy a piece of land on his plot and build and be a neighbour.

This offer just stopped me. I did not know what to say. I knew that I had just been offered something that very few non-Greeks would be offered. To say that I was emotional is an understatement. I got on well with Yannis and Kaliope and this offer was a testament to that. I am sure that Yannis asked about Helen and myself in the village, which of course is what an astute person would do. I had a tear in my eye when I said to Yannis that I was overcome with the offer and that I would speak to Helen about it. I stood on the hillside and took in the view again, looked at Yannis and smiled, shook his hand and walked down the mountain to think of the offer.

This was at a time when we had been living in Pythagorio about seven months. Whilst we had a large circle of friends our discussions of house prices and areas, which is common in Australia, had not been featured as there were no Real Estate Agents in the village and in the main town of Samos I had not seen any. There must have been some agents about but so far any knowledge of the value of a piece of land that was offered to myself was pure speculation.

Helen and I discussed the offer which was exciting in the thoughts surrounding a permanent move to Pythagorio. Eventually we agreed that we had to move to England to earn an income to perhaps return to Pythagorio to live one day. After explaining this to Yannis, he understood and said that he was in no hurry to populate his mountainside. When we returned the land would still be there.

It was a great compliment to be offered this and it said to Helen and myself that we had been accepted by the Greek community and that our ability to assimilate into a culture and country was very good. Of course Greeks and Australians had always got on well and this stamped that.

More Greek Customs.

After returning from Turkey one day where we had to go to comply with Visa requirements, we went to a newly opened bar in Samos town for early dinner. It is the custom in Greece to be heavy handed with the spirits when opening a new bar. Some good music was playing and I asked Louisa, who was visiting, for a dance as Helen could not dance Jive to rock 'n roll. Louisa and I danced OK and jived so well that the owner asked us to return in two days for the Saturday dance session and he would pay us via food and drink. We did this but could not take up the offer to perform regularly as Louisa was returning to Australia. We enjoyed the new opening and the custom of generosity with the drinks.

With the family unit being so important to the Greeks, when one of the very old family member dies she or he may be buried in a substantial cemetery. There was one such place of burial in the village. It overlooked the sea and one side of the cemetery facing the sea was built as a stone wall with an archway some 17 feet high. I got the message that a family was invited to rest their loved ones here by invitation from a council of elders.

Helen and I were invited to two such burials which took place in the evening. The cemetery was only about 150 by 250 feet and invitees only were allowed. The decorations were placed perfectly and the lighting was such as to make the scene quite surreal. It was a celebration for the people there with the children in traditional clothing to add to the custom. Drinks were had and each of us left in a glow and I am not talking about the lighting.

We repaired to the Sail Inn taverna operated by Gary who greeted us and suggested that we join a group where some of our friends were seated. There were about 15 of us and at this time in 1992 and the topic turned to the Olympic

Games and the soon announcement of the city which would win the bid to host the 2000 Games. As Gary was a Greek Australian, he knew that Sydney had bid for the 2000 Games along with Berlin, the capital of the new Germany which had now been united from the previous East and West Germany before the wall was pulled down in 1989.

There was a very tall German fellow in the group and he assured all of us that Germany would win the bid as they had Lufthansa and Mercedes behind them. I of course disputed this as I knew that our bid with Sydney was prepared very well. The person who chaired our bid was Rod McGeoch who was also Chairman of the College of Law in New South Wales. He was a sports "nut" and could tell you who ran third in the first 200-metre heat of the 1952 Olympic Games in Helsinki. He also happened to be a great organiser of the herculean effort to prepare this bid. The computer software that they designed for the bid was also used in 2004 in Greece.

After listening to the arrogance of this German chap I proposed a bet that Sydney would win the bid against Berlin. I suggested that Gary hold the money which could be paid to either him or myself. This chap did not take up this bet! Just as well for his wallet as I wanted to bet $100.00. We all know the result as announced by Juan Antonio Samaranche.

Greeks and Australians have fought together in World War Two. Their comradery is well-known and when a Greek hero from the Second World War was due in the village I was invited to meet him. The occasion was a remembrance ceremony for an event which happened on the island of Samos during 1943 when the island was inhabited and controlled by first the Italians and then the Germans after the Italians asked for and were granted an Armistice by the Allies in September 1943.

This Italian capitulation created some problems for the German High Command and reprisals were carried out in many places where the Italians were to be found. One such place was the island of Samos and in particular in the village of Pythagorio.

The ceremony was for remembrance of the killings of many Italian soldiers and Greek people in different places on the island. Some of the Greek soldiers at the time had formed themselves into a Parachute Regiment after escaping to British held Egypt after the Germans had invaded mainland Greece. One soldier had parachuted onto Samos during 1944 to help the Partisans fight the Germans who were in command of the island. I met this soldier who was dressed in his uniform with the Parachute Insignia on his battledress. Stavros was a tall and sturdy fellow with an iron handshake. After the ceremony, he was feted around town by many villagers and no doubt the conversations lasted well into the night.

Leaving Samos Island.

We had arrived in Samos early in 1992. We intended to leave in late September to go to Helen's sister's wedding in New York and then return to England to get jobs. Before leaving Samos I was due to meet a famous Greek painter who had a studio here in the village. One of my lady friends knew him well and told him that I was a painter and that I would greatly appreciate visiting his studio to meet him. This took some arranging as he was quite popular and he was busy getting ready for his first showing of his paintings for 1992.

Soulenaise was his artistic name but I met him with his real name of Aristateli. His studio was located on the first floor of his home which overlooked the Aegean Sea. He really did not need any more inspiration than that. His housekeeper showed me into the studio and I waited to meet him as he was painting a large seascape.

Aristateli turned around and smiled and extended his hand. He immediately had my friendship forever. He told me that his theme for this year was the sea and wave shapes. I looked around the studio and could see 20 to 30 paintings all completed. Some others were still to be completed and this should take a few more days to do. The theme of the previous year was the human form and I noticed a few paintings hanging high on the mezzanine floor of this genre.

I asked Aristateli why he chose only one theme each year for the collection. He replied that he chose one theme each year as it was easier to repeat the brush strokes for many paintings which were similar and which he would undertake at the one time in studio. Also the colours would be similar for the many different paintings in oil colour that were painted in any one period, be it a morning or a week. In other words, it made sense for one theme to dominate the effort in order to produce more paintings in a given period. These are the best reasons.

I understood Aristateli's rationale as my paintings were mostly of seascapes containing similar shapes and colours. I left his studio feeling rather buoyant and went home to my watercolour paintings.

During that week I noticed a sailing yacht come into the small harbour of the village. It tied up stern to, on the town key. I approached the yacht and met the owners who were flying a small Australian flag on the port shrouds. This meant that there were Australians on board.

Pete and Paula were the owners and they certainly had a story to tell about how they came to be in the Greek Islands in August 1992.

Their boat was an Island Packet 42, which was American made. It was a ketch which Pete converted to a single masted Bermudan sloop after the purchase. They lived in the suburb of Newport just north of Sydney and bought the boat from a broker in Pittwater which is part of the northern beaches of Sydney. I knew the area well as I grew up at Narrabeen which is part of the northern beaches. Helen and I were amazed to meet Pete and Paula as they were to meet us.

The four of us had a lot to discuss. Over the next week this was done and Pete and Paula's story goes something like this.

After buying the boat, they decided to sail to far north Queensland and of course stop at various places on the way. This took some months and after reaching Cairns they decided to try to make Darwin. They spoke to their grown-up children often and told them of their next port of call each time.

When they arrived in Darwin they spoke to their children who thought that they might be heat struck and to start to sail back to home waters. Pete and Paula were experienced sailors and decided to sail to Sri Lanka. This was a long passage which they made and they then decided that they could sail to the Mediterranean Sea. This they did sailing north through the Suez Canal and into the Aegean Sea and the small port town of Pythagorio on Samos.

All through this their children were demanding their return as they thought that their mother and father had finally lost it! That was not the case. They were simply having too much fun and adventure. It was their intention to stay until the following year and sail across the Mediterranean Sea, then sell the boat and go back home.

Pete and Paula were great company for that week and on the day before they left to go on further west, we went for a day sail. At one time, I sat down and said aloud, "I wonder what I would have to do to live like this?"

Pete answered back, "Well, first you need to buy a boat."

I did not know it then but those words were to become quite prophetic!

Our last visitors from Australia were Helen's parents. They had come to see why we had left perfectly good jobs and moved to a place where English was not the first language.

I picked up Jim and Jean from the airport in a borrowed car and stopped at our street where the walk uphill was about 100 metres. Both large bags were taken by myself and my in-laws were happily ensconced in their bedroom just before lunch. Helen had prepared lunch and we sat outside in our street and regaled them with our domestic, social and work life since our arrival.

This was a lot of fun for us to tell them and after two hours we still had not finished. However it was time for Jim and Jean to have the afternoon nap and recover from the traveling. They slept for some time and they stirred at about seven o'clock. Jean mentioned that it was late for them to now have dinner somewhere and I mentioned that they were in Greek time and dinner would be somewhere at a Taverna along dockside about 9 pm.

Jim and Jean were English and at dinner Jim wore a shirt and tie as is the English custom and Jean wore a conservative dress. Such are the English habits even in a semi paradise with relaxation marked on everyone's manner. They enjoyed their stay with us with the highlight being an evening sail to Posidonio for dinner.

Posidonio is a small bay on the southern side of the island of Samos. It is about a 50-minute sail from Pythagorio. We all went in a Greek fishing boat owned by a Greek fisherman who was part of the "Three Brothers" entertainment trio who would perform that night at the Taverna.

The night was balmy on the wine dark sea with almost a full moon and the reflection on the water from the coastal homes giving a wonderful effect. We had a drink or two on the way and by the arrival time we were all relaxed and ready for the night's entertainment. After the seating, we ordered some wine and beer. It was about two hours later that our food arrived and I said to Jim and Jean that tonight would be one to remember and this is how it went!

Much wine and beer was drunk by us and by the music had us up and dancing to the bazouki Greek music and joining the groups on the dance floor for the circular jig which was our groups contribution to the traditional Greek dance. It, sort of, looked like Greek dancing and about a dozen of us laughed at the end of the song, Zorba the Greek. Some Greek patrons congratulated us on our effort. They then got up on the floor as we retired and showed us how to do it. We clapped them and the bonhomie was complete.

Our joy through the night suggested to Helen's parents that they understood why we had returned to the Greek island where we had first sailed some years before. It was a simple and magical night and finished with one of the "Three Brothers" dancing and approaching the edge of the dance floor and picking up one of the tables on the edge of the dance floor with his teeth and balancing it as he stood upright with one of the legs of the table balanced on his gut. He completed the dance and of course we all stood and applauded for some time. He could take that effort to the Moulin Rouge in Paris!

We returned to our village on the same fishing boat some two hours later with same skipper who just happened to be the Greek chap who had just entertained us with the table dancing. The boat stopped about half way back with some engine problem and the skipper, showing great hospitality, produced a bottle of Ouzo and a couple of bottles of water for us to enjoy whilst he fixed the problem.

If you are going to break down in a boat, then make sure that you are returning from a great night out and are sitting on the glassy wine dark sea before you get going again about forty minutes later.

The following morning, I took a stroll along the dockside and approached the same fishing boat with the same skipper preparing to go out fishing with his crew. The crew were a bit dusty from the evening before and were very slow to the orders shouted by the skipper. He was one special man, this skipper! Multi-talented was an understatement.

Our happiness whilst living in Pythagorio was more than the fabulous night just gone. It mostly involved the people who were our friends and the village atmosphere that was evident from the start. The family togetherness extended to all people who wanted to contribute to the joy of life in the village. Work was an aside.

It was however time to move on and find some work in England. Some friends organised a party at the Iliad Bar of Tony and Sandy's place. It was an embarrassing roll up of people and plenty a tear was shed that night. We had given love and were loved in return by all.

Helen and I had to attend a wedding in New York and I left a few days earlier to travel through Europe and do some sketches of what I saw. I had sold a few watercolour paintings and was keen to continue with this new self-taught pastime. Helen and her parents left to fly to New York for her sister's wedding and I was to meet them in about two and a half weeks.

Chapter 4
The Interlude

I boarded the boat to Brindisi which is on the east coast of Italy, to start my time on the European Mainland. It was an overnight passage and I went as a deck passenger. The weather was still balmy and I found myself a cosy lounge in one of the saloon rooms and fell asleep. It was a cheap and cheerful way to travel with my fellow passengers.

Arriving at the port of Brindisi at 8 am, I immediately went to a pizza cafe and ordered a pizza and some Italian coffee. The pizza was so good that I ordered another and another coffee. The Italian coffee was a far cry from the Greek coffee and good coffee was about the only thing that I missed whilst living in Samos.

After breakfast I took a train to Monte Casino where I stayed for two nights. Monte Casino was the site of fierce fighting during the Second World War. The mountain was very high and atop the mountain was the Monastery of Monte Casino. During the fighting, the monastery was used by the German Army as a lookout post. From here they could command the countryside for many miles with artillery. The Allies could not make any headway whilst this mountain was in the hands of the Germans. Allied soldiers tried many times to take the mountain but were repelled each time with great loss of life.

The Allies then called on the US Air Force to drop bombs on the Monastery to kill the Germans in residence. Whilst the US Air Force did kill a lot of Germans they all but destroyed the Monastery. It still had to be taken by foot soldiers. The American soldiers tried and failed, a Scottish regiment tried and failed and it took a Polish regiment to take it with their usual doggedness. It was a similar effort with the Polish airmen during the Battle of Britain.

After a breakfast at the hotel where I stayed in the town of Monte Casino, at the foot of the mountain, I took a bus to the Monastery at the top of the Mountain.

It was a slow climb on the bus with many tight turns. I visualised the fighting by the soldiers as we ascended. What an horrific job it must have been.

About four or five hours later, after walking around the rebuilt monastery and marvelling at the Italian craftsmanship. I thought it was time to go down the mountain. The last bus was leaving however I decided to walk down the Mountain. At this time in the afternoon, there had formed a blanket of cloud well below the mountain top and completely shut out the town of Monte Casino. It was strange walking through the cloud cover and imagining this peaceful place was once a place of death. After some three hours, I reached my hotel. Repairing to the bar, I met some people who had been on the bus going up the mountain. We enjoyed a drink together and they commented that I was late getting back. I told them of my trek down the mountain and I am sure they thought that I must have been affected by the heights. I laughed as well as I am sure that not too many people do that.

The following day, I visited one of the Museums of Art and tried to gather some impressions of Italian art. That in itself is a large call. Rome beckoned and I got the train to Rome the next day.

The train station in Rome is big. I decided to seek accommodation as close to the station as I could. I found a cheap pension which was old but clean and would do me as a base. Walking was fun so off I went. Near lunch time I was at the Spanish Steps where I discovered that Lord Byron had lived for a time in an apartment. Why wouldn't you as it is a hub of activity with many restaurants and museums. Lunch was quick and easy and I tried the scaloppini for the first time for this sojourn. Sitting in what was a trattoria at the foot of the Spanish steps, people watched for an hour with some wine. It is always a delightful exercise.

At the start of this lunch I noticed some coloured people arriving at the foot of the Spanish Steps carrying what turned out to be musical instruments. After about a dozen people arrived, they moved about fifteen steps up and set up the band on the Spanish Steps. The band was a Cuban steel band and they entertained a big crowd which had gathered. Great music and where else would you go to hear a Cuban steel band! I had more than my share of wine and returned to my room at the pension for a good night's sleep. I had not seen much of Rome but what a day! The joys of travelling.

The next day, I visited the Trevi Fountain and duly deposited a coin over the right shoulder with the required wish. Some of the adults were urging each other to think seriously about what they wished before throwing the coin. Obviously this wishing exercise is thought to be at a substantial place where the chances of your wish coming true are enhanced. Some people even waited for a better position to throw a coin as it is recommended that you should stand at the edge of the pool to throw the coin. Everybody then wanders away to take a cafe or early lunch.

While looking for a lunch spot I came upon the Piazza Barberini. What a wonderful spot for viewing life in Rome. It is a five-way road or via junction with a fountain and a place for a horse and carriage to stop and alight passengers and take more. I looked over this scene from my small trattoria table outside. It was perfect for a sketch. So I set up my pad and ordered a glass of beer. There was a lot of movement in this piazza and I had to wait each 30 minutes before I could finish the sketch of the horse and carriage calling at the Piazza Barberini for tourists.

A break for lunch and I continued with the sketch. I am always surprised at how many people stop to look and comment favourably at my sketches and here was no exception. Ultimately it was a good sketch and its eventual home is later told.

I stayed in Rome another day and got the train to Urbino. Urbino, I hear you say? Well let me tell you how I got to want to go to this town. During the travels almost a year ago, I purchased a book called "Let's Go Italy" It was a thick book and detailed almost every town worth visiting in Italy. Hence its size. Each section of the book was written by a different travel journalist. One such section was for the mid-east coast of Italy flanking the Adriatic Sea. In this section, was the town of Urbino. The recommendation was that if you see no other town in Italy then you must see Urbino. That was enough for me.

Upon leaving Rome rail station I was seated next to a girl who was also travelling through Europe, much the same as I was. She was going to Sienna in Tuscany. She tried to talk me into going her way as there was a lot more to do and see in Tuscany. Whilst I agreed with her, my timetable and Urbino awaited. I changed trains to go to Urbino.

The train pulled into a station on the Adriatic coast and I boarded a bus. We arrived at Urbino and the bus parked outside the walls of the town. Urbino was once a principality and the walled town was at its centre. About 20 kms from the coast it stood alone in the landscape.

I walked with my roll-on bag and looked for a hotel to stay a couple of days. I chose a small hotel and had a little difficulty making myself understood as nobody at the desk spoke any English. This was OK and I opened the door to a small studio room overlooking many houses within the walled town. It was perfect.

Today Urbino is a University Town and after lunch I started to walk around its perimeter which was about 1.5 kms. I stopped for lunch at the edge of the large piazza and vowed to return there later. Two museums were on my list to see and these took about three hours to wander. After returning to the piazza, I settled with a drink to watch the passing parade. People of all ages came onto the piazza to simply walk around, stand and discuss, wait to be joined by friends and in the case of the students, to walk or stand and remonstrate their point which they no doubt had confirmed at that day's lecture.

I had just had a very cultural day and not a word of the English language was heard. I returned to my studio.

The next morning, after breakfast, I noticed that the light on the rooftops outside the window was showing a superb scene. I sketched this look over the houses and toward a larger multi story villa and the wall guarding the town. It took some time as the detail was involved with some curves that are mostly only seen with boats. The sketch became a water colour and was later sold.

It was time to leave after three days and I had visited a travel agent the day before who spoke a little English. She got me a ticket to Vienna in Austria on the train which would leave the coastal station and travel through the night to Vienna. We laughed at my ability to converse and she said that I should improve before my next visit which will happen one day.

The train was on time as is the Italian punctuality and I found my seat in a cubicle with my seat near to entrance door. Next to me were two girls who were both attractive. After a while, it was time to bring the hinged middle section of the seats up from under to make a comfy bed for the journey.

It was very difficult to sleep that night as the girl next to me would occasionally turn over and put her arm partly over me. Her girlfriend sometimes removed it. Very strange and funny sleeping format as we all laughed at the next morning when we pulled into Vienna rail head.

When in doubt for accommodation I always go to the big "I" in a city or regional town. Vienna had two of these and my stay at a hotel was soon arranged.

The coffee society in Europe has been established for over a century and is very prevalent in Vienna. They have some of the most beautiful coffee and tea houses which are a match for Paris and that is saying something. I came to one such place after checking into my room and then walking towards the centre. I had coffee there three times in my two nights in Vienna. The coffee was always accompanied by cakes of my choice and is a habit for me that is still in play. Do I have a sweet tooth? Go figure.

As I entered one of the park areas in Vienna and rounding a line of trees, I came upon the gold statue of Joanne Straus. It stopped me in its magnificence. Straus is revered here and I noticed an area nearby which was preparing for a concert with a small permanent stage where only the seating needing to be placed for the outdoor music. I returned here a little while later with a sandwich for lunch and listened to the concert of classical music. What else!

After the concert I moved away a little way and sketched this scene. What a delight this place was with the beautiful buildings and the habits of a nation on display.

Moving around Vienna the following day, I sketched the Vienna Opera House and one of the Piazzas. The Piazza scene became a sepia-coloured watercolour and was given as a Christmas present later to a family friend. They understood the sepia colour.

Travelling alone allowed me to do things in my own time and let the character of the place wash over me. It is a good feeling and one which thousands of people experience. I still look at some of the sketches of Europe to be turned to watercolour and live the moment. It is totally different to a photograph.

Time to move on again. By rail to Coblenz which is on the western border of Germany at the junction of the Moselle and Rhine rivers. After checking into my hotel room, I turned the television on for some local news, hopefully in English. This I found and then scanned some other channels. I found to my astonishment "The Paul Hogan Show" dubbed in German voices! There I was on the other side of the world watching two comedians, Paul Hogan and Strop Cornell making the Germans laugh. I do not know what Paul Hogan would have made of this but there it was and rating well as prime time.

I visited Cologne the next day by rail and came up the railway entrance by escalator, to be confronted by the Cathedral of Cologne which was still untouched by damage even though the city was bombed extensively during the Second World War. Divine intervention or perhaps divine exclusion.

By rail to Paris, through Brussels in Belgium and then to Paris was my next move.

Chapter 5
The Night in Paris

The train journey to Paris was uneventful except for a teenage girl who I was trying to talk to but with some difficulty. She was German and could not speak English. Somehow we managed to converse in French as both of us knew enough of that language to understand each other. She was good company and a few laughs were enjoyed as we both had not booked any accommodation in Paris after we arrived. We were winging it, as so many travellers do.

During the journey we were the only occupants of the compartment and our regard for each other increased over the five-hour trip. One might even say that it took on a romantic tinge, which was not so strange as we were headed for the most romantic city in this or any other world. Inez let her hair down and we were both very much at ease with each other. Paris was ahead.

We arrived at the rail head, Gare du Nord in Paris at about 4 pm. I helped my traveller friend, Inez with her very large bag from the train and proceeded to wheel both my bag and hers towards the exit gates. She had two other bags and was grateful for the help. After emerging from the rail station, I noticed a small hotel on the opposite corner and we both headed towards that.

I presented myself at the front desk and asked the attendant for a room for one night only. She assumed that the room was for both of us and amid some laughter from Inez I said that we needed two rooms. There was only one room available and Inez invited me to take it as they only had a vacancy for one night and Inez was staying longer. Inez had indicated that the one room for the first night was okay with her if I invited her to share with me.

I did not think that would be a good idea as I was married and showed Inez my wedding ring. We both laughed at that, although with a shrug of the shoulders from Inez, it was clear that Inez did not care about my marital status. In any case, the attendant made a phone call and found a hotel close by where Inez could stay for her week in Paris. On the footpath outside the hotel, I bade goodbye to Inez as a chap from the hotel where she was to stay came and helped her with her bags, which was a nice touch. She kissed me goodbye, which was even better—ships in the night.

I then returned to the hotel and was given the key to my room on the fifth floor. It was then a wait for those impossibly small lifts in hotels in Paris that can only take one person and a large bag. Whilst I was waiting I helped myself to some free coffee available in the foyer of the hotel and tasted a nice flavour which was better than a Starbucks coffee that I had in Brussels.

Arriving on the fifth floor, I opened the door to my room and then smiled. It was like a studio room with a slanting window overlooking a busy street scene. It was reasonably large for this type of room and I wondered if some of the Impressionist painters started in a room just like this. Some of them, of course, did in fact rent rooms like this when they arrived in Paris in the second half of the 19th century. Picasso, Monet, Mattise and Pissaro all started as struggling artists from attic rooms just like my room. I had just come across Europe, making some sketches of my wanderings and I was certainly a struggling artist but gratefully not relying solely on my paintings to live.

I was happy to be in Paris where I had visited twice before and realised that if there is a benchmark city on this planet, then Paris is that benchmark. After unpacking some gear, I was anxious to walk Paris and see this part of this city, have a drink and a little food. As the lift was too slow, I walked down the five flights of stairs and out onto the thoroughfare opposite the train station.

There was a small map of the area which I had from some literature in my room. A westerly direction looked to be of interest and as I started to walk I had no idea that in an incredible two-hour period that evening I experienced Paris…just being Paris. It went exactly as follows.

Firstly, crossing the intersection, I continued in an amble and saw that it was a busy area where the pedestrians were mostly well dressed. The buildings were of the architectural design which had all the hallmarks of Baron Eugenie Houseman and his work in designing this beautiful city from the middle of the 19th century. He is still revered in Paris as the one person who took on a job to transform the slum areas particularly and design the centre and outlying areas to present to the world an urban beauty, built by the best trades people available in Europe. Quite an achievement.

After about 30 minutes, I came upon a six-street intersection with a small roundabout. The streets met at the roundabout with an apex separating the streets and traffic lights for each as you entered the roundabout by vehicle. As I turned around to survey the scene, I noticed a Brasserie behind me with large windows and many tables and chairs outside as well as inside. I decided that I would stop here and have a drink and maybe some food at one of the two chair tables outside. I walked along the entrance way separating two groups of table areas and into the Brasserie where I ordered a small carafe of vin ordinaire as their local recommended wine and then walked outside and settled at a small table with a great view of the whole intersection.

Chapter 6
The Scene is Set

What happened from now on was simply Paris doing its thing.

On one of the apexes there was a telephone booth in front of me, about 20 metres away, with three glass sides and the rear being solid. After about 10 minutes, a guy entered the booth and made the call. Meanwhile, I noticed that three people sat down at a table of eight just across the entrance way from me.

Table of eight and three people. Two guys and one girl.

It was then that a most bizarre thing happened. My gaze was towards the telephone booth and as the guy in the booth was talking, the door to the booth totally shattered and the glass fell with a loud noise. The guy in the booth was shocked and then started to shake the small glass cubes from his feet as a lot of the glass landed inside the booth. By this time, he held the phone at his side and he started to laugh. What the person on the other end of the phone thought can only be imagined. Eventually he put the phone to his face and was trying to explain what happened and laughing quite loudly as he explained. How cool was this dude!

There were thousands of pieces of glass all around the booth and after a couple of minutes he finished the conversation and gingerly stepped outside because if he had slipped over he would have cut himself in many places. He walked a few paces to a safe area on the apex and shook his feet again, looked back and smiled and walked from the scene.

During all this commotion, I, of course, was laughing and looked across at the table of eight. Another girl had arrived and saw the result of what had happened amid her and her friends' laughter as well. She looked at me and with a circle of her hand, she was saying how crazy was this! She sat down with the merriment and the company of her friends.

Table of eight and four people. Two guys and two girls.

As the place became a little quieter, one of the waiters came from inside the Brasserie with a dustpan, broom and bucket and swept up the area to gather the shattered glass into what looked like a glass prism similar to the Pyramid in front of the Louvre Museum. In a few minutes, the place of catastrophe looked normal, but for the door of the booth.

There then arrived a girl on the scene who stood at the apex of the intersection behind the booth. She looked at her watch and was obviously waiting for someone to arrive. At this time, another guy arrived at the table of eight.

Table of eight and five people. Three guys and two girls.

The traffic was busy and more people arrived at the Brasserie, mostly to sit outside. The girl on the apex looked at her watch again. Whoever was due to meet her was late. Then the second bizarre event took place. The traffic lights next to us had gone red and the wait for the green lights would take time. It was then that a guy in the third car back from the lights opened his door and with a bunch of flowers in his hand, he raced over to the girl standing on the apex. As he approached her, she was very surprised and took a back step as he stopped in front of her. He spoke quickly as he gave the flowers to the girl. The girl however, from my gist of the conversation, did not know this guy. He invited her out for a drink with himself and she smiled, looked at her watch, and agreed to go out with him. He said he would be back soon and raced back to his car and caught the green lights and was off to the right as he passed the lights.

I was smiling and then laughing whilst all this was taking place. The night was warming up in Paris. Then I looked across at the table of eight and they were laughing as well. I looked at one of the girls and she said, "C'est Paris!" It was then that the guy sitting closest to me, at the table of 8, beckoned me to join them at their table. I grabbed my small carafe and glass and walked across and sat down.

Table of eight and six people. four guys and two girls, including me.

Introductions followed. Us four guys were seated on one side of the table with the two girls on the other side. This was how things were sorted here. At the end of the table were Pierre and Yvette sitting opposite him. Then there were Bruno and Carmen sitting opposite each other. The guy who invited me to join them was Rick and I sat next to him. Sorted.

They all spoke good English and I thanked them for conversing in English. I was still intrigued about what had just happened with the guy in the car. Was my understanding correct, in that the girl, who was still waiting on the apex did not know the guy in the car. Carmen confirmed that my assumption was correct as did the others. For me, it was just fantastic. For the others, it was a little odd but, as they explained, this sort of thing happens in Paris. You must be kidding…but then again.

At this time, the guy from the car turned up and he escorted the girl across the lights and away. I thought that he had arrived very quickly and had probably been lucky to get a parking spot. Rick then explained that Pierre and Yvette had just met each other at this table and Bruno and Carmen were out socially for the first time from their work place, an advertising agency, where they worked on the same floor. There was romance in the air. The two girls were a little coy across from the guys sitting opposite. It was just wonderful to see and hear the conversations of people who were attracted to each in early days of any relationship to develop.

For the people at this table, the guys were of good style and the girls were very attractive. The conversation turned to me and I said that I was from Australia and this was my third visit to Paris. Yvette asked me of my impressions of Paris and I said that I would love to live and work here as I had always been at ease with Parisians, even though it is the most visited city in the world and all that goes with that.

Stories continued of the work and sporting activities that they all followed and it was a joy to hear that they recognised Australia as a formidable sporting nation.

There arrived then another girl on the table. She was another beautiful French girl named Simone and she was Rick's sister and sat down opposite him.

Table of eight and seven people. four guys and three girls.

Simone had a beauty that was a little diverting with a smile that was soft and genuine. How did I finish up at such a place on this wonderful evening amid such company? I took a quick check and an inward smile as I realised how lucky I was. The romance in the air was accelerating. The looks on the girl's faces was impossible to describe, the look for some comments was effusive and subdued for others. A potpourri of emotions. There was nobody sitting opposite me but I need not have worried as what was to happened next was to top out the night completely.

From around the corner there appeared a girl carrying a basket of flowers. She was a flower seller with the regulation single red rose in a clear tube. Her basket was mostly full and she walked straight over to our table. Rick, who was still sitting next to me grabbed his wallet immediately and bought a rose which he then gave to his sister sitting opposite. The flower seller then introduced herself as Catherine and I beheld standing next to me another beautiful girl. Rick was smitten straight away. I looked at his face and he was gone for all monies. I then bought a rose, as it seemed to be the thing to do and also gave the rose to Rick's sister Simone. Bruno did not buy a rose for Carmen and I guessed that he did not want to show his hand too soon, given their working relationship. Pierre, however got a rose for Yvette…beautiful. Then Simone gave one of her roses to Carmen and so the four girls had a rose each, perfect.

Rick then did something extraordinary. He said to Catherine, the seller, that he would like her to join the table and he would buy her a glass of wine and would like her to join them later as they were going onto a club for dinner. Catherine was delighted but said that she was working for her mother, who owned a florist shop and she had to sell all the roses this evening. Rick had pre-thought this and said to Catherine, "If I buy all the roses in your basket will you sit down and join us for a drink?"

Catherine demurred then smiled and said, "But monsieur, I have a lot of roses here."

With that Rick asked her to count them and Catherine came up with a 36-rose count. I did a quick calculation while Catherine got her calculator out. It equated to about $240 Australian dollars or about 120 English pounds. Rick gave her the money in French francs and I said to Rick that I would go inside a get a large carafe and a glass for Catherine. Rick said, "What a good idea, John." Catherine was dumbfounded and smitten. You could have cut the romance in the air with a knife…or should I say, machete.

Table of eight and eight people. four guys and four girls. How good was this!

I walked into the Brasserie shaking my head. These people were so good at this! I returned to the table and Rick poured a glass of wine for Catherine, who could not take the smile off her face. It was then that Rick did another wonderful thing. He owned the flowers and stood up and walked around me and picked up the basket of flowers and proceeded to go to each table and give away the roses to all the girls sitting at the tables outside and inside and one each for the girls on staff. Catherine was just blown away with this act and Rick returned to his seat with a few flowers left over. He, of course, gave them to Catherine.

Rick then introduced everyone at the table and Catherine asked, "And Rick, what is your work that you can afford this generosity?"

Rick then said that he was a lawyer and Catherine replies that she was studying law at the Sorbonne, whilst working part time for her mother's florist shop and doing some part time modelling. The smiles on their faces were absurd. If this was a movie that I was in the middle of, it would stretch credibility. Everyone was partnered up except myself and Simone.

As the romance continued at the table, Rick asked me if I would like to join them when they went for dinner. I had to say no as I was catching an early flight to the United States for a wedding and had to leave my hotel at about 4 am to catch the flight. It was a pity all round. Eventually, after those two hours of magic, I stood to leave and kissed each of the girls goodbye and shook hands with the guys. I also thanked for their company and bonhomie and walked away towards my hotel.

I floated along to the hotel with the thought that for all that Paris has to offer with the culture, style art, fashion, buildings and the layout of this city, it was the people this night that made it such a place. It is always the people who shine through.

If anyone would relate this story, then 'tis best to first relate it to a Parisian when you are next in Paris. When speaking to a local, the response from the female or male will go as follows:

The listener will nod and a little later will smile, as you tell the story. A nod will be repeated and a smile with maybe a wave of the hand. This will continue until the story is finished, with bigger smiles from the listener as they are reminded of where they are. At the end, the Parisian will say "Yes, yes, yes!" with a wave of the hand and with a welcoming smile both you and the listener should embrace each other and kiss, male or female, when you then immediately become an Honorary Parisian. You should treasure this mantle during the rest of your stay in Paris. This title is not easy to gain and will enhance your life, for the rest of your life.

Chapter 7
To the United States

I made it to Charles de Gaulle Airport the next morning, having booked my flight sometime during my sojourn through Europe. There was a problem with my passport at the airport as it had been stamped in Italy on my arrival there with no further stamp until my arrival at this airport to go to the United States. My passport may have also looked a little odd as it was twice stamped in Turkey when I had to leave the Greek island of Samos and travel to Turkey for a day as part of visa needs. I explained these circumstances and was off to the US to attend Helen's sister's wedding.

The contrast between Europe and the US was stark. There is little difference to notice at the airports but driving around was different. For a start, there is very little that is old and the pace of life was faster. I arrived at Helen's sister's home in Ridgewood NJ. And all was quiet in the neighbourhood. I had arrived a couple of days early so the place was quiet no longer as I was given a beer by Joe who was to marry Judith and the reason for the visit.

After having a couple of drinks I went for a walk around the neighbourhood and returned about 30 minutes later. The only thing that I saw that was alive were a few chipmunks playing on the front lawns of homes. Judith had said that it was a well populated kid's street. Then the reason emerged. It was of course, computers! They had captured the minds of the children and no outdoor activities were to be seen. It was the same as the home that I was staying in. Three children and two adults shared three computers. For me, this social pastime has done more harm than good.

Helen and I attended the wedding and the reception was where I thought of the name of this book. I was standing in a group of people where the scene could have been out of Stepford Wives, the movie. In this group of husbands and wives was Chuck, the Director of CNN, New York. He and a few other people in this group had heard that Helen and I had both left good jobs in the IT industry to live on a Greek Island and had just arrived from same.

Chuck then asked the question which everyone was hanging on. "John, how do you leave two well paid jobs and do that?"

I considered the answer for a moment and then said, "Well first, Chuck you have to 'just go to the airport'." Everyone went hush and I interrupted the pause and added, "Of course, it is a mind game, Chuck. And if you can understand that then you will succeed and perhaps do something similar." This broke the expectation of an involved superficial answer and we all laughed as we went to get another drink. A couple of the wives stayed behind and said that it was a perfect answer and would have their husbands pondering for a long time, about the two Australians they met at a wedding.

A couple of days after the wedding we heard that Sydney had just been named as the host city for the 2000 Olympic Games. We celebrated and then packed our bags the next day to go to Newport, Rhode Island.

I had wanted to visit this place as it was the place where America had lost the America's Cup for the first time in 132 years. I think that this was the longest time that any country had held an international trophy in a sport. It had been held that long by the Americans with some very unsporting like behaviour and cheating in some of the defences of the America's Cup. This fact was revealed in a book some years later by Doug Riggs, an American, who wanted to tell the truth about the New York Yacht Club who held the Cup and were the financiers of each defence of the Cup.

Australia, of course, won the Cup in 1983 with John Bertrand as the skipper of the yacht Australia II. Australia was down in the best of seven races at 3 to 1. When interviewed after that fourth race, the designer of Australia II, Ben Lexen, said that we came here to win four races and the rest is history!

On our way to Rhode Island we stayed at a beautiful town called Mystic. I drive into a motel which was flying a Greek flag from a pole at the side of the building. I greeted the owner with "Kalimera" [Greek for good morning] and we had many laughs with the Greek couple who owned the motel.

We drove to Newport, Rhode Island the next day and arrived just before lunchtime. After depositing the bags in our room, I went to the bar for a drink while Helen stayed in the room. The manager poured me a drink as he relieved the barmaid for her lunch break.

I said that I had seen a sign whilst driving into Newport which said, Visit the World's First Naval College here in Newport Rhode Island. This seemed a bit far-fetched, even for the insular Americans, and I said that I wondered where the English, Portuguese, Spanish, Dutch and Italians had learned their sailing and navigation trade if not at a college. The manager looked at me and smiled and said, "If it is on a sign, then we believe it!" Enough said.

Newport was a delightful place to visit with a Tennis Museum and of course a great harbour with an Australian bar on the Marina. Apparently the same Australians run the bar that were present when we won the America's Cup.

It was time to return to Judith and Joe's home in Ridgewood NJ. We caught the train into New York twice during the next week and visited a couple of museums and aircraft carrier in the East River.

Saying goodbye, we boarded a flight to Paris and stayed one night as we got our correct taste buds back again with a lunch and dinner of good food.

Then a short flight to Heathrow Airport and England.

Chapter 8
England

After getting our luggage from the carousel we proceeded to the rail connection to London. We were staying at Karl and Roz's home at Hammersmith which is in West London. An early flight into Heathrow Airport suggested to me that we might stop off at Earl's Court which is a suburb of London where many Australians have made home.

At the start of the train journey to Earl's Court a couple of English chaps started a conversation in our carriage where they bemoaned the past week and their disastrous romantic adventures. This conversation between two guys dressed in suits had everyone in the carriage in fits of laughter as the stories unfolded. One of the stories went along these lines. One chap had a first date with an attractive girl that he had met at a trade exhibition and he dropped her at her home after the exhibition was over.

The date was for Saturday night and she was to be picked up at 7 pm at her home. Whilst walking to the car park station to pick up his car, and dressed in a new suit, he stood at the side of a road to cross and was swamped with water by a truck passing and driving through a large puddle. He was furious as he would be late for the first date of a good-looking girl. Back home he went and changed and rang and left a message on the first date's mobile phone.

He then burst out of the house to try the pick up again. When he was over half way to the date's house he realised that he had left his wallet in the wet trousers at his flat. Meanwhile, his phone had gone dead and he could not ring the date to tell her of the bad luck. At this stage of the story, the carriage was in uproar and hanging onto the finish of the story. After arriving home, he plugged in his mobile and called her to leave another message of his further lateness. Nothing could go right for him! He arrived to pick up his date and she, by this time, had listened to his messages and thought that this fellow had been in the pub all day and was making excuses for his lateness. She had got into her jeans and was about to join her girlfriends at the local pub.

For his penance he joined her at the pub and was made to buy all drinks whilst dressed formally amongst girls dressed in relax gear. Whilst walking his first date home he tripped over a running dog and twisted his ankle. His first date kept walking. At this, we all were nearly on the floor. He was going to call her in a few days and say God knows what!

I had arrived in the country of humour and it was time to leave the train.

Helen and I did not walk too far as we had plenty of luggage and we came upon a pub with the typical interior of the cosy English pub. We had lunch and then met some Australian locals who were very pleased to be able to drink Foster's Lager beer here in London. It was a very famous beer in England at the time and had come from Australia and landed in England in the late 1980s. That is to say the name arrived, as the taste was different in Australia with the brewers catering to English taste buds. This was late 1992 and tastes were maturing with each country designing the taste to suit.

During this pub visit, I asked a local where in greater London, would be a good place to live? I got quite a few answers and the best answer was to live somewhere in north London, not too far out.

We were back on the train soon and heading for Hammersmith to stay with Karl and Roz whilst looking for jobs and somewhere to live. Helen had always wanted to do a writing course so she enrolled at the London Open University and then she started to look for a job. She did not want to apply for a high-powered job as was her position in Australia. She applied for a position as the PA to the Managing Director of a very large European drug company. To say that she was over qualified would be an understatement. As her future boss interviewed her, he asked her typing speed and this was up to speed needed. Her shorthand speed was however non-existent. She assured her future boss that she could type as quickly as he could speak.

And so it proved to be with her boss dictating at Helen's desk and much to the amusement of the other people in the office, as was her ability to handle both PC and Apple formats. An amusing incident happened one morning in the office where Helen's boss came out of his office and asked "Coffee?"

Helen was busy doing something on the computer and replied without looking at her boss, "Yes thanks, black with one," much to the shock of the other staff. The MD then simply went to the kitchen room and delivered said coffee.

Helen also managed also to correct some of her boss's English wording and he would comment and agree. Another Australian at large in London and doing well!

I did not find it so easy to get a job. During an appointment with a Personnel Agent, he said that he wanted to see some references on letter heads from my last two employers in Australia. I advised this chap that we generally do not ask for these as a phone call is always a better way to find out about a person's previous track record. This did not best please another personnel agent who also wanted references. I was getting nowhere until I was given an interview with the Human Resources Manager at the Dorchester Hotel in London for the job of Events / Conference Manager.

The Dorchester Hotel in London is a five-star hotel and an Icon in London. However, it was suffering from lack of business from the corporate sector. The job was quite an important one for the hotel and came with salary and a bonus for overachieving. The interview was going along very well with the HR Manager impressed with some of my ideas for generating business for the hotel. After some time, I enquired about the salary and that quickly ended the interview. I told the HR Manager that the salary was far too low in my opinion for the job at hand. He replied that the position was with the Dorchester and the prestige of such a position should suffice. I politely disagreed and thanked him for his time.

It was then that I decided to contact Canon UK direct to see if there were any positions available. I had previously been told by one of the personnel agents that there was a head freeze for no more staff for Canon UK. I rang the Canon HR department anyway.

There was a head freeze, that was correct, except for two positions in the Imaging Division available. One in Manchester and one for the London area. I applied straight away for the London job. The job assessment was a long process and after the third interview with the General Manager and Operations Manager, the later emerged to say that they were impressed with my skills and that they would be in touch in a couple of days. I retorted that three sessions should be enough to select the correct person. The Operations Manager agreed and went back to the interview room to speak to the General Manager. They both emerged and the General Manager offered me the job. I congratulated them on their decision and assured them that I would not disappoint them.

And so it turned out to be.

Whilst driving home that night I reflected that Helen and I had been here for two and a half weeks and both of us now with jobs. It was now time to find somewhere to live.

I remembered the previous advice about north of London and Helen and I set off one Saturday morning on the Northern Line by rail. This was great fun as we got off the train often at certain stations, sometimes recommended, and went to the local pub. There we asked the locals what they thought of the area and its liveability. Some of the comments were very funny as the locals were taking the piss out of themselves whilst describing how they were still there after 10,20 or 30 years. It was a wonderful morning with the British humour on display everywhere that we stopped.

Eventually we alighted at the station of Finchley Central. The local pub, the Four in Hand were serving a good late lunch and we then went for a walk up the high street and onto a park area where we spoke to some local residents. This suburb felt good and we decided to look for somewhere to live here in Finchley.

The following week we inspected a three bedroom [two up, one down] residence located two streets back from the high street. Of course it was fully furnished and in a quiet part of town. It was quite expensive at 180 pounds per week when the average wage in London was about 290 pounds per week. We certainly needed the two of us working to afford the rent. My salary was quite good at about 600 pounds per week but once you had gone out for dinner once per week there was not a lot left over. A trip to Covent Garden for a show and a meal was a treat unless we wanted to dip into savings.

Still, we were living and working in London and that was just superb.

We decided to spend the New Year in Scotland and see what this reputed Hogmanay [New Year's Eve] was all about. Some friends from Australia, John and Louisa, were visiting family in England and decided to join us. Our accommodation just north of Edinburgh was a resort complex with cabins on the estate. It was naturally very cold at that time of year but I had never felt the cold very much anyway, so for me it was mild.

I had driven all day and Helen and I stayed for an afternoon nap whilst John and Louisa went to the local pub at 3.30 pm that afternoon, New Year's Eve. The phone rang in our room at about 5.30 pm and John was on the line to inform me that I needed to get down here to the town pub as soon as possible as there was a two finger of scotch whiskey free with every beer purchased! Helen and I rushed to the local pub which was only a few minutes' walk away.

When we got there, John and Louisa were in great humour and we soon joined in the fun. About an hour later I had two finger scotch glasses lined up. I poured them into one glass and drank them straight. They certainly hit the mark as we continued to try to talk to the locals with their broad accent and getting broader by the minute.

At about 7.30 pm, we left the pub and walked back to the resort to attend the dinner in the formal room. There was a fine display of local clan colours and all present were primed for a good night.

And what a night it was. I had purchased some lucky door tickets where the prizes were from local traders and I managed to win a bottle of good scotch whiskey. I had a small tipple and did not need any more and neither did anyone else. I noticed that the next table were a little short of scotch so a gave my bottle to two elderly sisters who immediately started to drink the bottle. After some dances with one of the elderly ladies who was 82 years old, I saw that the scotch bottle was almost empty. Pretty good, and what is more, they were still sober. The octogenarians were showing us up. We did have a head start in that department but nobody could deny that Hogmanay and the new year was brought in in great style with the Scottish Pipe Band reducing a few of the locals to tears as the clock struck midnight.

The evening was a cultural "tour de force".

Hangovers are also cultural as they appear in every country where fun is had. We visited St Andrews, the home of golf, and walked the course as it was closed due to the icy conditions. I stood by the "Road Hole" with its wicked fairway bunker and wondered how any golfer would ever try to get out of this bunker in a forward direction, where many golfers had tried and failed. A visit to the Black watch Museum had to be postponed as it was closed over this period. I had been a soldier in the Black watch Regiment in Sydney when I was part of the Army Reserve for a couple of years. The Scottish Black Watch Regiment is the most famous in Scotland and its very proud history can boast some of the toughest and brilliant soldiers ever to go to battle.

We returned home late on New Year's day and realised that we had to pay the piper for our fun.

My Job:

I joined the Imaging Division at Canon UK. This division at Canon sells an office machine which scans paper of A4 to A3 size and records this on disk. It is used to take a filing cabinet in the office and scan all the documents in the filing cabinet to disk and remove the filing cabinet. Each document or group of documents can be filed in eight different places electronically and retrieved under subject heading or by looking at the eight different filing headings and drilling down to find a document or group of documents. In this way, you can create the first relational data base for your documents.

That is how the product was explained to the corporate companies that I visited. The problem of paper storage was a world-wide problem. It was getting to be a huge problem in England. The English love paper and records on paper. It was even asked of everyone that if you wanted to cancel your electricity account, then this had to be confirmed in a letter to the provider. A lot of paper was generated because that is how they had been doing things for hundreds of years. The state of inertia in business and life per say in England is very hard to change.

Tradition is fine but this part of tradition had to change. Companies were growing with the attendant cost of storage of paper reaching unmanageable heights.

On visiting all the companies in my area of business I pointed out that the paper war had been lost some time ago. By ordering more filing cabinets or sections of floor-to-ceiling compact units, the organisation was simply adding more weight in the saddle bags! It was costing a lot of money to continue with present methods of storage to say nothing of the cost of finding a document that had gone missing from the filing place.

I took to the job with some gusto and humour. The bluntness of my delivery in the boardrooms sometimes set some of the people back on their chairs. I always took off my coat and occasionally rolled up my sleeves to indicate the gravity of my message. I also joked about the loss of the filing cabinets and closing of whole floors of records to be replaced with a gym or games room for staff.

This division started to deliver and install a lot of Canofile units which was the marketing name of the scanner and storage unit. I helped in this record period of sales for the division. The English had adopted this technology very quickly compared to past innovations.

My best contribution was when after the weekly sales meeting at Crawley in Sussex, I remarked audibly in the office that the state of inertia in England was negating the sales of our product. I was of course in some humour when I said this and my secretary, Maureen, said that the Concord aircraft was built with

English pragmatism and French flair. She was of course defending English ability and its eventual success with new technology and design.

After this I said to Maureen that some Seminars in the cities would help to make the Canofile product visible and produce more sales. I appealed to Maureen to help and I composed the proposal to our divisional head, David Aylward for the budget approval.

I knew that Maureen held some sway with management and I eventually got the approval for the first Seminar at Luton, north of London. It was a morning event with breakfast supplied and then the product time. The success was, as a few orders ensued from this Seminar and product awareness had started in a different way. The first Seminar for this division had been a success.

The second Seminar, a month later, was a similar success. I had by this time been accepted in the division even by some of the chaps who had stood back from me at the meetings and social events which were now at Henry's Bar overlooking Green Square. They supported the crazy Aussie who refused to wear the full English coat and did not feel the cold. It was a nice feeling to be part of a team again. That year the Imaging Division of Canon UK were in front of the United States for product sales, which was a first for any division.

Fun was the order of the day now and Helen and I visited places around England and Wales. One weekend, we visited Wales to attend a Welsh Choir recital near Snowdonia. We stopped at a town near the recital and walked into a hotel to stay for the night. Without any exaggeration, within one minute, I was in conversation with a chap at the bar and his son about the state of Welsh Rugby. He was bemoaning the loss of the nuggety half and five eight combinations of past Welsh Rugby teams. It seems that since the closure of most of the coal mines in Wales the tough men who worked them and went to play sport were no longer being produced. I could only agree with him and we had another drink after I found out that the road over Snowdonia that I had to take to get to the Welsh Choir recital, had been closed due to ice on the roads. It was a nice place to get stuck as the company was good and the food hearty.

Helen and I liked Wales so much that we went back a couple of weeks later. This time it was to Hay on Wye. This was a small town on the Wye River where, it seems, all the books go to die. There are large barns in this quaint town filled with books of all sizes and an honesty system of paying from 50 p to two pounds. In the village, there are many shops selling books of the vintage type and some of the prices were in the thousands of pounds. It was wonderful to stay the night in the village and go and have a full English breakfast at about 9 am and continue to troll the bookshops. I did buy two second hand World War Two books which I still have.

Time to return to work and during the week, I had to attend Canon's city showroom for an appointment with a corporate group of people who wanted a demonstration of the Canofile product. Usually, I would demonstrate the product at the customer's office boardroom or meeting room. I concluded this demonstration with the news that the status of paper was now legally accepted in an electronic format with a benchmark case just being completed with stored documents in this format as acceptable at law. The corporate community was happy with this decision.

The people left the showroom and I started on my way home on the train to Finchley Central. Before I reached the station I passed the Camper and Nicholson shopfront showing sailing and motor yachts for charter and sale. The images were magnificent and little did I know then that I was looking at scenes that were to be very familiar.

Also, on the way to the station, I visited the Ritz Hotel near Piccadilly, to walk through this icon of hotels in London. One of the British Parliamentarians, Alan Clarke, has a table booked permanently there for morning or afternoon tea. It is in a cafe and a very stylish area as you would expect. My visit could have gone on much longer as I imagined the joy that this place has given since Cesar Ritz opened his first Hotel Ritz in Paris in 1898. What fun this was to visit places that I had only read about.

The following weekend I went to Portsmouth alone to see the Maritime Museum and other places. Portsmouth is the home of the Royal Navy and is large in area. As you enter Portsmouth Harbour, there is Hasler's Marina to your left. Blondy Hasler led the raid on Bordeau Harbour in France, during the Second World War. The group of people which he led became the "Cockleshell Heroes" and a film was made of the same name.

I entered the Maritime Museum and started to inspect the exhibits. I eventually came to the display case showing Admiral Lord Nelson's uniform on the day that he died on 21st October 1805. There was the bullet hole on the right shoulder of the uniform where the bullet entered his body from the yardarms of either a French or Spanish Ship of the Line. On this day, the ships fighting the Battle of Trafalgar off the Spanish coast were locked in a broadside shooting fight and a grapple between the ships where the marines come into their own.

Nelson was taken below deck and died a few hours later and was taken to Gibraltar and eventually to England.

Nelson remains England's greatest hero in any of the services.

I then went to a tour of HMS Victory which was Nelson's Flag Ship on his last day. A group of about 12 of us boarded HMS Victory for the tour. We traversed two of the lower decks and saw the guns which fired the broadsides in any battle. The gun recoil area was evident and the height of the deck would have seen me permanently bent over to carry out the orders.

After inspecting the aft cabin which was where Nelson spread the charts and diagrams, we went up to the top deck and to the quarter deck. I stood back whilst the tour guide explained that this was where Nelson was killed. He paused a moment and said that he was shot exactly where I was standing above a brass plaque screwed into the deck. When this happened I virtually jumped aside so that people could read the small plaque. Wrong place at the right time.

The naval history in Portsmouth is extensive and I would return to this city again very soon although not as a person wanting to see the history.

It was now coming into summer in England and May /June is the start of "The Season". It is a time when the important social events take place. Events such as the Royal Ascot races, Wimbledon, The Grand National Steeple Chase, The Oxford/Cambridge Boat race with the last event being the Yacht Race around the Isle of Wight.

Helen and I decided that we would go to the start of the Oxford/Cambridge Boat Race, which starts at Putney Bridge on the river Thames. We went by train as a car would have seen us parking far enough away to get a train anyway. It was a bright sunny day and both sides of the river were packed with people dressed in boater hats and clothing almost from all eras of English history. What a great tradition this race is.

We spotted a large table outside a pub with two vacant seats at the end of the table and opposite each other. I asked the other people if they would mind and was straight away invited to sit. After getting Helen and I a drink, we introduced ourselves and our Aussie accent was accepted by all except the chap sitting next to me. His name was John Crawley and he was 21 years and the current opener for the England Cricket team. He had his back to me and so his dislike of Australians was palpable.

Helen and I were getting on well with the other people and the conversation was lively and friendly. During the conversations I heard John Crawley say that he hated Australians and as Helen and I rose from the table to leave after a couple of hours I turned to John Crawley and said that if hating Australians caused you to score a lot of runs, then good luck to you. Needless to say John Crawley was singled out by the Australian cricket team and did not score a lot of runs, being dropped after the first two tests of that year's Ashes Series. It was a silly attitude to have for such a young person and he was marked by the opposite team as any team would do.

The Boat Race was the only event that Helen and I went to. We next visited some of Helen's relatives in Leicester. They were fine people and we stayed one night. We told them of our New Year's Eve in Scotland and they said that they had never been to Scotland. I urged them to go as it was very different to England with the architecture, people, countryside and traditions. From Leicester it was not far. The English are sometimes such homebodies.

I am sure that everyone looks forward to summer in the UK. A heat wave is 28 degrees C. People go to the beaches for their one or two trips per year and gather a tan which probably lasts a week. That's OK because it is such a change from the rest of the year.

Another joyous occasion was going on a couple of "The London Walks". This is where you meet an official Guide who takes the group who turn up on an historic walk. It was usual that the walk started at a station. Our first walk was around Hamstead which is north of London. We passed the homes of Daphne Du Maurier and Vladimir Lenin when he briefly lived here. It was a great way to see some nice suburbs and take the history.

During a conversation on Friday night at Harry's Bar, after a day at the Canon City showroom, one of my colleagues said that he was going to Calais on the coast of France for a booze run. This was a very popular excursion as the purchase of alcohol in France could be brought back to the UK as duty free. The limit of your purchase had it that you could fill a van of beer, wine and spirits and no duty! Bargain!

The following weekend Helen and I took my company car to Dover and drove onto the ferry for the brief trip to Calais. On arriving, we booked into our hotel and went to explore the surrounds. Dinner was up to the French standard and we loaded our booze from a local warehouse. It was a delightful weekend with the bonus of saving a packet on the cost of buying alcohol in England. The two larger supermarket chains in England, Sainsbury's and Tesco, soon opened supermarkets on the coast in France to make up a little profit from what they were losing in England.

It was good to be an Australian in England at this time. In the sporting field, we held the Rugby World Cup, the Ashes in cricket and we had recently beaten England at Football [Soccer] in a Friendly at Wembley Stadium. Not all of the English were pleased with us.

I mentioned this to a visitor to our home one evening and we had a good laugh. He was Bob Keir and a friend of his who were in England to do some business in buying jewellery. I accompanied Bob to Portobello Road in Notting Hill one morning as Bob was to buy Rolex watches from a distributor. Bob had been buying for some years and was in the inner sanctum of this business. I had been to Portobello Road a couple of times and this time I purchased six brass navy shoulder buttons and the braid of an officer for the sleeves of a shirt. It served as a fun shirt to wear with all these additions attached.

After lunch, we left this great market area and if there is a better one in the world then I have yet to see it.

During this time, I was taking up the English language with more interest. I had my office at home and some of my business proposals were being used as a template by some of the chaps who I worked with. What I did not realise at the time was that my accent was changing to an English accent. I had known people whose accent would change with a mere month of exposure to an American or English accent and I did not think that this would happen to me. So here I was after nine months and I was sounding British. That was OK as there was nothing that I could do about it.

Helen and I got through our second winter in England and I, as usual, did not feel the cold as much as Helen. Then one night over dinner Helen said that she really did not like living in this climate and with the traffic on the roads she could spend two to three hours each day in the car.

She wanted to leave England and the only option was to return home, or so she thought. That night, I gave the circumstances some good thinking and had a suggestion the following evening which she thought about.

Chapter 9
A Fork in the Road

What I suggested was that we could leave England for better climates aboard our own sailing boat and sail to the coasts of Europe and eventually down to the Mediterranean Sea. I did not want to return home at this point as I wanted to stay and accommodate Helen's needs whilst continuing the adventure.

We had come through the first fork in the road in leaving Australia and the second fork was now before us. It was as big a call or even bigger call than the first call as this time it required us to do things that most people would not or could not do.

To buy a sailing yacht was a task that neither of us had ever done. Sailing the yacht was something that neither of us had done. Navigating the yacht was something that neither of us had done and big boat handling is an exercise that would intimidate everyone.

After discussing all the difficulties in order to do what I had suggested, Helen said yes, let's do this! It was quite a moment. The realisation of our decision sank in during the night after we went out for dinner to celebrate our prospective adventure. It was a blast and still today gives me goose bumps whenever I think of that night. After dinner that night, I rang a friend in Sydney who was a real estate agent. I asked him to sell the house as we were going to buy a yacht and needed the money. He said that I had too much to drink and call him tomorrow. I called John Woods the following day and said that he was correct about my sobriety but we still needed to sell.

Assisting Helen with her confidence was a reliance on me which gratefully I did not disappoint and vice-versa.

We returned to work on Monday morning with a gleam in our eyes. Helen was good at making lists and so she started to make lists of all the things necessary to achieve our goal, which was to sail out of England on our yacht towards France as a start to a new life. There was a lot to do before that could happen!

Christmas 1994 was approaching and work was busy. In the month of December that year, the team in my division at Canon UK achieved their best sales to date. Tony Wills who was our divisional manager and a New Zealander took us all out for dinner with partners to Harry's Bar for celebrations in the true Christmas spirit. The company paid and we could get a taxi home and hit the expense account. Helen and I once again met Tony's wife who was the true Blueblood from an Aristocratic line, a Sloan Ranger as the comment went at the time. She was lovely and contrasted so much with Tony's rough and ready manner that his wife Phoebe would say each day "Oh Tony you shouldn't say that". It was a match made in heaven.

In the new year, Tony asked me to go to another Canon UK Branch for three to four days and work from their Barnett offices. This was where the Facsimile Division had their headquarters. I was invited to sit in at their meetings and see if I could float the idea that we could share our databases and use each other's influence to help with corporate sales. It was nice that Tony had the confidence in me to ask me to do this. I must have made some sense as some months later the two Divisions combined electronically and eventually located to the one premises.

Meanwhile, Helen was busy preparing lists of what we needed to do and to research what we needed to know. I had in this time been told by a friend that we were proposing to do this sailing bit in the most difficult navigational and sailing areas in the world with tides of up to 12.5 metres and the attendant problems that this delivers to the sailors. I did not tell Helen this as we were both daunted by what we did not know at this stage and there was no point in adding to Helen's concern.

We needed to do some sailing courses, that was obvious. The world's leading organisation for all things sailing is the Royal Yachting Association in England hereafter referred to as the RYA. We started with the Competent Crew Course of the available curriculum at the RYA and its Authorised Agents. We found the Solent School of Yachting [SSY] on the Hamble River near Portsmouth as our base of learning and a well recommended Agent of the RYA.

We both applied for 1.5 weeks' holidays and found a B & B near the SSY. The B & B was with a family with two young children. Our first breakfast morning was in their kitchen with everyone scurrying about to get ready for the day ahead. I was sitting at the kitchen table and little Diane, one of the kids, was standing next to me and asking her mother to tell the story. What story I asked? Mary, her mother, offered the story.

When Mary started her labour pains during breakfast one day, her husband raced around to gather the hospital bag to get going, Mary called out that it was too late to go to the hospital. Her water had broken and the baby was coming! She dropped to the floor and baby Diane was born on the floor right where I sat on my kitchen chair. As Mary told the story there were tears and laughter. I stood up and joined the laughter and moved away from my chair. So too did Helen. Her husband, Bruce came in to the kitchen and the whole family was in laughter. What a story! I will never forget little Diane leaving to go to school and laughing all the way to the front gate.

They were a wonderful family where they had told the story for the first time to some strangers. Helen and I stayed with this family many times over the next few months to complete our sailing courses.

To start the Competent Crew Course we were briefed in the lecture room at the SSY and then boarded our yacht with four other people. We sailed down river and came out onto the Solent which is that body of water between the mainland and the Isle of Wight. What a glorious sight it was. This part of our sailing courses was where we were shown all the parts of the yacht with explanations of what all the bits do to make the yacht go through the water. There were seven of us including the skipper/ instructor. After sailing around the Solent for the rest of the day and taking turns to be on the tiller, [sometimes a wheel on other yachts] we tied up at Cowes on the Isle of Wight, for the night.

Part of any sailing day is the joy of reflecting on the day's sail when you go ashore to the pub and this we did with our fellow crew members. It was the theme for what turned out to be a 12-week period of courses for the advanced sailors. We did not know it then as that was to come. We completed the week of sailing and into ports each night, one being a very busy Southampton harbour where I was skipper for the day. I was very apprehensive in bringing the boat into harbour and alongside with most of my orders to the crew being done correctly. The skipper or that person on the tiller or wheel is God and he or she calls all the shots.

For the week that was, it was cold but sunny and as we drove back home both Helen and I were very happy with the start of a totally new learning curve.

We returned to work which was busy. Looking for a yacht to purchase was our next job. Helen had made a list of check points that we needed to know. It was extensive and ran to about three and a half A4 pages. There were many boats to look at, although we were advised that we should look at boats that were around 38 feet or bigger. This was quite large as our Competent Crew boat was only 34 feet. The rationale was that if we were to live aboard then we should need some room to live. It was good advice. Helen and I being the only people to sail this size of boat was called being short-handed. That is to say that there is a lot to do on a boat of 38 feet plus and the two people need to be rather proficient at sailing to do this with safety. Ultimately it was a mind game and we were both up for it.

Each weekend we travelled to marinas all over England and two marinas in Wales. We were becoming good at what we wanted in a boat. The ambience around marinas is wonderful. Everyone that we spoke to gave us a bit more knowledge and confidence. Each marina had a bar to gather at and good practical advice was delivered by the locals. Everyone thought that we were rather game with our plan and all wished us well. I got the understanding that nobody had ever attempted this, coming half way around the world and embarking on an adventure in the waters that we were about to tackle. And so it turned out to be. We were unique! More of why later.

Meanwhile, our home in Sydney had been sold, so we had the money in the bank. Our budget for the boat was about $80,000 Australian dollars.

During our search for a boat we inspected a few moody yachts which were the largest manufacturers of production yachts in the UK. Moody yachts that we looked at were either too small or too expensive if they were the right size. At last, we saw an ad in Yachting Monthly for a Moody 39. It was up on the hard at Swanwick Marina on the Hamble River. We knew the marina fairly well as we had visited it sometime during our look around England. Swanwick Marina was the Head Office for Moody Yachts.

We travelled south early one Saturday morning to have a look. On arriving at the marina we were shown to the Moody 39. It was a Bermudan Sloop and quite beamy at 13 feet six inches. The designer of the Moody 39 was Angus Primrose whose mandate at Moody's, as he was their chief designer, was to take the prototype for a sail across the Atlantic Ocean and discover any faults which he could then adjust.

After climbing the ladder to the deck of this boat we discovered the boat that we wanted to buy! It was a centre cockpit with a forward double cabin and an owner's double cabin at the rear or stern. It also had another cabin with two bunks with one bed up and one down. The saloon was large and could seat seven to eight people in comfort.

The name of the boat was "Tequila Sunrise" and I will say no more!

Helen and John The Team Players

The Enabler

S/Y Tequila Sunrise

Chapter 10
Preparing for the Departure

Having decided that this yacht was our choice we asked to have a test sail. This was agreed to and the cost of slipping it into the water was at no cost if we wanted to purchase it after the test sail. One of the B & B's that we used when in this area was with a couple of married people and Brian, the husband, was an ocean master which was the very best accreditation with the RYA. I asked Brian if he would come with us and look and listen as we sailed the yacht about the Solent on the test sail. Brian agreed.

During the sail, Brian asked all the right questions of the Broker and listened to the boat as we put it through the various points of sail. Tequila Sunrise came through with flying colours. We agreed the price with the Broker and repaired back to Moody's Marina. That night, we took Brian and his wife out for dinner to celebrate our purchase. I had given the Broker a deposit to secure the sale.

We still had two extensive courses to complete with the RYA before we could get going that summer of 1994.

To do this was a 12-week period with a break of one week between the Day Skipper Course and the Coastal Skipper Course. We were to have most Sundays off to relax. The format was a week of sailing and then to the classroom for lessons of navigation and knowledge needed to gain a pass for both courses. Then back to the sailing.

I needed to resign from my job at Canon. I did this with a regret as I was enjoying my time with Canon however if we were to do these courses then we should start as soon as possible. I was taken for dinner with quite a few of my colleagues including my boss, Tony Wills, the Kiwi. On my leaving their company that night, Tony gave me an envelope with a reference. I opened it on the train ride home and he said, "Is Tequila Sunrise the name of your boat or the state of your health?". It was a grand farewell.

Before we started the courses with the SSY I joined the Cruising Association [the CA]. This is a superb organisation which supplies information and advice for the activities that we were about to undertake. Their members notify them of any problems they encounter not only around the UK but also in sailing throughout Europe and in fact around the world. Members also supply information of the great times to be had at certain destinations and good wintering places to stay. A monthly newsletter is sent to each member and both Helen and I looked forward to receiving this at certain ports where we notified the CA to send any letters as we could use them for this as well. The CA had thought of everything.

I attended a night at the CA when the clubhouse was located by the Thames River in London. The feature speaker at this night was Sir Robin Knox-Johnston who had won the Golden Globe Race in 1968, which was the first single handed, non-stop, round the world race. He was the only competitor to finish after a Frenchman, Bernard Moitessier, pulled out of the race going east in the Pacific and well in the lead. Sir Robin spoke of his Mediterranean adventures and his advice for any would be sailors was to take different types of anchors to suits the sea bed holding. It was good advice and I purchased another anchor to add to the inventory aboard Tequila Sunrise.

The CA's wealth came from books and charts that were left to them by sailors in their Wills or by benefactors who were old members. They sold some books and a chart or two at auction to move to Limehouse, further down the Thames River, but still in London, and build a new Clubhouse with some accommodation for members who were visiting London. That is how much money old books and charts can fetch!

The first course that we did was the Day Skipper Course. The Solent School of Yachting was on the Hamble River and the classrooms look out over the river. The first week was spent in class going over the names of parts of a yacht and simple navigation knowledge. For the unaware, it is totally different to say, driving a car and noticing signs. For a start, there is a dictionary of maritime words that runs to about 3200 words. It was not necessary to know them all but it will give you some idea of a completely different type of travelling or passage making, from one place to another and the knowledge needed to do this safely. After the first week spent in class, we were to go aboard a 34 feet Westerly Yacht for the first week of training. Helen and I were on different boats during the whole training period of 12 weeks and came together during the last week on the one boat.

The course at sea involves sailing, boat handling, navigation and "Doing things in a seamanlike manner" which was a new expression and was to become very real in time. A pre-requisite was to be safe and to do things quickly which was safer because the boat is moving and it demands that you do things when they need to be done and hopefully in the right sequence which gives safety to crew and boat. This is at least the theory which I adhered to like the need to breath.

One of our overnight stays was at the village of Beaulieu on the river of same name. Going north out of the Solent we sailed past Buckler's Hard which was one of the ship building yards which built England's Wooden Walls, the Ships of the Line, like one of Lord Horatio Nelson's ships being the HMS Agamemnon. A fabulously historic place.

With our instructor, we repaired to the local hotel which was owned by Lord Montague who also owned the surrounding land for as far as the eye could see. On entering the hotel in late afternoon, I noticed that the fire place was so big that inside the fireplace was placed a small table and two chairs. As the evening approached, they were removed and a large fire was lit. I then remarked to the manager, that there were very few people here in such a large hotel. He said that it was off season and too cold for some people. Most other hotels in the area were closed as trade was slow. In the case of Lord Montague's hotel however, he kept it open for the few locals and the odd traveller, but his main reason was to keep all the staff employed during the slow season.

This was the same Lord Montague who gave over his Chateau and Manor Houses to the British military at the start of the Second World War. It was on his properties that the Special Operations Executive [SOE] people trained the agents sent into France, Holland, Belgium and other countries to gather intelligence.

Some of the English Aristocracy are very generous.

Each day we would sail to different parts of the south coast of England and occasionally call at Cowes on the Isle of Wight which is the Mecca of English Yachting. It is here that a club known as the Squadron is located. It is a yacht club and probably the most exclusive club in the world. For membership of this club, you must be invited by the Board of the Squadron. Prince Phillip is a member; however, Prince Charles is yet to be invited to be a member.

During one visit to Cowes I noticed a lot of people setting up chairs and a platform for some function later in the day. As we came into dock later the same day from our training yacht, I visited the boy's toilet and emerged from another door to see Prince Charles on the platform in front of me delivering a thank you to a charity group. I was seen conspicuously sneaking away from the platform and the TV cameras. I did not look at the news that night on the TV.

As the weeks rolled by we all, as crew, began to gather the knowledge and experience to do what we had come for. There was a bond between people from one month to the next with different crew members, all in love with the romance of the sea. I loved the beauty of sailing and in all weathers. It is worth repeating some words of Bernard Moitessier, the French romantic adventurer, who said: "I am a citizen of the most beautiful nation on earth. In this limitless nation of wind, light and peace, there is no other ruler besides the sea."

This was to be our "Raison d'etre" for what was to be a defining period of our lives for both Helen and myself.

On one of our weeks in class for the theory, our instructor, John Forsythe, directed our attention, at morning tea, to the yachts under sail on the Hamble River. They were sailing onto the Solent for the first race of the season. It was a beautiful day with the wind at about Force five on the Beaufort Scale or about 25 to 30 kmph. John noticed that most of the boats had their large sails up. He commented that using their number one sail set was a bit too much for the wind which was expected to increase slightly. He also mentioned that by afternoon tea, as the boats returned, we should see the results of some skippers choosing too big a sail set for the wind. Sure enough when the first boats started to return after the race, some boats had broken their masts, whilst others had busted spars. Bravado at the first race of the season had overcome some skippers and they paid for this with the cost of new masts and spars.

Back on the water for sail training, we had to do a night sailing exercise as part of the qualification for Coastal Skipper Certificate. It was part of the RYA course and where I found that a young Italian lad was to join us on our passage to Cherbourg on the coast of France. Helen was to join us on this trip as well and we had not been on the same boat for two months.

Helen was asked to do the calculations for our Passage Plan. This was without any GPS to assist. We set sail late one night for Cherbourg and encountered a little fog as we approached the coast of France. We emerged from the fog and straight ahead was Cherbourg. Helen had done a good job to get us right on target calculating boat leeway and tidal stream. Motoring into Cherbourg Harbour we were looking forward to a hot breakfast, a little sleep and a look at the town.

As Helen and I were walking along the harbour front there was a large statue of Napoleon Bonaparte. He was sitting astride his horse and pointing towards England which was the enemy of France, on and off, for many years. In any case, Napoleon never made it to England and it was mainly the French navy which failed France in its efforts to get to England. They also had to contend with a fellow named Horatio Nelson during their efforts, so they can be excused a little.

Our instructor, Paul for this exercise in night sailing, asked us in late afternoon time the following day if we wouldn't mind returning to Cowes on the Isle of Wight within the hour. We all agreed and I was made skipper for the passage back to England. Paul said that the weather forecast was for Force 6, slashing 7. I thought this a little strong, bearing in mind that we had two teenagers on board who looked a little inexperienced for rough weather.

As we motored in the Marina towards the open sea some of the people on the other boats in the Marina stood on deck and applauded us as we went by. I smiled as we went past these good sentiments, however it was a portent that was worthy of their bon voyage signals.

Paul knew that the skipper for the day, who was me, could call the shots and return if I considered it too rough to stand on with the passage. It was pretty bleak as we set sail to return and the sea state had the boat pitching up and down. About an hour and a half out of Cherbourg, I remarked to Paul that I think that it would be a good idea if we returned. Helen and the two teenagers were looking uncomfortable and our Italian youngster was looking a little queasy. Paul persuaded me to keep going as he thought that this was experience where we could all benefit. The two teenagers went below at about 10 pm as they were not feeling chipper. We had to tack or change direction a few times and during one tack our Italian crew member was thrown from one side of the cabin to the other side. Helen went to his assistance and stayed below. At this time, the wind was getting up towards a gale strength. I remarked to Paul that whilst he and I were okay, the others were a non-event and that I would have to bring the boat in to Cowes with Paul on the helm for a few hours whilst I handled the sail set.

As we approached the lights of Portsmouth and the eastern side of the Isle of Wight I noticed that a ferry that was emerging from Portsmouth Harbour was pitching noticeably and that Paul should warn our crew, who were below, that it may be a bit rougher for a little while. We got through this night and entered Cowes, on the Isle of Wight at about 9 am. The wind had gone and the sun was out. As the morning went, I was still on a high from the night passage from France and sat down to have a large coffee. It was then that Paul walked by with two people that he introduced as his parents.

Helen and I had a great chat with them and it was easy to see that they loved their son and what he was doing. I said to Paul, after his parents left to book into a hotel, that he should have mentioned his rendezvous with his parents as the real reason for making the rough night passage from France. It did not matter to us as it was all part of our adventure and we had learned things that you would not normally learn, as the guidelines of the Solent School of Yachting were that sailing will not happen with a weather forecast above Force 6.

Helen went back to the boat for a rest and I went for a late breakfast as I did not have any coming into Cowes. As I ordered my breakfast and went to a table to sit, I said hello to a sailor who was sitting in this cafe. He answered back very pleasantly and I said no more as he was in the middle of his breakfast. His name was Dennis Conner and he was the American who had skippered a yacht and lost the America's Cup in 1983 to Australia and John Bertrand as skipper, with Alan Bond and Ben Lexen as designer. The Cup had been held by America for 132 years and the New York Yacht Club, who held the Cup, were not impressed and Dennis Conner disappeared for a couple of weeks whilst making his way back to San Diego.

For now, in 1994, Dennis Conner had just competed in the Whitbread Round the World Race as a co-skipper. During that race and whilst near in the lead, he received a mayday call from another boat. As he was within 200 miles of that boat's position, he had to, in this case, turn his boat around and go to the assistance of the boat in distress. He and his crew did this and saved lives.

It is of course a Maritime Law that requires boats to go to the assistance of other boats when it does not endanger their crew or boat. In any case, Dennis Conner resumed the race but finished down the list. He was in Cowes for the World Etchells Sailing Championships, where boats of a standard length of 24 feet, race with crew of three. He was the consummate sailor.

At the end of the week of sailing we returned to the classroom for more tuition for another week. After a couple of days of this new week, we were set a simple task by our instructor John. To start the exercise, we had to do a simple fix on a chart. This involves reading along the top of the chart to find the longitude point and coming down the chart on this line to meet the latitude point which is read on the side edge of the chart. Simple, you thought?

Well, I was having some trouble doing this and I had done it a dozen times during the previous weeks. I looked to a fellow sitting near me and asked if he was having difficulty doing this. We both smiled as John, our instructor, approached us. Our difficulty was explained by John who said that our brain was filled to capacity with information which was new and some simple tasks were hard to do. Over a beer or two that evening John assured that our minds would be back to normal by the morning. He was right!

Our last week of sail training was with the Principal of the Solent School of Yachting and as our instructor he was to grant to us our Certificates of Competence at the end of this week. It was a fun week with all on board having plenty of experience and practice over the preceding months. Even our man over board drill went well. The Principal of the SSY was all smiles through that week. The last port that we entered before returning to the base of the SSY, was Portsmouth. Helen had the tiller that day and brought the boat alongside for us to get off and go for drinks. This she did, but we were about a metre from the dockside wall. One of the guys jumped ashore and we tied the bow and stern lines. Helen tossed her misjudgement aside and I gave no further thought of this until about a year later when it almost was our undoing.

On the following day, back in class, we were awarded our Day and Coastal Certificates with a couple of the Americans allowed to write their names on the ceiling of our main classroom. They were excited as we were on our future activities on the seas and oceans of the world.

As we left the Hamble River to return to our home in Finchley Central, north of London, we still had plenty to do before leaving England. Tequila Sunrise was in the water at Moody's Marina at Swanwick and we returned there after a couple of days. Helen went off shopping for some supplies whilst I moved TS by myself to another marina further down river. It was a heart stopping time but I did it with some nervous moments. It was here that I started to unload the cockpit lockers of all the items in them.

As I started to place these bits on the floating fingers of the marina, I thought that the previous owners have made a mistake and left these items on board. They intended to charter yachts in the Mediterranean as they figured that their experience did not run to getting TS there. I phoned the Yacht Broker to ask him to call the previous owners and tell them about the items from the lockers which were not on the inventory. The broker called back to say that all the gear from the lockers was ours. It was worth a couple of thousand pounds and of course was welcome as we would have purchased similar items to get going.

It took us about a month to prepare TS for sailing and departure from England. During that time, we invited some friends to go sailing one bright Sunday on the Solent. Karl, Roz, John, Louisa and John's parents arrived for the day. I quietly asked John if his mother and father were okay with the sea sick thing and he said that his father was okay and his mother said that she did not know. We entered the Solent and I looked over to John's mother, Susan and she had her eyes to the front and smiling. We stopped and had lunch in Osborne Bay where Queen Victoria would come down from Osborne House, her holiday home, and go swimming. The small beach huts as changing rooms were still there.

On the way back the wind picked up and TS was heeling a bit. Susan asked if we could go faster so I tightened the sails as Helen was on the wheel. TS heeled over even more and Susan was loving this where her husband was a little shell shocked at the action and his wife's joy. At dinner that night, Susan said to her husband, "Why did we not buy a yacht years ago?" There was no answer.

It was time to leave our marina in the Hamble River and move along the south coast of England to Brighton Marina to then cross the English Channel to France.

We sailed into Brighton Marina in late July 1994 and I jumped onto the floating finger platforms to tie the lines. Helen and I had a lunch ashore near Brighton Pier which is an iconic landmark on the south coast of England. On returning aboard TS, another yacht was slowly motoring to a berth next to us. They turned their boat into the berth and the lady on the bows lassoed the bollard on the pontoon. I was amazed at this as the guy on the wheel left the wheel and lassoed the stern bollard and within a minute they both had drinks in their hands. They were an elderly Dutch couple and I congratulated them both for their skill. With that, they invited us to share a drink with them on board their yacht. Eventually I met many Dutch people during our odyssey and they all were very good sailors.

    It was time to leave England.

Chapter 11
France

We left Brighton Marina to cross the English Channel It was just before midnight on the first of August 1994. On this date, each year the Isle of Wight race is held and is the last of the events for the social season. The reason for leaving at this time was to catch the high tide at Dieppe on the French coast at a reasonable time of the day.

There are Maritime Rules for crossing this very busy area of the English Channel. You must sail or motor your boat at right angles to the shipping lanes to enable you to get to the French coast as soon as possible so that you are not in the lanes any longer than you need. There are fines for any boat seen to be not doing this.

It was very exciting to be making our first passage to another country at the start of our lifestyle change. There was joy, apprehension, expectations, curiosity and other emotions, most of which were to be experienced during this night.

We set sail into the night and all was going well until I saw some lights off to port. By the lights of the lead boat, I saw the silhouette of a fishing boat and another boat following at a constant distance of about 200 metres. We were on a convergent course and I could have sailed between these boats but something told me that the lead boat may be towing the second boat although the lead boat did not show lights to indicate this. So I sailed to the stern or underneath the second boat and as I looked back I could see the tow rope against the lights of Brighton in the distance. The fishing was not showing the correct lights for towing activity and my track had been the safe one to do.

We sailed on with a cup of tea in hand and a snack. At about 4.30 am, we were sailing into an area of fog. It was light at first and then became thick, a real "pea souper". This was the first time that we had sailed in this type of heavy fog and it was very spooky. I made a bit of a joke for Helen's sake and mine, as I went for the claxon horn pressure pack can to make the audible sounds for vessels travelling in fog. It consists of one long and two short blasts of the horn. I stood near the mast of TS and the sounds came from the small trumpet attached to the pressure pack can. I could hear ships in the distance and just hoped that they had TS on their Radar screens. Soon, the pressure-pack can ran out of puff and I grabbed the plastic trumpet and continued making the same sounds manually. If it wasn't so serious an exercise it would be comical I thought. Helen was a bit blasé about it all so I relaxed a little.

From the cockpit you could see our Radar screen and the little blips shown on the screen could be heard as ships passing and heading at 90 degrees to our course. I remembered our Instructor, John, who said that the first two instruments that you put on a boat are a depth sounder and Radar.

We emerged from the fog at 11.40 am that morning and saw land. France was dead ahead. I did have one can of beer to celebrate but we still had some way to go. At 13.45 pm, we sighted Dieppe on the French coast. An hour later we rafted up to the visitors' pontoon to await the lock to go into Basin Duquesne, Dieppe, France.

There are many basins on this part of the French coast. They are built because the tides for this part of the world are big in range. The basins allow boats to go in at near high tide and stay. If you walk to the edge of the basin the tide drops away to the sea floor for some metres. You can leave the basin at near to the next high tide which is about 12 hours from when you entered.

We took TS into the basin at about 18.10 pm and came alongside the town quay. We celebrated with a nice bottle of French wine [Have they ever made a bad one?] which Helen bought at the local Carver [bottle shop].

As we were enjoying our wine and baguette with cheese a yacht entered the basin and motored up harbour. I remarked to Helen that I recognised this boat, although I could not see its name on the transom. The basin was full and as this boat motored past us I invited the skipper to raft up to us. He agreed to do this and turned his boat to come alongside. I still could not see the name of the boat but I said to Helen that we had been on board this boat when we were looking to buy. The bow and stern lines were thrown to us on TS and we had this boat rafted up to in no time. I said hello to the skipper and introduced Helen and said, "Is the name of your yacht, 'Canouan'?"

He said yes and I replied that Helen and I very nearly purchased this boat as we liked it so much. It was lying in the marina at Medmenham in the Medway east of London. The skipper Sean and his wife Dianne had purchased Canouan and then got married and this passage to France was their honeymoon.

The first of many coincidences in these years, was played out with celebration of their marriage and the four of us crossing the Channel in fog.

We stayed for a couple of days in Dieppe to see the town and enjoy French food. We had been on an English cuisine for over a year and French food was a step up in taste experience.

During the lead up to our leaving England, my mother had told me that she was coming to France to see our Auntie Ria who lived near Agen, in the south of France. I was now to go to Paris to bring her to our boat for a week of sailing, before she continued to the south of France. As you do. We left Dieppe basin at 9 am to go to Le Havre which is a large harbour and port near the entrance to the Seine River, the same river that runs through Paris. The forecast for this day of sailing was not perfect but seemed okay.

As we approached Le Havre roads, [lanes outside harbours] I looked behind to see a dark horizon with the wind picking up a lot and the glass dropping. Helen and I dressed into our oilies for the expected blow. It was then that a large water spout formed out to sea and appeared to be following us. It was a very big water spout! We dropped the mainsail and furled the headsail. The motor was turned on and I kicked it up to about eight knots towards the harbour.

The rain came down in torrents as the wind and sea state went awry. The thought of what this water spout could do if it reached us was not worth thinking about. After entering the harbour at speed, I turned to port and slowed. Visibility was poor and we needed to get in somewhere. As I spotted a place on a pontoon, three chaps jumped from their boat to catch our lines as we came in to berth. We did this successfully and I jumped ashore to thank them very much. This was the help that we all gave as much as we could in this fraternity of sailors. A wonderful tradition.

We had escaped the water spout and the rain eventually eased. It was a bit of a harrowing time that day as Helen and I sat aboard TS to contemplate our travels so far. The count was, 1. fog in a dangerous place and 2. a large water spout. All this on two out of two days sailing!

The following day, we dried out some of our clothing and went into the city of Le Havre to have dinner after basking in the French sun during the day.

Our dinner was of Moules [mussels] with a wine and cream base in a large bowl with the garnish of onion and perhaps some other vegetable, depending on what part of France that you were in. I will always say that the best food consistently, is to be found in France.

As we were waiting for my mother to arrive in Paris, a yacht arrived in the Le Havre Marina. It was about a 32-footer and in poor condition. There were four sailors on board and they were met by the Port Capitan as they secured to a pontoon. Their boat was about six boat spaces from us and we heard the Port Capitan order them to stay aboard. Soon after, the immigration officer and a doctor arrived. The crew of this boat had to stay aboard whilst their story was checked.

The four sailors claimed to have sailed from St Petersburg in Russia to permanently escape. They had no charts, but some torn out pages from an Atlas book. They were not in good health and thought that they had landed on the Isle of Wight! It was an absurd scene and I felt sorry for them if their story was true. They were removed from their boat for quarantine a couple of days later.

Meanwhile, I had to get the train [RER] to Paris to retrieve my mother for her visit to TS. After arriving in Paris, I went to Gare du Nord to find my mother who was getting the train from the airport. I found the platform and duly saw mum alight from a carriage. We were both over the moon to see each other as it had been some time.

On return to Le Havre Marina my mother was settled into the peak double cabin at the bow of TS. Helen gave her a cook's tour of the boat and we went ashore for dinner. The following morning, we slipped our lines and sailed across the Bay de Seine to Deauville and Trouville Harbour, a little further south. It was a sunny day and the short passage took about four hours. We came in to our berth at mid-tide and were almost in the middle of Deauville town. After a walk through the town which was a very pretty and was known as the Riviera of the west French coast, Helen cooked a great dinner and we sat in the cockpit around a small table that I had made attached to the binnacle which is the post where the wheel and compass are located.

My dear mother was fascinated with everything nautical. She had brought with her a large flag. On this flag, was the image of a boxing kangaroo with the flag of Australia. It measured about one metre by 70 cms. It was big. I ran it up the port shrouds underneath a small Australian flag and if anyone was in doubt about the nationality of those on board, then this flag could be seen from a long way away. It was a hoot, and we laughed a lot as we enjoyed our after-dinner drinks on TS.

The following morning, we went ashore after breakfast to further explore. I noticed a sign in the town announcing that the Deauville Cup was being run in a couple of days' time. As my mother was a horse racing fan, we decided to attend. It was a major race on the French racing calendar so the three of us dressed for the occasion. There was great food and wine and of course even better fashion form the ladies attending. My mother was excited to see the famous American jockey, Willie Shoemaker, riding that day, although he didn't ride the winner of the Cup. At the end of the day we walked back to the marina in somewhat of a happy state as we had drunk too much good French wine, if there is such a thing.

Inner basin Honfleur – John and mother, Corinne

A couple of days later, we got the bus to Honfleur which is a beautiful town about a 20-minute ride from Deauville. During this morning, I sat on the inner harbour of Honfleur and sketched part of the buildings flanking the harbour. It was a good sketch and took me about two hours to complete. I presented the painting to my mother after I returned home and it hung in her home in pride of place.

Lunch that day was near the boats in the harbour. As we sat for lunch, we noticed that the table near us sat two ladies with their two Poodle dogs seated on chairs at the same table. Dogs in France are accorded the status of people in most areas of social settings. This is probably unique to France and if you don't like it, then move on.

We returned to TS and the following day I took my mother back to Paris for her journey to the south of France. Slipping the lines in the harbour of Deauville, next day, we sailed further along the coast to Ouistreham and came alongside the visitors' pontoon in the river leading to the town. This was one of the towns that was taken on D-Day, the 6th June 1944 by the Allies or more to the point by the British. The town was featured in a film of D-Day and as we walked into town I recognised some of the footage of the film.

It was high summer in Europe and the next day we set sail for St Vaast. A better sailing day could not be imagined. We sailed all along the D-Day beaches and I imagined what it was like to come ashore and do battle with the Germans. Our course was almost due west with a following wind which was brisk. On this day, England were playing a Cricket Test Match at Old Trafford. I turned on the radio to listen. One of their opening bowlers was a chap named Devon Malcolm. He was a good quick bowler and started taking wickets. On such a glorious day, I celebrated each wicket that this bowler got with another can of beer. He took eight wickets in the first innings. By the time we reached St Vaast on the French coast and turned into the wind to anchor I realised that the wind speed was about a force 6. We had to wait for the gates of the harbour basin to open before we could go inside and secure TS for the night.

Towards the gate opening time, I noticed about eight or nine yachts coming up to enter the harbour. It was time to move. With a little trepidation, due to the state of my sobriety, we entered the harbour. It is always intimidating when one is to find a finger berth on a pontoon in a harbour that you have never been to before. I turned into the second channel and saw a berth. I turned TS at exactly the right moment to come alongside. A chap caught the bow line and I jumped onto the pontoon to secure the stern line. Perfect! As I went back on board I looked at Helen and all she could say was "well that was lucky wasn't it, considering your state". I did not brush it off and apologised. I never did something like that again. Still in all we celebrated a great day of sailing, if a little risky.

Ashore, we had dinner and some more moules with a fresh baguette. What a feed! St Vaast is a good stop for meeting all sorts of people. The English will go there for a weekend on their boats and we enjoyed their company for a couple of days.

Then it was onto Cherbourg where we had left for that night sail back to the Isle of Wight during our sailing course. We were in Normandy and the next day set sail for the Channel Islands.

I wanted to make Guernsey that day but a strong wind blew up and we were taken slightly off course by the tidal current which was running at about nine knots. I knew about this and decided to make for Alderney and get out of the weather. As we entered Braye Harbour on Alderney, we secured the very last visitors buoy in the harbour. I radioed to the Port Captain and notified our arrival and he suggested that their tender service would pick us up and take us ashore. It was a long way to the shore and this was a welcome relief.

When we arrived on shore we went to the local Chandlery to see the owner who was also the local representative of the Cruising Association, of which we were a member. The first question that I asked him was, "What was that?" referring to the weather. It was not forecast when we left Cherbourg. I had listened to the Shipping News that morning at 6 am and no mention was made. His reply was short and sweet, "Local condition." After a jolly conversation, he directed us to the local hotel for dinner. As a bonus, a Lord of the House of Commons, who lived on the island, was expected that night at the hotel and it was worth the visit just for that. We repaired to the hotel.

The hotel called 'The Anchor' was very pleasant and we had a beer each of the local brewery. It was good to relax after another eventful day. We talked about where we should next head to and decided that we would sail to both Guernsey and Jersey which were the main Channel Islands. We were not in any hurry and in any case we would have to put TS up on the hard for the coming European winter as sailing then is not a recommend especially in the northern Atlantic Ocean.

After about an hour and speaking to some of the locals we decided to stay a couple of days to see some of this island. It was then that Lord Rothermere arrived with his wife. They were a lovely old couple who obviously loved company as they greeted their friends. It was then that the Lord Rothermere spun around, then looked around, then waved towards the bar with a circular motion. This signified that everyone present was to get a free drink. What a wonderful gesture from a grand chap who I said hello to and thanked a little while later.

Two days later, we slipped the mooring and headed to Guernsey. We entered St Peter Port and the Victoria Marina. The lanes here were very narrow and I really had to have my best boat handling skills at hand. The weather was sunny and we went ashore late afternoon. The atmosphere at dockside was perfect with plenty of visitors who were there for the British Power Boat Championships. Some English people joined us at our bar table. They were tragic power boat people, quoting horse power and capacity numbers. When they found that we were sailors there were more questions than we could answer. Boat people are good company.

The next day there was a procession through town of the boats to compete. They were very large and most carried a crew of three as a person for steering, trim and navigation. A visit to the home of Victor Hugo later in the morning was a delight and since this famous French author was expelled from France, in the 19th century, I thought that there were worse places to be exiled.

That afternoon at a cafe overlooking the harbour Helen and I met a lady named Lucia. She was a lone sailor and her 30-feet sloop, named after her, was in the marina. Her intention from here in France was to sail to Seville in Spain and then sail around the world, repeating the feat of Magellan who left to do this from Seville in the 16th century. She was certainly upbeat about her prospects and we met again over coffee to wish her well.

We then sailed to Jersey and the marina of St Helier. It was only a leisurely five-hour sail. As Helen was steering TS into harbour, I set about tying the fenders onto the railings to hang down the side of the hull. As I tied the second or third fender and went to the next one, the same fender dropped into the water. I had tied it incorrectly. Luckily a boat following us picked it up and came alongside and tossed it aboard. I then did the same thing again! But this time we had to go back and retrieve the fender ourselves. I must have been in daydream mode as I was doing this and it was not hard to work out why.

In St Helier that week, the Battle of Britain Flight was expected. It was to fly over the Marina and along the beach. A Spitfire fighter, a Hurricane fighter and a Lancaster Bomber were expected to fly over with some other aircraft. Early in the morning and before the main flypast, I was sitting in the cockpit of TS having a cuppa, when I heard a familiar sound. I recognised the sound of the Rolls Royce Merlin engine in the Spitfire which was just about to fly over the Marina. What a glorious sound it was. I had heard it a few times at Duxford Airfield near to where we lived in England. The Spit fire sounds different to the Hurricane yet they both have the same engine.

The Royal Channel Islands Yacht Club beckoned us for lunch and it was there that I picked up their information booklet on tide times for the islands. One article in the booklet said that the biggest tidal range for that part of Europe was 12.5 metres. It explained some of the tidal streams of nine knots in this area. In other words, do not try to sail against it as that part of the coast that you see as you sail against it, will still be there in half an hour.

We left St Helier and Jersey and headed to St Malo on the French coast, near where I intended to put TS up on the hard for the European winter. Les Bas Sablons was our brief stay before moving to Chantier Naval de la Landriais. It was here that two extraordinary co-incidences happened over the next two days.

St Malo is a superb place to visit and live. The walled city was heavily damaged towards the end of the Second World War; however, little evidence is to be found of the damage now. There is an off shore island that we walked to at low tide before finding a restaurant within the city walls for lunch. Lots of tourists there in mid-September. We returned to TS to await the arrival of the Cruising Association local representative M. Jean Louis Fabre. It was at his boat yard that I wanted to locate TS for the European winter.

I had been practising my French now for some time and I could just get by speaking to the locals in French. I hoped that M. John Louis Fabre could speak some English, otherwise it was going to be a long conversation. I need not have worried. As Jean Louis walked along the pontoon towards, I walked of TS to greet him. As I thrust my hand out he did the same and said, "Jolly good to meet you, old chap" in perfect English.

I laughed and stood back and said, "How do…?"

John Louis said, "I attended Oxford University for most of my education,"…say no more. We got his information and directions to his yard up the Rance River, through the barrage lock. This was to happen late the next morning. Then the first of the co-incidences happened.

An elderly sailor walked along the pontoon and stopped at TS. He was a short, stocky Englishman with a wonderfully chiselled face of great character. His name was Norman. He asked if he could come by in the morning at 6 am to listen to listen to the BBC Shipping News for the weather report as he and his brother were returning to England tomorrow and his own radio was not working. With the comment "Norman, I have a better idea than that", I invited him aboard. He had some trouble getting aboard due to age and his height, but once in the cockpit he settled for a coffee. I offered to give him my Marine Transistor Radio to listen to in the morning and return to me then.

Norman enquired of our background and why we were here. He smiled when I told him of our plans to join the small group of cruising travellers to make it to the Mediterranean and sail to the Island of Cyprus in the far east of the Med. I of course asked of his background and Norman revealed that he had been a Merchant Navy Captain most of his life. During World War Two, he had sailed the Atlantic Ocean and the North Cape around the top of Norway to deliver all manner of war items to the Russians for the war effort against Germany. I then asked of his memory of the North Cape convoys to Russia, as they were the worst, and he smiled when he remembered that it was on one of these outgoing convoys, and loaded to the utmost, that he brought down a German float plane which was scouting the sea after being launched from one of the German battleships roving this track of sea and searching for convoys.

I asked him to go into detail of this achievement. As his ship was sailing in convoy, a float plane scouting the area at sea, flew down close to his ship. The plane attempted to do this again and this time Norman and his crew had something waiting for this plane. They had rigged a large net between two barrage balloons, which they had inflated, and as the scout plane was approaching his ship, in the line of travel, the crew, on Norman's signal, released the balloons and netting. The plane flew straight into the netting and crashed into the sea. Norman said that the float/scout plane had been catapulted from the German Pocket Battleship, Scharnhorst. With that, I said, "Yes, of course" and dashed below to get a book from the bookshelf in the saloon and raced back to the cockpit to show Norman a book titled "Scharnhorst and Gniesenua" a history of these two German ships.

I related to Norman that I had purchased this book before we had left England and the incident just described by Norman was in the book! Here I was sitting with a chap who was as brave as any soldier, because the passage to Russia was as frightening as any during that war with German warships and submarines decimating most convoys. Being unarmed as most merchant vessels were, Norman and crew had managed to do something extraordinary. I felt very lucky to be talking to him. He signed the book and was off to get a good night's sleep before leaving the next morning where I waved goodbye.

We then prepared TS to go up river to Jean-Louis' boatyard and put TS on the hard [on land] for the winter. John-Louis, who had a degree in Engineering, had designed and made a travel lift which could take a large boat out of the water from a ramp and supported by six steel arms, transfer the boat to any part of his yard. This he did and there we were looking out over the Rance River from the best view point in the yard. Wonderful. Helen went into the village to get some provisions for our stay and I did some work to prepare TS for the winter.

Helen and I were sitting the cockpit that afternoon when the second coincidence happened. I saw a sailing boat, coming up river under motor, and soon heading to a small bay. It had a kedge keel so that it could settle on the river or bay bed when the tide went out. It was common to see many kedge yachts sitting on the sand or mud in a lot of harbours in this part of the world. Sometime later, two people got off this boat with the girl walking towards the village and the chap walking, in his gumboots, towards us perched on TS. The chap arrived beside TS and I said hello. He introduced himself as Peter Cumberlidge and I suggested that he come aboard for a drink as it had been a bit of a haul from his boat to ours. He took off his boots and climbed the ladder.

With a can of ale in hand Peter sat down and I said, "Are you the Peter Cumberlidge who is a feature writer for the magazines, Yachting Monthly and Practical Boat Owner?" After he said yes, I started to laugh and said, "Not another one," and went below to get another book from the bookshelf. I had also purchased Peter's book called Secret Anchorages of Brittany before we left England. Peter laughed as well when I explained the story of Norman and the convoys of World War Two. Peter was most charming company and I asked him to autograph his own book. As he did this, he said that he had not shown his two favourite anchorages in his book. This was because he often sailed to this area for holidays or work and would stay. He marked the two best spots in his book.

It was then time for Peter to tell me of his own and odd funny story. It was this…when he had motored into the bay and settled on the muddy bottom he did so at a high Spring Tide. This happens about twice a month and the next high tide in the bay would not allow him to float off the bottom. The tide would be just short. He had not looked at the tide tables enough to discover this and his boat would be there for another two weeks before he would be able to sail it back to England. After much laughter, he swore me to secrecy. I kept his secret until now. After Peter left, I said to Helen that I took two books from the bookshelf in two days. Go figure!

Helen and I stayed on TS and got to know some of the villagers and visited the local areas of beauty and I painted a river and boat scene which I still retain.

Then it was time to return to Australia as Helen was to do some marketing for NEC Computers for the release of a new computer modem. We rented a flat in Avalon and I often went to a place called "Cafe for Obscure Avalon Artists." I was certainly an obscure artist.

Some months later, we returned to TS to prepare for sailing down the North Atlantic and eventually into the Mediterranean Sea. What a hoot, and it turned out to be a bigger hoot than I could have imagined.

As we cleared the Bay at St Malo we headed at 220 degrees towards Lezardrieux. As some possible rough weather lay ahead, we anchored overnight outside the town of Le Taureau. The tidal stream was running at about five knots so we took turns of four hours to anchor watch through the night. Sailing on, the village of Lezardrieux was up a river not far from the open sea and we secured a mooring near the village. We went ashore to a delightfully quiet village and had a late lunch at a small cafe on the town place [square]. There was a sort of enchantment that I felt with each new village that we were part of in our travels. People were always courteous with a smile to welcome us. The following day, a small market was found in the town place and we took some fresh food back to TS.

We sailed to and visited Trebeurden, L'Aberwrach and Camaret Sur Mer on the coast. At Camaret, the town surrounded the port and a good feeling of ambience was about. The following morning, we slipped lines to sail into Brest and the enormous harbour and bays attendant.

It was at this time, in Camaret, that a ketch motored into the marina and prepared to come stern to, onto the town quay. It was a fine-looking sailing boat with plenty of crew as it turned to come alongside us. It was about 10.30 am morning and Helen and I were having morning tea after doing some housekeeping which is always a daily activity.

As the ketch reversed and started its track to the quay, I noticed that the boat's name was 'Life of Brian'. The name of the *Monty Python* film immediately sprang to mind. So, there was the skipper, on the wheel, and the young crew of 8 teenagers, five boys and three girls. Well, it was just a delight to see this crew do their work to get the boat to the quay. They spoke to each other to do the jobs necessary and in the right sequence without the skipper having to say anything at all!

When the boat was secured safely there were smiles all round with high fives being the order of the morning. The teenagers were a well-oiled outfit and the skipper congratulated them all.

I stepped ashore to at least say hello to the skipper. I did this when the skipper came down the plank and I complemented him and the crew on the best job that I had seen done with one of the girls jumping ashore to secure the stern lines.

The skipper's name, of course, was Brian. His excellent crew were teenagers from a boarding school on the south coast of England where the teenagers were from disadvantaged homes and were permanent boarders at the school. Brian went on this sailing experience each year to give the kids a sailing holiday on his boat. It was all at his expense and he, like the kids, were enjoying every bit of it.

I was introduced to some of the crew at dockside as they were going ashore to discover the town. Each crew member deferred to Brian for everything and he gave his permission for most of their intended activities. The skipper was a most respected man for these kids and Brian was the perfect skipper to take them and teach them the way of the sailor. It was there for all to see.

I arranged to meet them for dinner at a marina-side restaurant at 6 pm.

When Helen and I arrived at the restaurant, we were introduced to the rest of the crew and we sat down to have pre-dinner drinks with only two of the teenage boys who were allowed to have a beer, the rest having Coca Cola or similar. During the meal I asked each of the crew their thoughts of this holiday. The superlatives ran throughout their replies and much laughter ensued. Occasionally one of the crew would refer to Brian for the best answer and you could see the love generated for each other and Brian.

The evening was a great reflection on the English lifestyle and character and of course for Brian. They still make people like that.

TS was happily sailing along and had just reached the approaches to Brest Harbour when I was alerted to a strange sound from the starboard quarter. I turned and saw a large thing emerging from the ocean depths. It shocked me a little and within a minute the thing turned out to be a submarine surfacing and making the same heading as TS into the harbour. Helen was making tea and toast and came on deck to see what my shock was all about. The submarine was going a little faster than TS and the usual etiquette was seen from each of us and as we came level with each other, we saluted the other and the submarine, which flew the US flag, steamed past. It was quite an eventful way to greet the day.

The main harbour lay ahead and another harbour that we had not been to. The Pilot Book is always a guide but it is always a little nervy entering a busy harbour to find a place to moor or come alongside. Brest was and still is a main base for the French Navy. The concrete pens that the Germans had built for their submarines during the Second World War are still flanking the western side of the bay. The Allies had tried many times to destroy them but they were built too well. We were surrounded by history and when I turned to port to enter the busy inner harbour there was a scene which was very busy. Ships slowly coming and going, day boats with the tourists on board and pleasure boats such as us.

I motored around for about five minutes and then I saw a vacant berth alongside a bust part of the many docks. There were a couple of other yachts there and I motored past where we might possibly secure TS for a couple of days. The space for coming alongside was small and I calculated that we could get in there if I could turn and come alongside to starboard using the prop-walk that was an effect that happened when I put TS in reverse and revved the motor viz: in reverse gear and briefly with plenty of power, the stern of TS would kick to starboard. This effect helped me here in Brest Harbour and as a chap caught one of the mooring lines as I jumped onto the dock, he said "well done" and I thanked him. However, without that prop-walk, I would not have attempted to go alongside. It was basic boat handling but only done well after a lot of practice.

Brest is an official port of entry in France. I was running a small French flag on the starboard shrouds as a salute to the country I was entering. However, above the French flag I was also showing the Flag of Brittany. I found this flag amongst all the signal and country flags that I discovered on TS when going through the inventory. As I did not recognise this flag, I took it to the local chandlery and they identified it as the Flag of Brittany. The advice was to run it above the French flag when in Brittany. Running the Flag of Brittany above the French flag was a bit of an insult to France but to the Bretton people, their flag is more important than the French flag. They have wanted to secede from France for centuries.

Moreover, flag etiquette is very important in Europe and the Port Captain, who saw the Flag of Brittany and our salute to this Provence of France, completed the formalities as did the Immigration Officer a few minutes later. The officials were very chatty and courteous. I think it had a lot to do with our flag etiquette and advice when we were in England.

The city of Brest has a decided nautical atmosphere which I could be around with happiness all day, every day. It has been a major naval port for centuries where Admiral Nelson, in the late eighteenth century, laid blockade to the port for months on end. We left Port de Plaisance in Brest and headed to Port Le Foret. After securing TS in the Marina, some single-handed sailors and their 32-feet yachts started to come into the marina and tie up at the finger wharfs just as we had done. We sat there and watched as some of the single-handed sailors brought their boats to rest. It was a lesson in superb boat handling by sailors who, in some cases, were still under sail when they entered the marina. As it turned out, it was a short distance sailing race along the coast of Brittany and these Frenchmen were perfectly adept at the concept of single-handed sailing.

In Brittany, there are numerous Sailing Schools where they offer accommodation, for the students, in buildings of 100-plus rooms. It is a serious business throughout the country and as the French were always known as daredevil sailors, they want to keep the tradition going, i.e., the Vendee Globe Race around the world for single handed sailors.

During the afternoon, a tender boat came into the harbour towing what turned out to be a 38-feet Westerly Sloop. English made and new, the yacht was gently coaxed into a berth. I walked to this boat to meet the owners, Brian and Cathy, and Brian told me why they were towed into the marina. They were approaching the port roads with the usual channel markers present when Brian decided to cut the corner and motor the short way to the channel. Soon after he did this, the prop picked up a crayfish marker with the attending rope and this rope wrapped around the propeller shaft and bent it. The engine stopped immediately and would not start. Brian jumped overboard and saw the bent shaft and called for a tow. It would be a big job to get it back to England for repair.

Meanwhile, Brian and Cathy invited Helen and I to their home in Port Le Foret for dinner. Here we heard why they had purchased their holiday home in Port Le Foret. It was a compromise deal as Cathy wanted it close enough to England to be able to drive back and see the kids and Brian wanted it as far away from England to deliver some decent weather.

Of course, most English people who we met out of England, close to their second or holiday home, were there to enjoy the better weather. After all, Julius Caesar in BC, and on his only visit to England, mentioned how bad the weather was.

We were really enjoying this new life style and it was living up to all our preconceived ideas of the total enjoyment of living and travelling in another country whilst being alongside the people of that country and sharing their ups and downs and joys. It was time to move along the coast to Belle Isle, outside Le Palais. Here we anchored under a skyline that was dominated by the Citadel on Belle Isle. We were right underneath it, near the shoreline and felt very insignificant. It was a spectacular anchorage and we did not leave TS as it was surreal being here and we were to leave early the next morning for an overnight sail to La Rochelle.

Painting by John Neale – Entrance to La Rochelle inner harbour

During the sail we had to pass through the Raz de Seine, which is a part of the Brittany coast and very rocky with a lighthouse off shore on a small area of rock. Between the lighthouse and the land is the stretch of water known the "Raz". In times of rough weather, the "Raz" becomes a heaving mass of waves, currents and is very dangerous to go through apart from the top or bottom of the tide. Photographs on calendars over the world show the lighthouse with waves hitting the sides halfway up the building. I planned to get to the "Raz" at high tide and as we sailed through this famous place I imagined what it might be like for the many ships that had been wrecked here. It was quite a serene feeling as we looked behind after the 10 or so minutes of this passage.

The solar heated shower on deck was used by us both at about 5.30 pm. Solar, that is to say, a black plastic bag that was hanging from the forestay. It contained about two gallons of water that had been heating through the day and with a shower rose attached, it was perfect. Although TS had two en-suites, I mostly showered on the bow part of the deck.

A most comfortable night's sail was had and we arrived at the very large Port of La Rochelle at 10.45 am the next morning.

What an enormous Port and Marina this was. We thought Brighton Marina in England was big but La Rochelle was twice as big. About 3500 boats lived here. It took me 20 minutes to walk the length of it and what an enjoyable walk it was too. After the visitors' pontoon, we were directed to our berth and went for a walk into the City of La Rochelle. We approached the inner Marina of the city which is a show place for the more expensive Yachts with a mooring fee to match. At the entrance to this inner Marina were two towers built many centuries before to stop invaders sailing this far towards the city. It was a beautiful scene and I sketched it some days later and then painted it as watercolour to make a good painting which I still have.

We had arrived on the 6th of July and I suggested to Helen that as La Rochelle was such a good place to stop, that we could stay for the French National Day on the 14th of July, Bastille Day! She agreed. As usual, we got the local bus to the places that we visited and as our French was improving the locals were very chatty. It was just good fun to talk to them, albeit in halting French.

One morning whilst on deck of TS, a small open fishing boat was motoring towards the exit of the Marina and out for a day's work. As the boat came nearby, the fisherman held the tiller between his legs and produced a trumpet from his seat and played the French National Anthem. All this while still steering the boat. The Anthem was a stirring rendition of an inspiring tune for all French people. He did this a couple of times again and then the 14th July arrived.

We had never been in France before for Bastille day celebrations, so we did not know what to expect. After breakfast, Helen and I walked to the old harbour at the edge of the city. People were going about their business at a slow pace, but with a lot more people carrying flowers. Perhaps the French were into flowers in a big way? We would have to wait and see. It may have been my imagination to notice everyone saying Bonjour and smiling from a genuine happiness of just being alive. The further that we walked into the city, the happier we became. It was strange and unique. I even purchased a Bretton shirt which I still wear.

After returning to the old harbour for a late lunch, we managed to get one of the last tables at a restaurant looking out to the harbour on looking about, the reason for the many flower carrying people that we saw earlier, was there to see. It was a sea of colour and since I love colour in any form, I was in a spot of heaven. Lunch came quite late but we did not care as we were fortified by some good local French wine and a baguette…of course a baguette goes with anything at any time of the day.

Evening came upon us and we were still there at the same restaurant, as time had disappeared from reckoning. To be surrounded by so many happy people for many hours, of course, is infectious and we stood at the table, a little unsteady, to move off to another happy venue. Some coffee brought us closer to earth and we joined late night celebrations until about 11 pm, when we returned to TS. A wonderful day and we had thousands of French people to thank for it. Our trumpet playing fisherman was a bit late the next morning and a little off note.

One of Helen's friends, Louisa, joined us in La Rochelle for our passage to the north coast of Spain. We slipped our bow and stern lines on 17th July 1995 and sailed out into the Bay of Biscay to the Port City of Bilbao near the corner of the borders of France and Spain.

It was an uncomfortable sail as the Bay of Biscay has a continental shelf running diagonally across it, which makes for a lumpy sea state where TS would pitch and toss. We entered Bilbao Bay and Helen and Louisa went forward to unshackle the anchor. There were a few building sites close by as I motored to our anchorage and six or seven workman stopped work and were waving to the girls who, of course, waved back. This was not our official greeting to Spain, but had a lot to do with two attractive girls in bikinis. The girls thought it great fun.

We anchored near to the Yacht Club and went ashore for lunch. We had made it to Spain and near to the Basque region. There was a totally different atmosphere here, although just as delightful as in France. The day was sunny and the seafood on sale on the streets was bountiful. We chose a restaurant and had lunch with some Spanish wine that we had not had before. It was good to be eating different food and the Spanish are as diverse in their range of tastes as the French were. It was here that we noticed some of the waiters pouring a type of alcoholic cider into a customer's glass where they would pour from the bottle, held over their head, into a glass held at about knee level. It was a scream. This was the traditional way, in this part of Spain, to be served this drink. Needless to say, most of the cider that we saw being poured did not make the glass. Nobody seemed to care so we ordered some and were duly entertained.

An after-lunch walk through the city brought us to the Piazza. It was a very large area with many fountains and sculptures. Louisa had noticed that quite a few people were wearing clogs. This looked a bit odd in Spain and then I remembered that Holland had once been called the Spanish Netherlands and the footwear had been retained here after Spain relinquished their rule over the Netherlands. The girls were thinking of buying a pair of clogs when we went to a shoe store the following day. We all tried on a pair but declared them too difficult to walk with.

After much walking that first day, we aimed up at a bar near to TS. We found a table to sit and I ordered some drinks. The atmosphere washed over us with the bold Spanish colours adorning the walls and the odd Dali print just to add a touch of realism.

And then it happened! A man of about 50 walked into the bar and ordered a drink. He was near to us and within a minute he walked over and introduced himself as Serge. He was pleasant and I asked him to sit on the last chair at the table. Helen and Louisa were complimented by Serge and toasts to the city of Bilbao ensued. We had been speaking in broken English, French and a little Spanish with some Italian thrown in. We all laughed at this and I then said to Serge, "Of course Senior, you are Pablo Picasso" and Serge demurred. This fellow looked the very image of Picasso and Serge knew this. It was extraordinary and the girls agreed after they got back their memory from school days.

It was a jolly afternoon and Serge invited me back to a club which he part owned with his brother whilst the girls returned to TS. Serge then wanted us to wait for the weekend as there was a planned Spanish BBQ at their family home which we were invited. I had to decline as we intended to leave the next day for Santander, further east on the north Spanish coast. More hospitality. It must be the salt air, I thought.

As we approached Santander there were some signs at the entrance of the new marina announcing the celebrations of the town's Saint's Day. This is the annual celebration of the founding of that town's establishment. It basically meant party time. After coming in quite late that evening to the marina, we walked to town and the main square. People were dressed in traditional costumes with Spanish music playing everywhere.

After leaving Marina de Cantabica in Santander and visiting San Vicente de la Barquera and Ribadesella, we arrived in Gijon on the north Spanish coast, for a break from the celebrations of Saint's Days of some towns just visited. Gijon is the largest town on the north coast and a very attractive town it is as well. As we arrived in mid-afternoon Louisa, Helen and I went ashore for a late lunch. The time did not matter as we had gotten used to eating Tapas Food for some time now. Tapas was always available at any time of the day. We melded a late lunch into dinner and discovered that the Saints Day for Gijon was in two days' time. As we were going to stay here for a few days, this was an even better reason to stay for a while.

After breakfast on TS the next day we went back to the town and I separated from the girls as I went to sketch a scene that was interesting. After lunch, I had to visit a bank and there was a branch in this town. I knew the address but the local map was not detailed enough to show it. So I approached a young girl walking in the main Piazza to ask for directions. She stopped and smiled and as she could speak English, I explained. As she was giving directions, she stopped and said it would be better if she showed me herself and off we went. About 12 minutes later we arrived at the bank and I thanked her very much. It was an obscure location and I wondered how many people would have been bothered to do what she had done.

On the day of the Saint's Day for Gijon we first went ashore for a Spanish breakfast. Afterwards, we sat at an outdoor theatre where there was a small orchestra. The MC came on stage and asked anyone in the audience if they would come up on stage to sing. With this, two chaps came on stage. After the first chap asked something of the orchestra, he started to sing. He was good. The second chap was very good and the third was excellent. I thought that most of the guys in this part of Spain thought that they were Hose Carreras who of course was part of the Three Tenors. The other two being Luciano Pavarotti and Placido Domingo. The thing is that they were all good to listen to and some of the girls were operatic.

We sat at the main Piazza at about 2 pm for Tapas and drinks and reflected that the day's entertainment was so good that we should return next year.

Sailing onto Cudillero, we motored through a narrow entrance to find pastel painted houses on a steep hill and moored in this great atmosphere. Onwards, we sailed west to Ribadeo which had a pretty river approach and there the town was perched on a hill overlooking all. Then on to Vivero, where fireworks were seen that night.

We made it to A Coruna on the far west coast of north Spain. Here we visited Santiago de Compostello and visited the Cathedral there. This is a place of pilgrimage for people from all around the world. They will come to Spain and choose a town to start a walk which gets them to Santiago de Compostello. Some of the faithful will walk hundreds of miles to finally reach their goal. The Cathedral is massive and the aura around it is thick. After returning to Coruna, we went to the Yacht Club which was very enjoyable with a fantastic atmosphere and a huge beach nearby.

After checking the weather forecast that afternoon I decided that it was not a good window to get out into the North Atlantic and head south. We tried the next afternoon but returned due to the conditions. The following day, we watched as a Spanish yacht entered the harbour. It had to raft up to a Spanish Coast Guard boat to wait for a spot. The lady at the front of the yacht was dressed superbly in navy /white and threw all the rope to a crewman on board the coast Guard boat. The crewman then threw the rope back to the fashionable lady and explained how she was to tie off her end to secure their yacht. This, of course, amused some of us looking on and when the yacht could get to an alongside spot two down from TS I did not look any further.

However, about 20 minutes later the family from the yacht went ashore for lunch. I watched the skipper secure the lines fore and aft before he went ashore with his family. I looked at the people on the boat next to TS and we both said at the same time "what about the tide" Unless the skipper returns to his boat, and as the tide drops, the lines will become tight and then snap and then the yacht will drift away. I guess it was about an hour later when I went ashore from TS to this Spanish yacht. I boarded it and released the lines to allow for the drop of tide.

Some hours later, the family returned. I saw them coming and approached the skipper with the news of his oversight. He thanked me very much but my reason for the advice was so that he would not do it again. It is very easy to forget stuff after a sail and you still need to do things to keep safe. That evening, I walked on to the mole jutting out of the harbour where about a dozen fishermen were doing their thing but not getting anything. I asked one fisherman why he stays so long and he and about half the guys there said that they are there because their wives nag at them too much. It even happens in Spain!

We eventually slipped our lines and left a Coruna at 9.15 am one morning to make an overnight passage to Vigo on the Spanish Atlantic coast. After lunch on TS, some dolphins joined us and they are of course wonderful to see as they effortlessly kept pace with TS which was doing about seven knots. [13 kph]. With the sun still in the western sky, we hit a gale at about 8 pm. It was not on the forecast that morning and I wondered what was going on. There was a scramble on TS as we got everything stowed and set a reef in the mainsail and furled the genoa in to reduce sail area. About an hour and a half later the gale abated and we got back to smooth sailing.

I then grabbed the chart of that area and noticed in very fine print, "Coast of Death". I was perplexed until a read in the pilot book that for this part of the North Atlantic which meets the warmer climes of the Bay of Biscay, a gale is prevalent at any time. The coast area was so named, as in the days of the square-rigged sailing ships, they could not sail away from the coast with the gale blowing them onto the rocks with loss of life and ship. It was just another local condition.

During the night more dolphins appeared and the water produced phosphorescence which was a different wake for TS. We tied up at the Vigo Yacht Club which was where the Spanish ship would go into when being chased by the British, especially Lord Nelson.

Portugal was not far away and we made Viana de Costelo as our first stop in this new country. The hospitality here was great and provided by David Lumley. He was pleased that we were flying the Portuguese flag on our starboard shrouds as a salute to this country. David was the Cruising Association Representative for this area and he gave me some advice for changing the water pump on TS. There was a trip into the hills to see a couple of small towns and it was then that we realised that Portugal was still coming away from the dictatorship rule of M. Salazar who had ruled from 1974 until recently. It was in many ways a third world country. The people, however were wonderful and very gracious in their manner. It was the same as Spain, only different food.

From the beginning of our travels, we met quite a few people who were going our way and they looked forward to seeing us again in one of the ports to come. I do not think that we met any of these people again as we were enjoying each port of call so much that we stayed longer than most. It was all due to that thing called hospitality. I made up a word for this, because it does not appear in the dictionary. We were being "hospitality-ised" and if you stay in this mode for too long it makes the world and its people seem like a movie of good nature. Still cannot explain it.

After six days we got out into the Atlantic again. It was a good day for sailing but soon after a morning coffee I noticed that our power had gone for the services on board. I checked the batteries for this and found that two of them were flat. We needed to make a port that day to have them charged and to check the generator. I looked at the chart whilst Helen was on the wheel and saw a port and anchorage at Pavoa de Varzim, where we arrived and anchored at 5 pm. We were the only yacht in the harbour, the rest being fishing boats.

The following morning, Helen and I went to shore by the tender and secured it near the ramp. It was about 9.30 am and we had waited until some shops were open for business. I called at a service station and luckily the chap spoke a broken English. He directed us to the Club Naval not too far away.

Club Naval was a fine building with a large bar area and dining room. The staff were preparing for opening later in the morning and one of the barmen, after briefly hearing our need for battery attention, said he would get the President of the club to come down from his office and try to help. We met Michael, the President, who gratefully spoke good English and we sat down at a table and Michael ordered some coffees from the kitchen. After explaining our predicament, Michael assured us that he could help and the problem would be attended to that day. With that, he made a phone call and returned to his coffee. He told us that TS was to be towed to the fishing quay in about 30 minutes and he then ordered some cognac to have with the coffee! It was about 10.30 am. Helen and I laughed and so did Michael as we had a further coffee and cognac. We then returned to TS and met a couple of young chaps and directed them to the batteries that needed attention.

Michael owned a large men's wear store in the centre of town and he invited us to go there for any help as his son, Balo, was the manager there and would help with anything. As so it turned out to be. Balo showed us on a town map some of the places to visit and an art gallery of seafaring paintings. We returned to TS to change for the evening and met Michael, Balo and their staff after they closed the store at 7 pm. Drinks were had at an ornately decorated bar, mostly in blue, white and yellow which seemed to be the national colours of design. Michael then invited Helen and I to dinner at his house. We accepted. Michael's home was near to the top of a mountain overlooking the town and harbour. The view over a drink was just European, that is all I can say. Before, during and after dinner, neighbours and other people kept arriving at Michael's home to meet us. It was a humble time for Helen and myself.

Michael's mother and the chef of the very fine meal that night, wanted to see TS, so I suggested that we drive down to the town quay and all get aboard for a drink and coffee. three car loads of people descended on TS and a cook's tour of our boat made our visitors very happy, to say nothing of the wine, which was a small return compliment.

The following morning, we were due to leave and I took a small Australian flag to the Club Naval and presented it to Michael, who said that he would put it in a frame and hang it in the club to mark the visit of Tequila Sunrise. To this day it is probably still there. Michael gave me a 25-year-old bottle of Port and there was no cost for the battery charges.

Sailing out of that fishing harbour later, we looked behind to wave to about six people. Once again, we had been 'hospitality-ised'. Some feeling, that.

We then sailed to a small marina at Leixoes Yacht Club near the coastal city of Oporto. This city is on a grand river and a large bridge spans the river at the centre of town. I sat down at a cafe to sketch this scene while Helen went exploring. After lunch, we went on a guided tour of a large distillery of Port which was one of the main products of the area and in the country of Portugal. The following day, we slipped our lines at Leixoes Yacht Club and were headed to Lisbon, the capital. It was an overnight sail and the forecast looked OK.

What happened during this night and day passage to Lisbon was both exciting and scary. The wind was slowly increasing in force and I had tried to reef the mainsail but without success as the wind was too strong and to turn TS around would have risked broaching. So we were stuck with the full main up and the wind increasing. I then tried to furl the genoa or large headsail and this would not work from the cockpit with the genoa sheet. Helen had the wheel and I clipped onto the jack-stay from my harness. The jack-stay is a length of webbing running either side of the boat from stern to bow. I moved forward to the bow and on inspecting the furling mechanism I could not see anything untoward. It was probably stuck somehow inside the drum holding the sheet. After I returned to the cockpit, I sat down to explain the situation to Helen and what we needed to do.

We could not reduce sail and it just so happened that the wind, which was increasing, was coming straight down on TS from the stern. This was the best direction that we could have. All we had to do was to steer almost dead south as the wind was from the north. The wind was now a gale and we decided to take two hour shifts instead of the usual four hours. Helen got us some tea and biscuits and I took the first shift.

Steering like this, with the sails pulled tight, was not easy and you had to keep your mind on steering because at the speed that TS was doing, to look around too long and not concentrate would have TS sliding sideways across a following swell and broach the boat. This almost happened to me after midnight and I just corrected our direction in time as I noticed that we were almost doing

12 knots across the face of the swell/ wave. The maximum hull design speed of TS was 10 knots.

I only looked behind me once and saw that we were at the bottom of a swell, in the gully, and the top of the wave following us was almost to the height of the mast. This made the waves, which were cascading at the top, about 50 feet high. Helen came up from the galley about two hours later with more tea and I went below. When I reappeared Helen looked exhausted and I suggested that she go below and sleep and I will try to do a few hours. After about three hours, I banged on the deck above the rear bedroom and eventually Helen appeared still rubbing her eyes. I thought that it best now to do one hour shifts as the concentration needed was exhausting. This worked well as sunrise came and we were hoping that the sea state would moderate. It did not and we continued to speed through the Atlantic on about a 160-degree course which was a little easier to handle as the wind filled the sails. It was also the course to Lisbon and the very large bay approaching Lisbon.

As we approached this bay the wind increased and it was now a Force 9, one notch above a gale. It did not worry me so much as TS was doing its thing and the sun was out. Then it happened. One of the shackles, holding the large headsail in place, came free and both the headsail sheets were in the water on the starboard side and doing washing machine impersonations in the water. The sheets were flicking all over the place and if one of these hit you it would cause some injury and possibly take an eye out. I turned a little into the wind to slow down and asked Helen if she could take the wheel while I worked out what to do.

I wrote down five things that I was going to do and, in the order, listed and went forward. The headsail was gathered in and tied to the bow stay on about a two-metre area of the stay. This took me about 20 minutes and the problem was fixed. The wind was still blowing the clappers but TS was now not leaning so much. We sailed into the river leading up to the Doca de Santo Amaro, the marina. We came alongside a berth and secured the lines. What a sail that had been! Helen and I opened a bottle of Scotch and with our adrenaline up we did not notice how much we had consumed until about an hour later. It was the best part of that bottle.

The marina was on the edge of the city and in a fabulous place to see the sights. After we settled down and got TS, in order a chap named Darius came to the side of TS and offered his services as a mechanic and boat fixer of most things. I arranged for the engine to be serviced by his young mechanic and the furling headsail to be repaired. We decided to stay for about two weeks, so there was no hurry. I checked in our passports and Ship's Papers and we walked into the city for dinner.

We walked through the very old City Gates and into a square which was very large. Lisbon is an impressive city and well laid out. Trams were still running and were English made where England is Portugal's oldest ally. After some days of sight-seeing, we decided to hire a car and drive to the south of Portugal which is called The Algarve. We wanted to visit various Marinas to decide where we would spend the winter that was approaching.

The drive south was like driving in the NSW countryside. It was amazing with eucalyptus trees everywhere and rolling hills. On visiting the last Marina at Lagos in the Algarve, we decided that this was the place to be for the European winter. We would sail there when we left Lisbon. The marina in Lagos was relatively new and was built by Camper and Nicholson, an English company who also managed it. It looked very inviting and we booked a spot with their office.

Returning to Lisbon we were treated that evening to a music concert nearby and the sound was fabulous. Dulce Pointes was the main singer and the next day I purchased an album of hers. Portugal was of course the place where Henry the Navigator, a Portuguese supporter of exploration, would send sailors away in the 16th century to see the world and hopefully return. Statues of him in the city were everywhere. They were and still are very proud of their seafaring heritage.

Darius, our fixer upper, was around the marina one day and invited us to his place for dinner. We did not have far to walk as his home was close to the main square in the city. Darius' home was large and his wealth had come mainly from being a mercenary fighter in Africa many years before. I was surprised what was paid to officers for that job.

It was then that Helen had an idea that could earn us some money. We went to see a Personal Computer dealer in the city and offered to conduct some Internet Seminars for anyone to attend. The Internet was new to Portugal Telecom and nobody in business knew anything about it, let alone the average citizen. Helen ran up the overheads to show on screen and we held some seminars during our stay in Lisbon. We did this again in The Algarve with a PC dealer from Faro, on the coast near our winter stay.

It was time to leave Lisbon. We set sail under the bridge as we left the Tagus River approaches and out into the Atlantic. The day and night passed with calm weather and a good sea running. At about 8 am, we came up on portside, to one of the great icons on the European mainland. It was Cape St Vincent on the south western corner of the Portuguese mainland. There is a large lighthouse at Cape St Vincent and this morning it was embraced with a flat cloud about half way up its height. It was a sight worthy of a painting but doing the sketch from a yacht is too difficult. From here we were to turn to port to reach Lagos, our wintering spot.

Cape St Vincent was so named after a famous sea battle which took place in these water in 1797. Admiral Sir John Jervis who commanded the British Fleet in this action, met and defeated a Spanish Fleet. During this action, Rear Admiral Horatio Nelson left the English line of battleships, against English Admiralty instructions, and destroyed two Spanish ships. He did this as he considered that his ship was in a point of vantage. He severely damaged two other ships. Initially, his commander, Sir John Jervis was aghast but watched as Nelson put his touch on the battle.

After this battle, the English Parliament bestowed the title of Lord St Vincent to Jervis. The Portuguese government, who hated the Spanish and wanted to commemorate this battle, changed the name of this cape to Cape St Vincent and still its present name. This cape was also the last bit of land that the explorers and various navies of Europe, would view as they got about their business, after leaving European waters. Many never returned of course, either lost in storms, or sea battles or to scurvy.

Lagos. Our winter home. We entered the channel and tied up at the reception pontoon just outside Marina de Lagos. I presented passports and papers at the office and in the excitement of arriving and the buoyant conversations in the office, the Immigration Officer forgot to stamp our passports. This would rebound on us a little later.

After finding our berth in the Marina we went straight to the bar for a well-earned drink. There were a few people gathered there and we introduced ourselves to as many as was practicable. Most people that we met that afternoon were wintering at the Marina as well. It was the 3rd of October and we did not leave until the 3rd April 1996, six months. The people that we met during this time all had very interesting stories to tell. After a while, we became a large family and helped each other in all sorts of ways. Such is the camaraderie of sailors.

Boats and people were arriving every week and one of the first yachts was a sloop called "Yellow Bird" which we saw reversing down the pontoons at, what

I thought was too fast, and then stern to and tie up in about a minute. It takes skill to do that and I walked over to say hello and met Aubrey Long, aged 82 years and his son Richard. Aubrey had been at the wheel on the fast manoeuvre. These two were English and were there for the winter as well. Aubrey had won a recent ARC Rally [Atlantic Rally for Cruisers] which races from the Canary Islands to Antigua in the Caribbean. About a two-week sail. They both were great hosts and at 5 pm each day anybody could go aboard their boat for drinks. Aubrey would ask Richard to strike their boat's flag at exactly 6 pm each day and fold it for the locker. Tradition never dies with some Englishmen.

There were lone sailors there as well and characters all. James, who made great pains to say that he was Canadian and not US nationality, had a 34-feet Catamaran and was good company. Sheldon was a US citizen and had been sailing the Mediterranean for about eight years. His wife had recently returned to the US to be with the family, but Sheldon Cohen stayed as he preferred this life. Derek was a lone sailor on a 32-feet sloop which looked like it needed a good clean and renewal of sails and standing rigging. He was a funny character and still drank rum as a staple. The last lone sailor was Dan Wilson, a US citizen, who I saw one morning approaching the reception pontoon in the channel leading into the Marina. I judged his Catamaran to be about a 36-footer and kept wondering when the crew were going to come on deck and help to come alongside. This of course did not happen as Dan jumped with the bow line, and threw the stern line onto the pontoon. I had done something similar but Dan looked a lot older to be doing it. Lone sailors need to be very handy people.

It was a short walk to the village of Lagos and it is a pretty village with an old church bordering the piazza. Lagos had been one of the main towns where African slaves would be auctioned in the town square and then sent to the Americas, in the main. One day, Helen and I were walking in the piazza and a police officer walked past. I suggested to Helen that we might follow him, as it was lunch time, and he might be on his way to a cafe to have lunch. We followed and sure enough arrived at a small family-owned lunch spot. We sat down and the lunch selection was of only three dishes. It changed daily and the three dishes tomorrow would be different. We ordered lunch and some bread and a carafe of local wine. It was delicious and very inexpensive. We had left some wine in the second carafe, when we were about to leave, and the waiter came across with the bill and deducted an amount for the fact that we had left some wine and two pieces of bread...How about that! We returned many times and told the others of our find.

Twice each week, we all gathered on the beach for a game of beach volley ball. The local Beach Bar had provided the net and ball to play with. six people on each side and rotating the serve etc. We gradually became better and better and later on there were some long rallies.

Lagos Marina, Our spot for the Winter

Ships log for one passage

The coast line on this part of The Algarve is dotted with small beaches and alcoves and one day whilst I was walking along the small beaches I came across a home overlooking the beach. The home had a sign on the wall saying Yacht Club, so I walked in. There were about a dozen people having a drink and I joined in the frivolity. After about half an hour whilst talking to one of these chaps, I mentioned that I had a Moody 39 and was wintering at the Marina. Then one of the chaps said "Of course that model Moody was designed by Angus Primrose, who was Moody's Chief Architect." I agreed and this fellow asked if I knew the story of Angus Primrose's death. He confirmed what I knew of his death. It was this…Angus would always take the prototype of any newly designed yacht for a test sail across the Atlantic and return to England having taken note of any faults and improvements needed. He would sail the prototype with his mistress as he had done previously. One afternoon, the prototype Moody 39 was brought into Plymouth Harbour, with his mistress as the only person on board. It seems that Angus had fallen overboard some nights before and was lost at sea. Angus was insured and the bulk of the money went to his mistress and not his wife.

This news hit the maritime headlines as Angus was a much-loved character. So this chap in the bar, we'll call him Alan, then informed me that he had seen Angus Primrose the year before in the Caribbean when he was working there for Sunsail. Alan had been sworn to secrecy but too much to drink and he let loose with this secret. He repeated his end of the mystery and I took to believing it. I then got Alan aside and said that I would not give up the secret. He was pleased and apologetic for the utterance. Angus would be dead now even if the story was true. I went back to the Marina and kept wondering.

Christmas was approaching and we were all very excited. One of the guys booked a restaurant for the Christmas lunch and we all had to buy a Secret Santa present for one of our large family. Christmas morning arrived and I was on deck having a cup of tea, when I could hear some music starting to resonate across our part of the Marina. I caught the tune soon. It was Waltzing Matilda. I stood up and looked around in wonderment, as did Helen when she heard the music from below and came on deck. Waltzing Matilda was coming from a yacht that had arrived that week. It was a Rival-Bowman Sloop, a beautiful boat. The yacht was named "The Piano" and the tune that somebody was now playing was on a piano.

You cannot imagine what it is like to hear your default National Anthem as an Australian, on Christmas morning, on the other side of the world and in such a beautiful place as we were. Tears started to roll down both Helen and my cheeks. At the end of the song, we both walked over to "The Piano" as the owner Charles, came on deck. We both thanked him so profusely that he was a little overcome, as we were. He was Dutch and he was a concert pianist, of course. His wife was not on board as she had gone to church earlier. We met her later in the day. Charles invited us down into the salon for a look around, as any proud skipper would. As I descended the companionway, I noticed a very large teak beam bracing the boat and from port to starboard across the ceiling of the saloon. I remarked to Charles that I had never seen anything like it and Helen said that it was a wonderful feature. There was also the superb keyboard on the starboard side, next to the chart table and surrounded by teak. This of course was a lead-in to the story as told by Charles of the abundance of teak on the boat. Charles had travelled to Thailand soon after the start of the build of the boat. Here he picked out the particular teak tree that he wanted. It was promptly felled and hauled to a port city, where he followed, and put aboard to be taken to Holland for the fitting out. I think that Charles was a perfectionist.

Why did Charles play Waltzing Matilda? He saw our Australian flag running on the port shrouds, which for flag etiquette in Europe, means that there is an Australian on board and amazingly he had the sheet music.

We met Charles' wife at our Christmas lunch. There were 28 people who sat down for lunch with nine nationalities represented. It was such a great mix that most of us had swapped lots of addresses by day's end. 82-year-old Aubrey played Santa Claus and he insisted that all the girls sit on his knee before they received their presents. The dirty dog! A lot of Christmas songs were sung that afternoon in the different languages, at the same time, which sounded absurd and with the accompanying tears that were the order of the day.

We returned to TS and some sleep as we were invited to Karl and Inger's boat for Boxing Day lunch. Helen and I were a bit dusty next morning but by lunchtime had recovered. Their boat was a Colin Archer designed "Double Ender Ketch" built in Holland. About a dozen of us went aboard for lunch. We first had some mead wine which Inger had made over previous weeks from a recipe that was handed down by her Norwegian grandmother. Karl, who was Austrian, cooked a BBQ of some Austrian origin and the day was completed when Charles played a selection of songs from a borrowed keyboard.

After the Christmas lunch, we became a closer family of international people. Helen had met Sara and Bruce a few weeks after our arrival and I met them at the community bar sometime later. After shaking hands with Bruce, he introduced me to his wife "Slug". I said, "Sara isn't it?" Sara corrected me and said that her name was always "Slug" and not to call her Sara. Now, Sara/Slug was a beautiful girl and to call her Slug was so incongruous that I found it difficult, as did anybody. They had even made a Battle Flag which is a personal flag to be flown in port. On it was the image of a Bruce Anchor [a design of anchor] and a large slug sliding down the shank. It was about one metre by

700mm. Very creative. Both Bruce and Slug had taken a year off work to sail with Sara being Nokia's top Salesperson in Europe on the corporate side. She kept getting phone calls from Nokia pleading with her to return, but she refused.

Ian and Steve were also wintering at Lagos and their boat was called "Lola", a Beneteau sloop. These guys were two great humoured Englishmen who decided to take time out for nine months whilst their girlfriends would fly in to visit when they could.

Ralph and Jeannie were two Americans staying at the marina. They conducted a small charter business when American visitors would be taken on a six-to-eight-day sail to Morocco or Algeria. Their boat was called "Battlestar" and Ralph would often ask me to look after the boat while they were gone. That simply meant that I would open the hatches to air the boat for the occasional day and keys supplied.

David and Jenny owned an old motor cruiser which was fitted out below like an English country cottage. It was meticulous. David proudly told me that he had found the boat up a stream on the south coast of England. He was told of this by a ship's chandler because it had been one of the little ships of Dunkirk which had saved many lives from the beaches of Dunkirk. Somebody needed to save this boat and it was David and Jenny.

David, who owned two small hotels, and a few friends, hauled the boat out of the river and started to work to restore. It was almost 2500 hours later and she was ready for sea again. The hotel profits took a pounding during that time.

When I was on board I noticed a small brass plaque that was screwed above the entrance to the companionway stating the Dunkirk experience and presented to David and Jenny by President Mitterrand of France for the 50th Anniversary of the Dunkirk evacuation in 1990. Quite an honour!

I minded this boat as well when David and Jenny went back to England to attend the hotels.

During the week between Christmas and the New Year a Moody 42 Ketch arrived in the Marina for an extended stay. It was a sister ship to TS and was owned by an affable Irishman named Paddy. With his mate Steve, he had sailed from Lisbon after some professionals had sailed it from Ireland. What a character Paddy was. He was a reformed alcoholic and attended the local AA Meetings whenever he could on his travels. He was married and had three children who helped in his business which was in scrap metal.

For some reason we became good friends quickly and Helen and I joined in a dinner with him and his wife Sally, in the new year. We were at a table of about a dozen as some of Sally's friends had flow down with her to join them for a holiday.

It was then that there happened the doozy of coincidences. I was seated next to Richard and his fiancée who were friends of Sally's younger sister. I eventually asked Richard what he did at work and he told me that he worked for Microsoft in London. I mentioned that a mate of mine in Australia who worked for Microsoft in Sydney should, about now, be in England to visit his parents in Oxford. Richard asked "Is his name John Levison?"

I replied, "Yes."

Richard then said, "Well, I had dinner with him two nights ago!"

I do not know what the odds for that sort of thing is, but it must be rather great. Richard and I were incredulous and the laughter followed. Paddy had heard the story at the table and we were all entertained with coincidences like mine but not to that degree.

In February, our new family were invited to Karl and Inger's wedding. The invitations arrived with a photo of intertwined legs of Karl and Inger underneath a small table. A nice touch. They were married on the beach with the reception at the beach bar. The bride and groom were going to get married in either Norway or Austria but could not agree. So they decided on Lagos as their new friends, their new family, would love to meet the relatives who flew down for the wedding. It worked like magic and some of the relatives stayed for a few days longer. The weather helped as it was always about 22 degree C, t-shirt stuff.

Aubrey was to return to his home near Plymouth in the UK briefly and Paddy was returning to Galway in Ireland to attend to business. They both invited Helen and I to visit with them. I had always wanted to go to Ireland and especially Galway, as this was where our family, on my mother's side, had come from. We booked our flights to London and arrived at the airport at Faro to depart. There was a hold up as our passports were not stamped at Lagos during that excited arrival some months before. It took a phone call to the Lagos Marina to prove our bona-fides and the plane took off about five minutes late.

On arrival at Heathrow Airport I hired a car and we went straight to Aubrey's home on the coast of Cornwall on the south coast of England. After driving through the narrow, hedge row lanes towards the Cornwall coast we arrived at Aubrey's home. All without a GPS. Aubrey lived in a charming two bed cottage next to a very large house which was Aubrey's family home for many years before his wife died. Aubrey moved into the cottage because he could not live in the big house because of his memories of his life in the big house and his wife's presence there.

I took us out for dinner that night at a local pub and the following day we went with Aubrey to the Royal Plymouth Yacht Club, where a large photo of "Yellow Bird", Aubrey's yacht, was on the wall as you ascended the stairs to the club. He was obviously very proud of his achievements and the lunch time members all said hello and introduced themselves to Helen and myself. It seemed that anybody who was with Aubrey was worth knowing.

It was then back to Heathrow for the flight to Galway in Ireland. Paddy's son, Patrick, picked us up at Knock Airport in Galway and we left to visit an Irish Pub before going to Paddy's home for dinner. But first, there was a pint or two of Guinness to be had and a dozen Galway oysters to be consumed at the pub. For those of us who have drunk Guinness away from Ireland before, and that was me, there is nothing like drinking a Guinness in Ireland. The taste is sublime. If it is with some Galway oysters, it is a heaven of taste bud revival. Patrick would not allow me to pay for any of this. It's that word, hospitality again.

The following day, Paddy pointed to a spare BMW in the five-car garage and threw me the keys. Helen and I were off to discover the Ring of Kerry in southern Ireland and then onto Dublin before returning to Galway. I did a number of sketches over the next three days and combined this with a confirmation of our family history, starting with the Mayor of Galway in 1774.

After returning to TS in Lagos, we met some friends from Sydney who had purchased a three deck Motor Yacht of 62-feet length. It was large. Helen knew both Ray and Pauline as both had worked with Helen in Sydney. They had also bought a home near to Lagos. Ray was in the Marina at Lagos to greet two mechanics from the US to service the two Detroit Diesel motors in their Motor Yacht. We visited their home for lunch and the home seemed to be made totally of marble. Marble looks great and was a very cheap building material in Portugal.

There was another power boat cruiser in the marina that had just arrived from England. The owner and skipper was Roger Carr who had purchased his boat, a Broom 44 and this was its first extended cruise. He and I hit it off straight away and dinners were enjoyed with his girlfriend, Felicity who arrived for the balance of the winter. Roger, who owned UK Fire Supplies, was fairly wealthy and he needed to be to pay for the fuel that this boat used. Roger and Felicity were eventually going into the Mediterranean and were going to coast hop along Spain, France and Italy. I painted Roger's boat and put it, in a scene, in a harbour that I knew that they would visit. It looked good in the frame and I said to Roger that he would have to find this harbour and anchor his boat exactly where it was in the painting. The harbour in the painting was at Portofino on the Italian Riviera.

It was time to start to prepare to move towards the Mediterranean Sea, past Gibraltar. About a week before we left I was approached by two men, dressed in suits, who were asking about Ralph and Jeanie and their boat "Battlestar". I said that as far as I knew. they were off on another Charter and would be back soon in the Marina. They seemed satisfied and went on.

It was a sad day when we left Lagos at 1.30 pm for an overnight passage to Puerto Sherry on the Spanish coast. There was an eclipse of the moon which started at about 11.30 pm and lasted for over two hours. We had new Autopilot Steering and this helped with a bit of relaxation during the passage. As the new day dawned, the swell was uncomfortable and we had to tack to escape the swell. We finally made it to Puerto Sherry in Spain at 11.30 pm that night. It was later than I had planned and the lights on taking up a course to enter the were almost non-existent and I had to go very slow. I had looked at the pilot book for this port and the sea bed was sand and mud so I knew that if we did run aground there would be no damage. We did nudge the bottom and I called out to Helen, who was forward, "Well we've hit Spain." I then backed off and we motored into the Marina and moored. We awoke late the next morning and had a swim in the swimming pool and walked to the town of Santa Maria.

We left Puerto Sherry for Puerto de Barbate and its proximity to the Spanish city of Cadiz. As we approached Cape Trafalgar, Helen slowed down TS and I then tried to explain the movements of the opposing fleets of ships in the Battle of Trafalgar on 21st Oct 1805.

A combined Spanish and French fleet under Admirals Gravina for the Spanish and Villeneuve for the French were faced by an English fleet led by Admiral Horatio Nelson. Nelson split his fleet into two columns with Collingwood in the van in one line and Nelson in the van in the other. This had not been done before and both columns sailed at right angles into the opposing fleets. It was a brilliant manoeuvre and destroyed the Spanish and French fleet's composure and they were defeated during this sea battle. Unfortunately, Nelson was killed and his body taken to Gibraltar in an alcohol cask and then sent to England on a fast Frigate. This battle told, that any thoughts by Napoleon of invading England would and could not be successful.

After a night in Puerto Barbate, we sailed for Gibraltar. We were joined by Aubrey and "Yellowbird" which was sailing to beyond Gibraltar. We started a tacking duel going east right into the Levanter wind. This wind can sometimes reach 90 to 100 miles per hour, but today it was about 20 to 25 mph. "Yellowbird" was tossing in big tacks whilst I was tacking closer to the wind. It was soon evident that Aubrey on "Yellowbird" was doing the better, sailing to the east. I called him on the VHF and bid him safe passage and hoped to see him some time into the Mediterranean. We made it to Gibraltar, that day and moored at Queensway Quay at 5.30 pm. We stayed about a week here as we had some minor repairs to the wind and speed instruments to wait. Gibraltar is populated with a mix of English and Spanish nationals and the two just do not look right here. They get on, but only just, as the Spanish have wanted this place forever.

John polishing top sides in Gibraltar

Another delightful encounter came on about day four of our stay here. We met an English couple who were in Gibraltar after sailing their yacht around the world. They were married and their story went like this.

Paul was 70 when we met him in Gibraltar and his wife was Australian named Catherine or Cathy as I shall call her. They met in 1944 when Paul was a Lieutenant on HMS Warspite, the largest British Battleship in their fleet. HMS Warspite called into Sydney Harbour to replenish and fit out for tropical duties with the US Fleet in the Pacific under US Admiral Chester Nimitz. This was to take a week or so and Cathy was a Nursing Sister over from Perth in Western Australia. She was there as Sydney was a major destination for soldiers, airmen and sailors to get medical attention from the war in the Pacific. Paul and her met and fell in love whilst Paul's ship was in Sydney. Paul and his ship sailed away to the Pacific and the war at sea. They kept in touch and were eventually married in England. Two of their children lived in Perth and the other two in England. They had always loved sailing in England and decided very late in life to sail around the world. It was a love story that was not to be beaten as they were clearly still in love.

Their achievement to sail around the world put what Helen and I were doing in the shade...a very enjoyable experience. To do that, at their age, was something special. I asked Paul what was the most dangerous time that they had. It was when Paul had to stop the boat for two days and clean out the toilet lines to the sea that had clogged up with salt and would not operate. Paul had not put the solution that takes away the salt in these lines on each flush. They stopped near the equator and it took Paul the best part of a day, in that heat, to find and release the lines for cleaning. The dangerous bit came when he tossed them into the ocean to clean. Whilst he was cleaning them some sharks appeared and Cathy had to warn them off with a point 22 rifle that they had on board. I couldn't stop laughing as that was truly the only time that they had some trouble! Cathy was flying back to England to see the kids and Paul was soon to follow after a bit of work on their boat. Paul then planned to return with one of his sons and some friends to sail back to England. Helen and I met many people who had sailed some long distances but nothing compared to the lovely couple that we met in Gibraltar where Cathy still had her Australian accent.

It was then into the Mediterranean Sea.

Chapter 12
Into the Mediterranean Sea

Our first port of call was in Estepona in Spain and Bruce and Slug were there on their Yacht "Lucy B" and it was good to catch up with them some few weeks after leaving our winter home. It was then that we heard some remarkable news. It was about some of our family of friends that we had wintered with in Lagos.

Estepona Marina

Firstly, Ralph and Jeannie on their yacht "Battlestar" which I had often been aboard in order to give it some air, had been arrested at sea sailing towards England. On board their yacht was 3.5 ton of marijuana. They were exhausted as the passage from where we were in Portugal to England is what we called "uphill" as it was into the wind practically all the way and a very tiring time. So the customer charters to Morocco/ Algeria were a cover for the collection of the marijuana. Apparently the Interpol police had rented a unit overlooking the Lagos Marina and were monitoring the comings and goings of "Battlestar" over a time. It was no wonder that I was interviewed by the two officers from Interpol with me having the keys to their boat. Of course at the time I had no idea that they were from Interpol. The last that we heard was that Ralph and Jeannie were in separate prisons awaiting trial.

Secondly, James, who was the solo sailor on his catamaran, had been arrested by the fraud section of Interpol. He was wanted in the US for financial fraud. We had a few parties aboard James' boat and his insistence that he was a Canadian national was wrong as he was a US citizen. This was no doubt to deflect any suspicion upon him. It may also explain James' request after he came aboard TS for a day sail along with two or three other yachts. Lots of photos were taken that day and James asked me if he could have the copy of the only photo where he appeared as he wanted to send it to his mother in Victoria, Canada. I could not find this photo among the others and James was disappointed. No doubt he did not want his image shown anywhere.

And so it came to pass that not all people are as described. In any case, the three people were good friends, for many months, on almost a daily basis.

During our next passage, I set about polishing the brass fittings and the stainless steel around the cockpit. When the wind was dead astern I rigged TS on a "Goose winged" sail with the mainsail out to one side and the headsail to the other. It is a spectacular point of sail but takes some care to keep the boat in that same attitude to the wind. We reached Benalmádena on the Costa Del Sol and were gob smacked by the buildings at the Marina. It was like being in the Arabian Nights with the spiralling tops to many buildings and the Moorish colours of gold, blue and red.

Benalmadena Marina

It was also here that we met a lot of young English tourists who collectively were known as "lager louts". They were here for a holiday to drink cheap beer. These lads and some of their girlfriends were good company and we enjoyed talking about how their lives were working out. A few of these chaps decided to get to the sunshine without the 30-plus sunscreen and at late afternoon when entering the bar, they displayed their blisters on shoulders and chests. The following day, however, they were in good spirits whilst still looking like an upright lobster. Benalmádena was a tourist heaven or hell, depending on choice of company.

Our next port of call, on the Costa Del Sol, was Marina Del Este. This place had won the European Marina of the Year two tears before and we were lucky to get in there as it was a very small place. It was a beautiful isolated area and all class. We stayed for over a week and played tennis at no charge and used their extensive facilities, as above the Marina were resorts, which were rather exclusive. And this on the Costa Del Sol, which is mostly known as a down market destination.

Tequila Sunrise in port at Marina Del Este

We slipped our lines at Marina Del Este and made Roquetas de Mar on the 8th May. Here is where we slipped TS for some anti-fouling and water pump repairs for the showers. It was the best value that we had come across for doing this work and a pleasant place to spend it whilst the work was done. Here is where we came upon another Moody 39 yacht. It was owned by two English people, Simon and Susan who were married. Simon was an Ocean master which in our circles made him the top-rated sailor who could skipper any vessel up to 200 feet long.

Aboard his boat identical to TS, it was the same until we went below. There, it all went askew There was an ornate cotton table cloth on the saloon table with place mats. Above the saloon table was a real cut glass chandelier. In the bunk room, instead of the cabinet, there was a washing machine. There was a microwave oven where the radar set should have been. I started to smile and Simon said that we should go up the companionway to the large cockpit and have a drink. Whilst we agreed that the roominess in the saloon was generous, the chandelier was a bit over the top.

It was also here that Helen and I hired a car to visit the great city of Seville. This city is located about 60 miles from the sea on a river. It is a classic city combining Moorish architecture with traditional Spanish. The layout of the city was superb and the parks were a delight to walk through. For a late lunch, we settled on an ornate bar which was in fact a well-known place where the Matadors, Toreadors and Picadors would come to after appearing at the stadium to ply their trade.

We stayed here as we were told that one of the most famous Matadors in Spain would be arriving at about 9 pm that evening. Our table was joined by some of the locals and fortunately some of these chaps could speak English. After briefly explaining our life cruising on TS, the topic was about Spanish Naval History. Of course I commented that the Spanish Main was the strongest area of Spanish sea dominance for over a century. I then mentioned Spanish Admiral Gravina at the Battle of Trafalgar and his bravery and our Spanish friends went quiet. They then smiled and were surprised that I knew of him and his status, at that table. More jugs of sangria were ordered. When the Matador arrived we all stood and applauded his entry to the place. The evening was a success for us, just out of a bit of history.

After returning to TS the following day, we sailed a short distance to Aguadulce which had a big harbour and quite a few English people who were still wintering. I don't think that they had noticed that Spring was marching on and they could safely move. But then again…who cares? We had done the same thing. There were a few Moody yachts here and it was evident that Aguadulce was a small English gathering spot for cruising yachts.

We stayed for six days whilst TS was hauled out of the water for two coats of anti-fouling paint, shower pump repair and back in the water after four days. It was good value here for the work and we conveyed a note to the Cruising Association to mention this in their next quarterly magazine. The town was a pleasant place to visit and on one of my walks into town, I was passing by a home which was being renovated and on the footpath, in front of the home, were some pieces of teak timber which looked destined for the skip bin. I enquired with one of the workmen and he invited me to take some, which I did. I subsequently built a small stand for our sound system on the chart table. It looked pretty good next to the other teak fittings in the saloon.

At this time, we were enjoying a different scene at each of our stops and to go ashore each time to explore, was a curiosity that was both revealing and enjoyable to experience how the Spanish lived here on the south coast. It was different to the north Spanish coast where the style of the people seemed more refined.

We left Aguadulce and sailed overnight to Torrevieja which has a large harbour and is another wintering spot for quite a few English people. There were also a few Moody yachts here and we spent a few days chatting with the owners and listening to their stories. It was here that I realised that our sailing adventures in respect of the gales that we had been in, were not common to the general cruising people who we met. It was not so much bad management, on my part, as some bad luck with the weather which is not always as reported on the radio. In any case, TS could handle it. We just had to hang on.

Torrevieja Marina

We slipped our lines at Torrevieja and sailed towards Arenal, further along the Spanish mainland coast. At 5.08 pm on the afternoon of 20th May 1996, we crossed the 0 Degree Longitude Meridian, which meant that directly to our north, a long way away, was the City of London. We celebrated this phenomenon with a glass of wine. Sunset that evening was at 9 pm and the following morning was our first sight of a sunrise over the Spanish Balearic Islands and at 9 am we were passing the island of Formentera, off to starboard.

Arenal Marina

There is always something special about an early morning at sea and specially when the weather is hot and sunny. If there is a chill in the air early, then it quickly disappears and you have to take off your oilies or you will sweat too much. The day then unfolds, as it did on this day, to be perfect sailing weather and we were joined at 7.30 pm with a pod of dolphins, the sailors' friends. Dolphins are a joy to behold and they seem to chatter to each other as they followed TS and occasionally I would try to mimic them and talk back. Totally absurd of course, but great fun as one tries to emulate Dr Doolittle.

Entering the Bay of Palma at 2.40 am at night was a little mysterious and we did not get into the Club Nautico Arenal Marina until 4.15 am and come alongside and tie off. After a brief sleep, we rose to have a good lunch and both Helen and I reflected on the passage just completed. It was very much a varied sail, with the conditions as sunny, then strong winds, then no winds, then good sailing and then no wind. As we were to find out, this changing of conditions was common for the western Mediterranean. In any case, we were in Palma, the capital of the island of Majorca. It was a very good marina with all the facilities that you could wish for with a swimming pool, hotel, shops and a discotheque. It was an expensive marina, so for a few days we were spoiled for some choices.

After five days of a different high living, we decided to visit the Archipelago De Cabrera.

For this short passage we were joined by some friends, Rob and Edna from England who, by chance, were in Majorca for a holiday. We got some fuel from Arenal fuel dock and headed out of the marina for Cabrera. It had been necessary to get a permit to go to this island as visitors were only allowed a maximum of three days stay with only a limited number of boats allowed in harbour. It was another superb day for sailing and we only had 24-mile passage.

After about two hours sailing, we came up on a similar sized boat to TS which was having some trouble setting their sails. I came up near them to port and called out to offer some help. They were two Spanish guys who had chartered this Beneteau yacht but were not too sure how to sail it. I suggested that they unfurl the mainsail a bit more to make it the size on TS and to do the same with the headsail. The headsail setting was a bit difficult for them until I told them what rope to uncleft and then pull to get the sail out onto the wind. After that, they thanked us very much and Helen, who was on the wheel, sailed away towards Cabrera. Rob and Edna were most amused at their lack of how to anything on board a charter boat and I remarked that it is too easy to charter these boats where, because you only have to be breathing to get a boat, which can easily put you in danger. In the meantime, Cabrera awaited.

`Tequila Sunrise – Anchored in the port of Cabrera

When we arrived at 5.40 pm, it was so much more than we had expected. The bay was almost round with the Fortress of Cabrera dominating the harbour and built on a small mountain overlooking the seaward side of the island and the harbour. We had to tie up to a mooring buoy as anchors were not allowed for the 11 buoys maximum allocation. The water was as clear as could be and we all jumped overboard into the bay after putting on our swimmers. The scene was another remarkable one with the surrounding forest coming down to the water's edge and some stone buildings at the eastern side. With the fortress, there it was like a postcard look and I sketched this scene the next day from our dinghy to show TS and the Fortress of Cabrera. That evening, the four of us settled into our seats in the cockpit area with the table attached to the binnacle and watched the sunset, which in this place was just special. I think that you prepare for sunsets whereas sunrises just happen. It was so special that Edna had some tears running down her cheeks with the beauty of it all.

The next morning was clear and I took the goggles and snorkel and had a good look at the bay and the sea floor which showed some parts of wrecks from other centuries. These Balearic Islands were used by a few navies, including the Royal Navy, where Admiral Nelson would direct that stores be kept on these islands for retrieval when needed. At one time here in the Mediterranean, Admiral Nelson did not leave his ship for almost two years as he stood blockading the French Naval Port of Toulon. So ship's stores were vital and these islands were very close by.

The four of us went ashore at mid-morning and discovered the very small village there was a taverna, a general store for provisions and a coffee spot where we sat and took in the atmosphere over a coffee. We spoke to a few of the soldiers who were part of a small Army Garrison stationed on the island and they were most helpful in pointing out some of the walks to be done and other activities. A recently completed Maritime Museum was open and we walked towards it. It was some 600 metres and on the way there we stopped to look at the holiday home of the King of Spain, Juan Carlos and his family. It was set back from the pathway that we on and was built of stone. A very simple four bed home surrounded by a white picket fence. Whoever did the landscaping here might have got the picket fence wrong. In any case, the home was perfectly situated and modestly built for comfort and access to the bay for swimming.

We continued on to the Maritime Museum and I lingered on here as the others went for a walk along one of the many tracks clearly sign posted. The

Museum contained a lot of artefacts from ships which had come to grief in these waters by way of battle or storms. It was quite a pleasant time for me as I had the Museum to myself for over an hour at one stage. In these situations, I tend to get lost in the history of what I am looking at and time just seems to go too quickly. I have been like this forever and have only met a few people of like fascination for this type of activity.

At dinner time we went to the taverna and the food was hearty with a limited menu. It was fine and washed down with some sangria and the local beer. The village had not changed for about 240 years and after a while it was easy to imagine oneself sitting here in 1796 waiting for square rigged ships to come into the harbour for a rest or to take on supplies. This National Park of Cabrera was different to any place that we had been and we were thankful for that with no hustle and serene surroundings. A lot different from the Costa Del Sol on the Spanish mainland but with the common denominator of Spanish courtesy and hospitality.

Bay of Mallorca

We had to leave after three days which was not enough but we need to make room for others who want to come here and enjoy this unique place. So we returned to Arenal Marina and the city of Palma on Majorca. We only stayed one night here and sailed to Port Andratz, in the morning, further along the coast. It only took about five hours and we sailed into a very attractive harbour and anchored to the north with good holding. About an hour after arriving at our anchorage, another yacht arrived in the harbour and the closer that it got to TS the more familiar it looked. It turned out to be our friends Jeff and Brownie aboard "Lola" a 40-feet sloop.

They waved to us and anchored nearby. They came over to TS for a drink and at about 6 pm returned to their boat for dinner. After they left, Helen said that our huge beef lasagne would be about another hour in the oven and then we could have this with some great fresh salad. Helen and I were enjoying the dusk atmosphere here when we noticed Brownie emerge from the companionway on "Lola" and hand Jeff a plate of food for his dinner. Jeff was standing in the cockpit when he took his first spoonful of Brownie's Green Currie and then announced, to all who could hear for about 70 metres "Brownie, this is shit!" He then tipped the plate of food into the bay and called out to ask us if he could come aboard TS for some of our lasagne. Helen said OK and Jeff jumped overboard and swam towards TS.

In the meantime, Brownie came from the galley with his plate of green curry and when on deck took a spoonful. He called out to Jeff, who was still in the water, "Jeff, you are right, this is shit!" Brownie then put his plate down and asked Helen if he could come across to have some yummy lasagne, and of course Helen agreed.

Whilst all this is going on, Helen and I were in fits of laughter and when both the chaps were on board TS, I gave them a beer and we settled down to listen to an animated conversation between Jeff and Brownie about who contributes the most on board "Lola". It was all in such fun as the two of them were great sailors and could handle anything within reason that the elements could throw at them. Brownie did, however, address his lack of culinary skills and said to Jeff that he [Jeff] had not died…so far. That set off another round of insults and the comedy that evening could only have come from two Englishmen who were in great form and spirits. It must have been about midnight when they swam back to "Lola", as we all got up rather late the following morning.

After breakfast Helen and I went ashore and walked to one of prominent cafe/restaurants on the waterfront. After ordering the coffees, I asked the Barista if Christopher Skase is seen here and to my shock he said that we had just missed him after his early morning coffee here. Skase, by the way, was wanted in Australia for very large fraud charges and was living in Port Andratx where the Spanish Government would not recognise the extradition request from Australia, due to health reasons provided by Skase's doctor. In any case, our Barista friend took me to the door of the cafe and pointed to Skase's home on the other side of the bay. If you need to convalesce as a criminal, then this was a great place to do it.

Helen then went to discover the village and I took my sketch pad and walked up a hill, along the shoreline, from the town quay. I stopped about half way up the hill, in front of "Villa Borghese". This was the name of the large home in front of me. I had seen about four or five villas of the same name, on our travels over the years and it seemed that to name your villa "Villa Borghese", it had to be large, of Italian design, have large landscaped gardens of a certain era and in a prominent position.

The villa that I was standing in front of, was perfect and I felt like opening the gate and perching myself on the deck around the house to complete a sketch. I demurred and walked across the road and sat on a rock looking down and across this beautiful bay. It took me well over an hour to do the drawing as there was quite a bit to show for this scene. I did not sell this painting which hangs on a wall in my home and each time I look at this painting I think of the two funny English chaps and an uproarious night.

We stayed for five days here and explored the area on foot and one day hired a bicycle each and peddled for a couple of hours to have a break at the heights of a valley which had most of the food fare growing on the flat with the tiered sides accommodating fruit and olives, what else! The morning that we weighed anchor was very hot and with little wind, so we motored to Cala Portinatx, which was a small bay and took about four hours to reach, when we dropped anchor. During this passage, Helen stopped TS and I went for a swim with Tagonago Island on our port bow. It was here, as I swam away from TS and as I looked back at her sitting beautifully on a calm Mediterranean Sea, on such a day, that I realised that I was a voyeur of my own design and so lucky to be here.

After a late lunch on board, I took Helen ashore in the dinghy and I returned to TS to do some housekeeping. Helen would be shore side in a couple of hours and I would go and get her. I had a bit on my mind that day, with a few overdue jobs to do and when I got back to TS, I stepped onto the stern ladder and did not tie off the dinghy. I was below for about 30 to 40 minutes and then went to the stern to do something when I noticed that the dinghy was missing. I scolded myself and looked around for the dinghy. No go!

Naturally, I needed to find it, but how? I then noticed another yacht anchored nearby and yelled out to the two chaps on board if I could borrow their dinghy to look for mine. They agreed, so I swam over to their yacht and dropped into their dinghy and I was off for the search. Our dinghy was not in the bay where we were, so I motored around to the next bay. Gratefully the prevailing wind was on shore and if our lost dinghy was anywhere, then it could be in this large bay, which was host to a couple of resorts around the bay. I motored towards a few dozen people who were swimming and one lady waved to me and said to me in Spanish, "Are you looking for your rubber boat?"

I shrugged my shoulders and she immediately repeated the question in English. Then I said "Si,"

The lady replied in good and clear English, "Well, I thought it was the Mary Celeste drifting into this bay, so one of my sons took hold of the line and it is over there, by the shore, under those trees." What a relief, and I thanked her and her son and motored over to get our dinghy and tow it back to TS after returning our neighbour's dinghy. What a great little adventure it was with Spanish courtesy once again in the mix. The reference to the Mary Celeste here is for a ship, so named, found in the Atlantic in the late 19th century drifting aimlessly and totally abandoned, as there was nobody on board. It still remains a mystery today.

I saw Helen waiting on shore, sometime later and I took the dinghy to pick her up. We then returned to TS to get our snorkelling gear and then went to some nearby caves to see the underwater world of this part of the coast of Majorca. It was another time that we did not expect to do this, but when we noticed the caves, we just had to look a little closer. That part of the coast had a small grotto which was not accessible from the land and we swam into this from the sea and sat on some large rocks and listened to our own voice echoes. It was all quite surreal.

The following day, we left this anchorage and sailed to Ibiza, another of the Balearic Islands. Here we anchored in the Bay of Ibiza town for the first night. Going ashore in mid-afternoon, we visited the Club Nautico to locate a trades person who could fix our alternator. We found the right person and the next morning moved into the nearby Marina Club Nautico to allow the electrician to come aboard TS and repair the alternator. After the electrician left, Helen and I walked into the town to have a late lunch. We were in a bay side restaurant for lunch and soon realised that the Ibiza reputation as a wild gay town was well founded.

It was a bit over the top for us, so we left after lunch and settled into the Club Nautico Bar when we got back to the Marina. We may have stayed longer here, but having had a few nights anchored off shore and loving the inherent beauty of the off shore anchorages, we left Ibiza and sailed to Espalmador Bay on the Island of Formentera, the southern most of the Balearic Islands. It was only a short sail of about three hours and a perfect day. When going south from Ibiza, I turned to notice a feature on the south west coast of Ibiza. It was where, in mythology, the sirens were supposed to have beckoned Ulysses to sail through a narrow gap near the coast and a rock spire. I saw the gap through the binoculars and I started to suggest to Helen that it might be fun. I was cut off with the comment, "Don't even think about it!"

Not to worry, it was worth a try.

On arriving at Espalmodor Bay, the whole world changed. This bay was like a South Pacific Haven with sandy beaches on all sides and tropical vegetation on shore. We were in the western Mediterranean and suddenly we were not. The bay was unique in this part of the world. We soon had the cockpit table set up and naturally, and as you would expect, the beer and wine came on deck with the cheese and crackers. Our music was given a gallop and once again we were enthralled. The sunset was calm, with the sheen off the water being too strong to look at. Where were we again?

Bay of Espalmador

In the morning I went for another swim around this small bay and I noticed that a few more yachts had arrived during the night. I walked ashore and lay down on the already very warm sand and was woken up from my rest by a dog. A dinghy was nearby and the couple who rushed over to me were most apologetic for the behaviour of their dog. They, of course, were staying on their boat and it seems the enthusiasm for this place was joined by their "puppy" as they referred to him.

I swam back to TS and after breakfast Helen and I were to walk into the nearby town to explore, shop and have lunch. We pulled the dinghy up onto the beach and did not need to dig the anchor into the sand as there was very little tide here. We got to the top of the rise on the walk and could see the town at a distance. There was however, a sea channel to be traversed before we could continue the walk to the town. On approaching the channel, we could see the depth and waded across the channel at a little over waist deep with our bags and towels held over our head. I said to Helen that a few wines at lunch would make this crossing a bit of fun on the return.

It was about a 40-minute walk to the town in the morning sun and we sat at a cafe and had a couple of iced coffees to refresh. The town was charming with all the basics there and the supermarket had all that we needed including the long-life milk which was now part of our breakfast with the cereals. The people in the shops were always polite and with a smile. I had judged the Spanish people, some time before, as a meet and greet race, with a handsome countenance for both men and women. It was and still is, a fine feature of their culture. After exploring the town, it was time for lunch and we chose a restaurant at seaside looking across to where we were anchored as you could see the tops of the masts in the bay where we were anchored. It was a good sight as the top of the rise was punctuated with about a dozen mast tops and the anemometers, which give wind speed and direction, showing along the line of rise.

After being seated, we ordered drinks and a nearby couple said hello and of course they had come from their yacht where we were. Helen and I joined their table. They were a Dutch couple, Hans and Jean who were having an extended holiday at this end of the Mediterranean on their yacht which lived in a marina in Sete, on the French coast. Like tourists and travellers, world-wide, we swapped stories of how we were here at this time and a few hours passed quickly along with a few bottles of good local light red wine. Our waiter that afternoon could speak English very well and he was joined in some of the delight at our stories. It was the first time that a waiter had done this and it was fun to enjoy his comments by way of advice sometimes and envy at other.

The four of us returned to our boats for a siesta and Helen and I rowed over to Hans and Jeans boat at about 6 pm. We were greeted with drinks aboard their ketch which was 42-feet Rival make. We were seated at the stern around a table with the dipping sun and some traditional Dutch food served. The scene and the company was memorable. At about 12.30 am, we carefully managed to descend into our dinghy and wave goodbye to our hosts. It was dark as I rowed away and I had not taken bearings from their boat to TS and so I began a lost meander amongst the other boats as we tried to identify TS, as the darkness and our happy frame made the job a bit tricky. We eventually found TS after rowing up to four or five boats and rowing away on our search. Whilst we felt a little dusty the next morning, a swim soon fixed that.

It was always going to be hard to leave this island as we had stayed in many towns, bays, cities and marinas longer that most people would have. However, now we were on a timetable to reach the other end of the Mediterranean before the weather turned. We stayed five days here as we knew that we would not see this sort of a scene again. Returning to Club Nautico in Ibiza, we had the wind generator refitted after the repair and then set out the next morning to sail to Minorca, which is the northern most island of the Balearic Islands.

During the morning, a pod of dolphins joined us and about half an hour later, we noticed a couple of whales, off to port and broaching out of the water. It was a great sight to see. We had however, been told that inquisitive and playful whales can approach a boat and come up underneath that boat and lift it out of the water. We both looked at the whales and told them to keep playing just where they were and not come any closer. The whales obliged and we sailed away and left them to their playground.

This was an overnight passage and in the evening the wind started to pick up. We started the four hour shifts with plenty of wind still around. The sea state was okay and we passed Mallorca to the west as we tacked into a mostly north wind. It was when we were changing four-hour shifts, that Helen and I could hear the waves crashing onto the rocks of the coast, off to port. It was then that a problem occurred. There was aloud tearing sound and I looked up to see the headsail was ripped along one of its seams. Most of this sail was now just flapping in the gale that had crept upon us. Whilst Helen tacked the boat to get away from the lee coast, I went forward to sort out the headsail. After furling it in and tidying the bow area, I came back to the cockpit and we kept on with a reasonable course to our destination. Calm seas returned at about 8.30 am and peace was restored.

The morning bird frenzy returned as hundreds of fish were devoured by diving birds into the water. The strong winds returned at 12.30 pm with a large swell which made it uncomfortable until we entered the Bay of Ciutadella and rafted up to another boat on the town key at 15.40. It had been another adventurous passage of 30 hours with enough sleep to keep us bright now that we were in harbour and looking forward to dinner ashore here at Ciutadella.

Piazza of Ciutadella – Fiesta of the Horses

After tidying TS and a change of clothes we stepped across to the boat inside of TS, on the town key, and went ashore. We walked to the Port Control Office to register our arrival. I presented the ship's papers and Passports. The Port Captain said that he would see us tomorrow to collect the fees and advise us that we would have to move out into the harbour as our position on the town key had been reserved for the upcoming Fiesta St Jean. I had noticed some posters on our way to the office and it seems that we had arrived just before a three-day Fiesta dedicated to the horse with a variety of events over those days. The Port Captain was busy and I did not mention that we had some repairs to do before we could leave.

We left the busy office and walked further into the bay to settle into a fairly big restaurant looking up the bay. The see-through blinds were in place all around this restaurant as the wind was still strong, although the temperature was fine, shorts and shirt. After being seated at a table, we introduced ourselves to an English family at the next table who were on the island for a two-week holiday. We told them of our gale experience in getting here and were told that this wind was out of a sudden low pressure in the Gulf of Lyon. Helen and I just looked at each other and shrugged. It was not forecast when we left and I did not listen to a forecast on the passage to Ciutadella. A little bad luck again.

So here we were, once again, by chance, at a town where something substantial was happening, a horse fiesta or festival involving 120 horses. The Spanish love horses and one of the biggest riding schools in Europe is the Spanish Riding School in Vienna, Austria. There are events and festivals all over Spain to celebrate the horse. This festival was to start in two days' time. On our walk back to TS from the restaurant, I told Helen that I was going to claim "Port of Refuge" which is a maritime legal term meaning that a boat can enter a port for reasons of repair and seaworthiness and not be asked to move until the boat is able to, in our case, sail. Apart from real repairs I told Helen that I was going to say that our motor would not start and that a friend would be here in a couple of days to fix the problem. This, of course, was not so, but it would allow us to fix what we had to do, in calm water and not out in the harbour at anchor with the gale blowing.

The following morning, our neighbours, who were on the town quay, inside TS, were on deck and we said hello. They were a French couple and the girl remarked that she did not have a good night's sleep as their boat was being pushed against the wall all night. As their boat was a lot smaller than TS, I offered to swap places, which they readily agreed to do.

With some fairly nifty rope handling work by Helen and myself we managed to not engage our motor while doing this and our inboard French neighbours squeezed out of their spot and motored around to raft up as we were before. Job done and the Port Captain arrived and I told him of my intention to seek "Port of Refuge" and naturally he nodded, particularly after seeing us manoeuvre TS without the motor. Maritime Law was part of our courses in England and it was handy to remember all of the laws, to our benefit, even if it was a fine line.

The following day was spent with some attention to the furling gear for the headsail, some stitching on the lazy jack, which cradles the mainsail when not in use and some glue onto our boarding plank which was now being used as protection outside of the fenders, which held us off the wall. The Fiesta of St Jean started the next day.

We rose early for the first day of the Fiesta and after a good breakfast which we had as we were not sure of food through the day, we started walking towards the town piazza. I took us about 20 minutes as the crowds were coming from all directions. Buses were unloading people and the resorts surrounding the town were emptying of their guests. When we arrived at the piazza, it was packed with people and some of the horses were paraded around with their adornments all over them. Many children were running up to them and shouting with excitement while waving their arms. These horses were so controlled by their riders that they must have been trained to be spook proof. I admired their calm as they proudly walked around the piazza.

About a third of the people there were dressed in period costume and the attention to detail for their dress, for both boys and girls of all ages, was something to behold. I had attended a number of festivals in Europe at this stage and the proudest people that I encountered during any of these festivals were the Spanish. For a number of girls that I watched during our walk around the piazza, when they realised that they were being watched, they would walk up to me or Helen and swoon past, as if to say, yes, we look great, don't we?

The colour and vivacity of the piazza that morning went on for over an hour, then slowly the horses and people left that arena to follow the scheduled events. We eventually saw a table at a taverna bordering the piazza and sat for a drink or two. A couple of small bands were still playing and the children were to be seen dancing their traditional moves across the piazza. What a wonderful culture these people enjoy and it seemed that each generation teaches the next generation on how to preserve their legacy. We sat at our table and let this all wash over us as we enjoyed the company of some very happy people. Our drinks were finished and we ordered lunch at the same taverna and a jug of Sangria. When in Rome…

By mid-afternoon, we were as happy as anyone had a right to be. Walking back to TS we stopped at one of the bars along the waterfront and sat at a bar rest and met a Dutch married couple, Peter and Angela. They also had a yacht here and had been to the piazza that morning as well. Their boat was called "Spirit of Delft". Delft is an old harbour on the Dutch coast facing the North Sea. Peter described how he had grown up around there and would sail and negotiate the shifting sands of the Dutch coast. This is not easy to do and there is a small business along this coast in rescuing boats that have gone aground on a sand bar. It is a point of Maritime Law that if the boat in trouble throws the rescue line to the rescuing boat then that boat has a salvage right to the rescued boat. A lot of money is earned this way as the insurance companies will tell you.

In any case, Peter and Angela's boat was well named. We swapped many stories over some drinks which Helen and I probably did not need, but the company was great and Peter and Angela would be in our company, occasionally, into the near future. We said goodbye and snaked our way back to TS.

Next day we went ashore to follow some of the events of the Fiesta. There was a race from the piazza along the narrow streets, down to the river bank and along this and back to a finish line. I marvelled at the horse's ability to run on cobblestones, which were slippery, then onto large pavers, then to bitumen and finally to the sand on the river bank. At each new surface, they would change their speed and a couple of the horses would almost fall but then regather their stride and go on. Marvellous animals!

The last event after three days was a race along the river bank and around some obstacles where the horses needed to be strong and the jockeys as well. Apparently an outsider won the prize and the bookies had a good day. Our last dinner, along the waterfront, was a celebration of the Fiesta and lots of sangria was consumed with hugs and kisses as people said goodbye to each other.

We also left the following morning to go to Port Mahon where I needed to get a report on the headsail which had been torn along a seam during our passage to Ciutadella. We only had a mainsail to sail to Port Mahon and left at 11 am and arrived into the harbour of Port Mahon at 2.30 pm, a short sail.

The harbour of Port Mahon is very big and we motored well into the harbour and saw a couple of mooring pontoons in the middle of the harbour. We came alongside one of these and got the bow and stern lines out and were tied off in no time. These pontoons were about 100-feet square and naturally secured to the harbour bottom. There were seats and pot plants on them. We had not come across this mooring type before, but it was a delight to be able to moor here as the town was only a short distance away. We saw the sunset over dinner on board and had an early night.

I had found out in Ciutedella that there was a sail loft here in Port Mahon and after a breakfast on the pontoon, I started to pull the headsail from its track and then fold it to take ashore. It was a large sail and TS got most of its power from it. The sail weighed about 60 kg of terylene and in some places, three fabrics thick. Helen and I loaded it into the dinghy and motored ashore which was some 300 metres away.

The vista on approaching the shore was clear to see. A high wall running for hundreds of metres had been built of stone as part of a natural defence of the town. Port Mahon, with its large harbour, was a good place to bring ships to repair, replenish and give crew a respite in the days of square-rigged ships. Admiral Nelson certainly used it with the English Fleet from 1794 to 1805. It was imposing for us to approach the wall and climb the steps to the town level. We found the sail loft and I spoke to a lady who owned the business. Her team of machinists would repair what was needed to be done and she would then give me a report of the state of the sail. I also left the lazy jacks with her for repair. This would take three days.

PORT DE MAÓ

So we had plenty of time to discover this area and the capital of the island of Minorca. The town was laid out in a fashion where there were many park areas and in each park was a sculptor or display of its heritage, particularly pertaining to the sea. I was busy for a few days looking and reading about the history of this town. For me, the joy of a traveller, is to know something of where you going to, and in this case, an opportunity to discover the history of a very interesting town in detail. The Town Hall, museums and art galleries all told the story of an island which changed hands a few times, as have many places in the Mediterranean.

Helen and I had lunch one day at The English Pub and I had Cottage Pie for lunch, very pleasant. There was a game of football [soccer] televised that night between England and Germany and I decided to attend. On returning to our pontoon, another yacht had tied up and we introduced ourselves to the owners, Boris and Susan who were German, which we realised from the German flag flying on the port shrouds. They were a very pleasant and outgoing couple and we had a pre-lunch drink together on the pontoon. These pontoons were a great idea. Imagine them in Sydney harbour. I mentioned the football game to Boris and of course he knew of it. We decided that we would both go to the pub and watch it live, as both wives were not interested. Besides, Helen's grandmother was German and there was a connection that the wives might explore.

Boris and I left at about 6 pm to motor ashore and walk to the pub. I did suggest to Boris that since we were going to The English Pub, then it should have its share of English lager louts that night. These lads, as Boris knew, were some of the worst football supporters in Europe and I suggested to Boris that he not show any exuberance if Germany score a goal. He agreed and about half way through the first half, Germany scored and Boris was about stand up and cheer when he realised that it was not a good idea. His restraint was painful for him, but I admired him and told him so. Germany won three to 1 and we left the bar to celebrate back on the pontoon. An international incident had been averted! Drinks all round please.

The next day Helen and I returned to the sail loft and met with the lady owner. The headsail had been repaired and a few other areas of the sail had been strengthened. The report on the sail was very good with a warning to keep an eye on the leech [back edge] of the sail and make sure that the double thickness here is maintained to allow for the sacrificial terylene to do its work against the sun's harmful rays.

We returned to TS and I got about re-rigging the damaged sail and adjusting the furling mechanism. I finished by late afternoon and we had a farewell drink on TS with Boris and Susan, as we were leaving next morning. I did mention, that afternoon, to Boris and Susan, that they were different to most of the Germans that we had met and we had met and seen a lot more of their countrymen when living on the Greek island of Samos. Boris volunteered that Germans were mostly insular and group bound when travelling. Boris and Susan were determined to break that habit and teach their compatriots to do the same. It was a very admirable attitude as the past couple of days had shown.

We slipped our lines the next morning for Sardinia, Italy.

The Italian Adventure.

The morning was fine when we left Port Mahon and the forecast was okay. The Mistral wind for that part of the Mediterranean was there and by the first afternoon we were making a comfortable four to six knots. Helen made hamburgers that evening which were very good with the fresh provisions from the day before. The night passed with our watch turns of four hours each working a treat. Morning saw a great sunrise with the wind picking up a little. By the afternoon I had put two reefs in the mainsail and furled in the headsail a little as it looked like we could get a little more wind. Our intended course on this four-day passage, was east south east and of course the wind was coming from exactly that direction so we were tossing in some tacks against the headwind. The sea state was okay and dolphins appeared on the second evening.

Meanwhile, on board TS, I was doing a small repair to the dinghy and Helen was sorting through the charts. We now had about 150 charts after buying about 110 charts in Gibraltar from an English chap who was returning to England after he had been sailing in the Mediterranean for some years. He did not need these charts anymore and we naturally did need them. They were Admiralty and Imray charts which are the two best available for reliability. All charts up to this time were based on coastlines from on shore navigation beacons and were not 100% accurate.

They were the best that they could be and besides, they were the only method of navigation that we had. The US GPS navigation units were just now coming available in the marine shops for us boating people to use. From now on all the charts were seen to be incorrect and this was obvious when you could take a definite fix on your chart. This might be done using three landmarks near a coastline, like a church spire, a lighthouse and a radio tower. When you could read your latitude and longitude on your chart, of your fix, you could then read the GPS reading of latitude and longitude and they were always different. In some cases, by a long way. So, what was happening now, was that all charts were being redrawn from GPS readings and this would take years to complete.

Helen had taken on the job of sorting through these charts and putting them in some sort of order for us to use. It was quite a job. At about 5 pm on the third day, the wind increased to gale force eight and we could no longer point TS to the desired direction. We could only sail off to points which were not getting us closer to our objective. I then decided to hove-to. That is when you tack and centre the mainsail boom and leave the headsail backed and not bring it across TS. It virtually stops the boat. I did this and we had an early dinner. Helen noticed that we were making some movement through the water and I agreed and went to the windward side of TS and dropped a tissue into the water. That tissue was leaving our boat at about a speed of a little over one knot per hour. Helen was worried that we might reach the north coast of Africa, as our drift was taking us in that direction. I smiled and calculated, from the chart, that it would take about three weeks to get to the African coast at this rate. We both laughed and had a beer each to wait for the wind to hopefully change direction.

The wind did change about four hours later and I could point TS towards the direction of the south coast of Sardinia. We were motor sailing for a while and then pure sailing and at 8 am on the fourth day we entered Teulada Harbour, Sardinia and came alongside the mole and secured the bow and stern lines. This place was safe and a lot quieter that recent weeks. It was a welcome atmosphere and were a little tired after the long sail. A short sleep later that afternoon and we left the boat and walked over the low rise to a beach where we had a swim in a crescent shaped bay. A town wasn't far away and we decided that we would go there the following day. On returning to TS, we were delighted to see Peter, Angela and their Spirit of Delft tied up a little further along the mole.

Drinks were taken on TS and dinner was there, courtesy of Helen. It was great to see them and hearing where they had gone from the Balearic Islands. We retired at about 10 pm. Some hours later, at about 1 am in the morning, I was awoken with the sound of loud voices. I scrambled up the companionway, in shorts only, to see a large fishing boat with the high bow just off TS. Through some of the crew on this boat, the captain wanted me to move TS so that they could land their catch into the waiting freezer truck at dockside. When I understood what they wanted I was very annoyed and it apparently was obvious to the crew and captain. I told them that I had no intention of moving. With that, the captain came down from the pilot house and remonstrated with me to move my boat. An argument started with the captain waving his hands, as only the Italians could do and I, in English, told him what he could do with his demands.

By this time, Helen was on deck and trying to understand what was happening. The noise got Peter up and he was at dockside. Other people were also awake and looking on from the decks of their boats, as dockside was full, hence the demand from the captain. I went from the deck of TS to dockside and said to the captain that I would see him here, on land and we would sort it out. I meant, of course that we would fight it out. With that, the captain went back to the pilot house, came back to the bow, waving a machete. Helen was next to me and trying to restrain me. I backed off a little as Helen was taking photos of the whole scene. It became obvious that the fishing boat was trying to land an illegal catch here. The captain then realised that the game was up! He then took his boat to the other side of the harbour and, with difficulty, unloaded his catch.

My blood pressure had probably gone up a notch or two during this episode and within a few minutes I was back on-board TS with a stiff drink in hand. I was soon smiling and wondering how a captain could really expect any person to move their boat after being woken in the middle of the night. I think that Helen's photos were the telling point. Then back to bed and looking forward to the morning. That was the first Italian adventure.

Next morning was sunny and we set about exploring the surrounds. After walking to the nearby town and having a coffee, which the Italians do very well, we chose a trattoria to have lunch with Peter and Angela. The previous night was declared a joke, but it was good to have Peter standing next to me in the farcical episode.

The following day, we caught the bus into a larger town in the hinterland. Arriving at mid-morning, it seemed that there was some event about to happen with barricades erected and a crowd arriving. We soon learned that the Tour de Sardinia, the bike race, was about to pass through this town. The Italians love bike race as much as the French. The four of us were lucky to get a table at a cafe overlooking the road. We then watched the procession of bikes ridden through the town to the cheers of all who were there. It was exciting with the team colours on display and the support vehicles following. It was here that the infectious Italian vivacity was evident and the four of us caught the mood of the day and laughed with the locals around us, although sometimes we had no idea what we were laughing at. Of course it was bon homie in the very best sense. A coming together for the spirit of life.

The next couple of days were spent, in the main, at a couple of resorts near the bay and but a short walk from the mooring. I had noticed these resorts earlier and on enquiring if we could use their facilities they said okay as long as we had a lunch or dinner there. It was a good deal and we used their pool and daybeds for two days. How very bourgeois it was.

It was time to head further to the east and to Sicily, so with the Spirit if Delft not far behind us, we left Teuleda, Sardinia, on a Friday at 10 am. The mistral winds promised good sailing for two days and that is exactly what we got. The sea state was a bit lumpy for a few hours and then changed for a comfortable passage where we came onto Capo St Vito on the north west coast of Sicily. We sailed into an impressive bay with a mountainous backdrop with stunning cliffs, beautiful beach and the water temperature just right.

Capo St Vito

It was Sunday morning at 9.20 am when we anchored in this bay, about 70 metres from the beach. Peter and Angela had decided to enter the marina here to do some cleaning of their boat. Meanwhile, I was making some tea and toast for us. We sat in the cockpit and saw quite a few paddle boats for couples coming towards us from one end of the beach. When these paddle boats were nearer to TS four or five of them formed line ahead and paddled around TS. At this, the people started to sing "Volare oh…oh…cantare…oh…oh…oh…oh" which of course is a very well-known Italian love song. Meanwhile, Helen was below making some more toast and I just had to tell her to come up on deck to see this scene. She did so and there we were, being serenaded on a Sunday morning by a lot of romantic Italian people. We waved to them and smiled a lot and blew some kisses. They paddled off waving. I turned to Helen and said, "There must be something in the air?" We laughed and looked at the backdrop here in this bay. It was just made for romance.

So this was our greeting in Sicily and how wonderful it was. I did not know it then but it was not to be all good here, along the north Sicilian coast. In any case, it was Sunday and we needed to get ashore and mix with our new friends. We dressed well and jumped into the dinghy and I rowed ashore to the beach, which was not far away. We pulled the dinghy up onto the beach and looked around. The sun was high in the sky and the beachside glare was strong, off the sand. Families were everywhere playing in and out of the water. We felt at home as this could have been anywhere in the world. Joy and laughter are contagious and we walked towards the town to find a coffee. At this stage of our odyssey, I think that Helen and I were hooked on a morning coffee. It just had to happen! We found a great spot near the town piazza and enjoyed the first of many Sicilian coffees, whilst cruising along the north coast.

We then walked around to the marina to find Peter and Angela working on their boat. It did not take much to divert them from their work and we soon repaired to the Bar Marina where we had lunch of scaloppini, an Italian speciality. I related the singing around TS that morning and Angela said that one of the boats in the marina had a young crew who were also singing that morning. That proved it. There was definitely something in the air!

After a couple of days here in this beautiful place, we sailed to Mondello Bay and arrived and anchored at 7.30 pm. An early night was had to greet another sunny morning. Here was a popular beach resort and we took the dinghy to the beach and had a day on the beach. The sun in the Mediterranean is nowhere near as strong as the sun in Sydney and its burning skin effect. You needed a little SPF sunscreen and that is all, for the day. We noticed that most of the Italians here were very stylish people, with the clothing to go with it. I had always thought that the Italians do for style, what the French do for cooking and food. Here was the proof.

Tequila Sunrise – Anchored off Cefalu

The following day, we sailed to Cefalu with Spirit of Delft not far behind us. To the west of the town is a large bay, where we anchored at 6.30 pm. After speaking to Peter on VHF radio, we agreed that we would all go ashore the next morning and spend the day in the town of Cefalu, which from TS, was picture postcard stuff, with a mountain backdrop and a large church fortress behind the town. It was just another great scene.

For some reason, the four of us arrived on the shore the next morning, really looking forward to our day. We were certainly not disappointed. It was an old Roman town with narrow cobblestone streets where you would expect to see people in Togas appearing around every corner. It was an attractive town and very friendly people. We all agreed, Sicily at its best. A morning coffee was had, compulsory, and we chose to have lunch at a restaurant where we sat outside, in dappled sunlight, surrounded by historical buildings and Sicilian hospitality. Were we spoiled? Yep, we sure were. As was our want, we shared a large carafe of local light red wine first. It was superb, so we ordered another with lunch. Some lunches that you have in your life are never forgotten, and this was one of them. The waiters jollied us along with suggestions of what to see here and we went to the eastern side of the town later that afternoon. Here we found some decadence in the form of bath houses and massage rooms, surrounded by cafes and bars. Once again, we were voyeurs of our own design.

It was dark when we found our two dinghies on the beach and slowly motored back to our boats for a good night's sleep. We weighed anchor the next day at about 5 pm to sail to Portarosa, further along the coast. There was a reason for leaving late that day. It was to see the Aeolian Islands at night and the volcanic scenes, on those islands, of a night. Mount Stromboli was spewing out its lava and smoke and as we looked off to port, there was the spectacle to see. Quite something, with nature a little upset. The colours of the night were changing. The moon was up and the atmosphere, because of the volcanic dust, was one colour at one moment and then another half an hour later. I was not aware until later, but Peter was taking some photos of TS during this strange natural night. It was all rather surreal really.

I was on the wheel at about 1.30 am into the night, when I looked down to our Garmin GPS and saw that it was not giving any reading of speed/direction or mapping. This was early years for GPS so I just waited until a signal strength returned to show our position. For safety, I got out the chart and marked a "fix" on the chart as my dead reckoning on where we were. I also radioed Peter on Spirit of Delft and asked him if his GPS was working properly. He said that his was not showing anything and that we should just wait and it should return. There was not much else that we could do. We just had to approximate where we were, every half hour.

It was about 90 minutes later when I noticed that the GPS was attempting to gain the satellite signals that we needed to boot the GPS. This took about 10 minutes and all was well again with our passage. Then, however, the second Italian adventure came upon us.

I glanced at the GPS about 20 minutes later and whilst we were sailing, we were not covering any ground. The sails on TS were full, but no speed. I stood behind the wheel then, as the auto pilot was still working, and looked about to see small lights above the water and spread out on the port and starboard side of TS, into the distance. When I jumped up to the stern and looked over the side I could see the problem. We had sailed onto a fishing net and were stopped. I looked around again and realised that I did not see the net because the lights on the water, attached to the net, were not high enough to see from our deck. I knew enough from the sailing course, back in England, that these lights should be 35 to 40 cms above the water line. The lights that I was looking at were about 10 cms. I woke Helen, as I may need her help with something, but at that stage I did not know what!

With Helen on deck, she grabbed the binoculars and looked off to port. There was a large fishing boat on the horizon, showing lights. I looked through the binoculars and this fishing vessel was slowly bringing in its continuous net on board and slowly coming towards us. In the meantime, we took down the sails, all bar a little bit of the headsail, to keep our direction constant, and sat there to await the proceedings.

It took about 20 minutes for the large fishing boat to arrive and lay off TS. As usual, the Italians were waving their arms and all speaking at the same time. This time, however the skipper came down to the bow and said that he would have to send a couple of divers down to release his net by cutting it. He was not happy but at least he was not carrying a machete. Helen, meanwhile was taking photos. Whilst the divers were preparing, a couple of the crew members, who were at the bow, were asking for a cigarette. I duly obliged and threw them a packet. They had no lighter, so I threw them a lighter. That kept them quiet. The divers went overboard and it did not take them long to cut the net and join the two ends for the fishing boat to continue hauling the net on board.

Before the fishing boat left the scene, the captain came to the bow and asked us where we were headed. I said, Portarosa and he said that he would see me there later that morning. I did not know what that meant and waved goodbye to him and the crew as they steamed away. In the meantime, Helen had raised Peter on VHF radio to tell him of our plight. He reckoned that he was about 45 minutes behind us and he would arrive and go and have a look underwater to see if the net was jammed around the prop, rudder or fin or all of these. Peter had scuba diving gear and could do this easily as he also had an underwater light. I could have gone down to have a look but without underwater lighting, it was a waste of time.

Peter and Angela arrived on the Spirit of Delft and Peter got his gear on whilst Angela controlled their boat, as Peter went overboard. It did not take Peter long and he resurfaced with a length of fishing net in his hands. The net was caught around the prop and rudder and was easy to free. That was a relief and after Peter was back on board we both sailed away from our second Italian adventure, to Portarosa.

We arrived at Portarosa Marina and moored between piles at 9.45 am. After a cup of tea and a quick clean up, Helen and I went ashore to have a breakfast with Peter and Angela, as arranged. Before that, however, I noticed the captain of the fishing boat having a coffee near the Port Captain's Office and of course I went to see him as the others settled into a great tavern for breakfast.

Bearing in mind the Italian passion, I walked towards the captain and prepared to do battle, if that was necessary. I should not have worried, as he stood up and walked towards me and shook my hand heartily. He laughed and said that I should not worry. I told him that I was glad that all was okay and after telling him that we would be here for a couple of days he wished me good luck. A nice ending to an interesting night.

Portarosa Marina was very expensive and after walking about the area and the resorts we decided to move after the second day, further to the east to a bay just before Palermo, the capital of Sicily. Helen's friend, Louisa, joined us at Portarosa as she was on holidays again in Europe. We left early, at 7.45 am and had a good sail along the coast. I looked in at the bay before Palermo and as there were no visitor mooring buoys, I decided to go on to Palermo Harbour and try our luck there.

As we approached Palermo I asked Louisa, who had an engaging VHF radio voice, to contact Palermo Port Control and see if we could get a harbour mooring for a few days. She did this with relish and a conversation soon started with a Port Officer who was taken with this conversation, to the extent that he suggested that both Louisa and Helen join him for coffee the very next morning! Needless to say we were appointed to a superb mooring, in the middle of the harbour, about 60 metres off the shore and in front of a large restaurant. I did however, have to remind Louisa and Helen that we were in the home of the Cosa Nostra, the Mafia, and they should bear this in mind and go for coffee in a crowded area. They both laughed as we secured to the mooring.

The table was set up in the large cockpit as we waited for Peter and Angela to arrive in the bay of Palermo. I had radioed Peter that we were bypassing the harbour before Palermo and going to Palermo instead. A little while later, the Spirit of Delft appeared around the point and pulled down their sails, to motor over to us, about 400 metres. As I looked across to Peter's boat, I remarked to Helen that I hoped that Peter had read his Pilot Book or had a detailed chart of the bay, as there was a reef, in the harbour, near to his position. Just as I was about to call him on VHF we heard a loud noise of metal against reef and I looked to up see that Spirit of Delft had gone aground on the reef.

I spoke to Angela on VHF and said that we would bring TS across and see if we could pull their boat off the reef. We arrived at the reef some 10 minutes later and I went in the water with goggles and snorkel to have a look. When I surfaced I told Peter that their boat was only just on the reef with the bottom of the keel about half way onto the reef. We rigged a tow rope from TS to their boat and with as much weight as possible to the stern of their boat, we successfully pulled their boat off with a loud screech. The only damage was the bottom of the keel and this was of little concern as it only lost a bit of anti-fouling.

TS returned to the mooring and Peter followed and rafted up to us and there we were, perfectly situated in the harbour once again. Peter and Angela came aboard TS for the afternoon drinks. We had saved each other from a predicament in the last couple of days and we celebrated that outcome. Dinner was also taken on TS as the night fell and we were greeted to the lights of the harbour and the large restaurant right in front of us.

It was obvious that the restaurant was preparing for a reception and the binoculars confirmed that a wedding reception was going to happen there as the staff were running around the final touches on presentation. Soon the Bride and

Groom arrived and the guests filled the two-story restaurant. It was to be a big reception. A band began to appear on the first-floor large balcony and set their instruments on their stands. A short time later a person in white tie and tails appeared on the first floor to lead the small band. He took out his violin and began what was to be three sessions that night.

I thought that I recognised this violinist and the binoculars were focussed on him. Yes, it was Stephan Grapelli, one of the foremost violinists in the world. The music was sublime and I turned to Helen who said, "I know, I know…again!" The four of us were just amazed that we had ringside seats to a very small concert by a maestro. And we probably had the best seats in the house, whilst floating nearby. Naturally we listened to the three sessions and the reception finished at about 1 am and we all retired after a rather big day, when you stack it up.

After breakfast the next morning, we all went ashore, with Helen and Louisa to meet the Port Official for a morning coffee. Peter and Angela were going to explore the city and I went to the two-story restaurant, the scene of our concert. The restaurant staff were cleaning and preparing for the lunch trade. With very few people in the restaurant, I looked out over the main dining area to our yachts, through the large sliding doors onto the downstairs balcony and that scene was something to remember. It would have made a good painting. Some scenes you just never forget. I met up with Helen and Louisa after lunch and their coffee with the Port Official went very well with an invitation to return to Palermo, at another time, for a tour of the city, courtesy of some of the officials of the Port Authority. A very polite gesture. Another two days were spent in the city and some of the museums and then it was time to move on.

We left the mooring early at 7.45 am and sailed in company with Spirit of Delft to Bagnara Calabra, on the toe if Italy. It was a pleasant 7.5-hour sail and we entered a mostly empty port with some strange looking boats at the far end of the port. With both boats secure, the four of us walked towards some buildings at the port and the town beyond. Helen and Angela carried on towards a cafe, whilst Peter and I were intrigued by these strange boats that we had seen on entering the port. We walked towards the or six boats which were stern to the wharf.

These boats were fishing boats, but not like any that we had seen before. They were about 70-feet long with about 60 feet of narrow walkway extending from the bow. This walkway was supported by many ropes from the mast. Very strange looking and it had Peter and I scratching our heads to work out what these boats do, until one of the local workmen, who could speak English explained. These boats were for catching sunfish or sailfish in this part of the Mediterranean. These fish bask on the surface of the sea and these fishing boats, with a man in the lookout seat at the top of the mast, creep up on these fish basking. A man then walks to the end of the walkway and with a large net, throws it over the basking fish and then the rest of the crew haul it on board. The trick here is to be as quiet as possible, hence the long walkway. These fish are naturally a delicacy in Italy and are very expensive. With our curiosity solved, we joined Helen and Angela for a drink and dinner, not far away.

The following afternoon, we sailed to Saline Joniche, further around the toe of Italy. But first, we had to sail through the Straits of Messina, separating mainland Italy from Sicily. I had read in the Pilot Book for Italy, that there is a current in the Straits and to be aware of this as it may be difficult to steer any boat. That was an understatement! TS had both sails up and we were sailing well until we reached that part of the Straits where the current was strongest.

Then the fun began. I was on the wheel and just could not get TS to sail in the direction that I wanted. TS was being tossed from one direction to another and the wheel was useless. We centred the boom, the foot of the mainsail, furled in the headsail a good way, and just sat back and watched as this short passage was to be like no other that we had encountered. It seems that the topography of the sea bed was tossing up a confused sea and currents that were bizarre. This passage lasted about an hour and we could then sail to the south east and reach Saline Joniche.

At the entrance of this almost deserted harbour, there were plenty of underwater rocks and the lead in was dangerous unless you could see these rocks. I had a pair of sunglasses that reflected both the sun's rays and the reflection off the water. This allowed you to see into the water. Helen had the wheel, while I went forward to the bow and guided us into harbour safely. It was a bit hairy, but safely done. We came alongside and tied bow and stern lines. I got Peter on the VHF and told him of the approximate track to take with him at the bow of his boat and he made it into harbour safely. Job done.

This was a reasonably large harbour as it was meant to service the manufacturing of a Union Carbide Plant at one end of the harbour. The Plant was now derelict, due to the Union Carbide Plant explosion in Bhopal in India, some years before. The Italians were not going to have a repeat of that! The four of us had dinner on board and reflected that the day had been another interesting one.

The morning was sunny and warm and I went ashore to have a yarn to the skipper of a large barge tied up next to TS. He was an affable Dutchman, who had brought his barge all the way from Holland, by river and canal through Europe. It had taken him about 15 months and he just loved telling me of the highlights of his trip with his wife. He passed a coffee to me as we moved forward towards the bow of the barge. There was a very big Tarpaulin over something forward and I wondered what it was. When he removed the Tarpaulin, there was a Morris Mini car on a turntable! After putting down two ramps from the barge to the dock, he drove the car onto the dock. His wife joined him and they drove off towards the town. Dutch people never surprised me with their creativity and skills.

Late in the morning the four of us walked into town for lunch. We had a beer at a bar and then onto a trattoria for lunch. One of the landmarks in this town was the home of Senior Garibaldi, the founding father of the United Italy in the 1850s. It was a grand home on a hill overlooking the town, with cannon shell damage on the walls, still visible from bombardment, from the sea. He was certainly a brave character and the Italians were very proud of him. We all returned to the harbour in the evening and slept well as Helen and I needed to. We were leaving Italy the next morning for the Greek Islands.

To the Greek Islands.

We said goodbye to our sailing friends, Peter and Angela as they were going to go to a few more ports in Sicily. They were great people to know and we kept in touch by mail. The forecast was for stronger winds as were to cross to the western side of the Greek mainland and the Ionian Islands of Greece. There was an easterly wind and we were sailing to the east, so tacking was the order of the day. After about 90 minutes, we were passed by two yachts going the other way. I noticed that one of these yachts was anchored with us along the north coast of Sicily. The wind was apparently too much for them and they decided to return somewhere to shelter. That surprised me as their yacht was a Bavaria 38, a good sea keeping boat.

Helen was a little worried with the conditions and suggested that we might also return and await better weather. We then turned TS around and were sailing in the opposite direction. The wind was caused by a northerly wind coming off the heel of Italy and whipping and increasing in speed and becoming an easterly.

The more I thought about it, it seemed that this phenomena was to be experienced all the time, at this time of the year and at some time, we were going to have to make this passage. I jumped up onto the deck proper and then up to the boom and perched there with the binoculars. On the far horizon, to the east, about 30 miles away, there was a single yacht, sailing north. It was not bobbing around and it appeared that the wind was okay as all its sails were set.

I then convinced Helen that all would be okay if we could make it through the next few hours with a bit of discomfort. We then turned TS around and got cracking. Sure enough, a few hours later, the wind abated and smooth sailing prevailed. It was just perfect sailing conditions, with auto pilot engaged, that we both laid back on the cockpit cushions and read our books. After a little while, we heard a dull noise from behind us. That noise soon became louder and as I turned around to see what was happening, a jet plane flew past us to starboard and very low to the sea. The noise was deafening and about 20 seconds later another jet flew past and more deafening noise. I caught the second plane in the binoculars with the Greek flag under the wing, whilst raising my fist from being interrupted in such a dramatic way. The Greek pilots were having a bit of fun and possibly thinking that we'll wake these guys up! They sure did. We were yet to make Greek waters and this was a good omen, albeit a different one.

The wind was brisk through the first afternoon, with plenty of white caps and a glorious sunset at 8 pm, just to remind us why we were here. The dawn saw dolphins at 8 am, whilst we had a hearty cooked breakfast. We always looked forward to a cooked breakfast as it set the day just right. Many times this was not possible and while the galley had a belt to place around your bottom, we did not light the stove in rougher conditions, as a rogue wave could upset the whole galley show. It became quite hot that afternoon as the wind backed to a northerly direction. This allowed us to be at a point of sail, being the best for TS. It was a bit forward of the wind on the beam. It was hot and the sunscreen was on under the hats.

The moon rose early that evening and it was almost full. Another picturesque night followed and great expectations for reaching the Greek Islands the next day. It started to become light at about 6.30 am. However, by 7 am, fog had descended and around 9 am there was cloud and mist. This was really strange as my Pilot Book made no mention of this condition. All was okay as it was not as bad as crossing the English Channel. Helen turned on the radar set and we could not see any blip within 20 miles. We were still making four to five knots, so all was well.

Before we left The Algarve in Portugal, our winter place, those of us who were then going into the great expanses of the Mediterranean, had agreed to put out the occasional VHF Radio call for any one of us within hearing distance. In this way, we could meet up again.

Whilst we were in this mist and cloud on the sea, Helen put out a VHF call on the Emergency Channel 16 and asked if there was a known respondent, then she could chat on Channel 28. The first call got no response, but the second call about 20 minutes later certainly got a response. We were just coming out of the mist when yacht Yellow Bird with Aubrey and Richard Long, answered. We were within sight of the Greek Island of Lefkada and they were just coming away from the port of Vasiliki, on the south coast of Lefkada, heading south, on a day sail to Fiskhardo on the island of Cephalonia.

Yes, we had found that vagabond Aubrey again. In 10 minutes, we saw Yellow Bird in the binoculars and we were almost on a convergent course as we sailed east and Aubrey sailed south. We must have been about 100 metres away from each other when Aubrey got two of his nephews on board Yellow Bird to get on deck, turn with their bottoms towards us and pull down their shorts to show you know what! This was their salute and welcome for us, to the Greek Islands.

I got on the VHF to Aubrey, the 82-year-old captain and thanked him for his kind greeting and as we were going into Vasiliki, he would see us tomorrow when he returned. He also mentioned that Bruce and Slug, on Lucy B, were stern to in Vasiliki. That was also great news. The wind had died down considerably as we approached the run to the north to reach Vasiliki, at the end of a bay, flanked by mountains on both sides with a valley at the end of the bay. Another postcard scene, as the wind then increased and we had to tack a few times to get to the marina to moor.

Bay of Vassiliki

There was a peculiar wind phenomenon around Vasiliki Bay. With the mountains on either side and not a lot of vegetation to give shade, a Katabatic wind is generated in this bay by the heating of the mountainsides and the valley at the end of the bay. The wind starts to generate at about 9.30 am and increases to a peak at about 1 pm and dies off at about 4.30 pm. It happens like clockwork each sunny day. The wind over the islands can be almost nil, but Vasiliki Bay will have wind. If I had not known this coming into Vasiliki I may have thought that a giant wind turbine was at the end of the bay.

We approached the Marina and saw Lucy B's Battle Flag of a Bruce Anchor and a giant Slug sliding down the stem of the anchor. It was always distinctive. As we were now in Greece, our mooring type would change. Here, in the Greek Islands, we needed to go stern to or bow to the dockside, mole, town wall etc. It would be stern to, most of the time as it is far easier to jump from the stern toe rail to the dock, to secure both port and starboard stern lines, than it is to jump from a high bow to the dock. Either way, it is a tricky exercise.

On rounding into the marina, I motored around and saw that there was only one spot available for TS. On inspection, we noticed some rocks, under water and protruding from the dock. A stern to mooring was not on as it would have damaged the rudder and possibly the prop. We went in bow to and Bruce and

Slug, who meanwhile had seen us, caught our bow lines and put them through the stainless rings on the dock and threw them back as return lines. Job done and we rigged the plank from the bow to the dock, at a rather steep angle and both Helen and I were soon ashore and rejoicing with Bruce and Slug. It was still difficult to call beautiful Sara, Slug.

A celebration was the order of what was left of the day and we sat at a habourside taverna and ordered drinks at about 2 pm. We were back in Greece and our spiritual home here in the Greek Islands. It was a wonderful feeling for both of us. The taverna and all manner of things around us were familiar. Wicker chairs, plastic tablecloths, ouzo everywhere, smiles, tacky souvenirs and the inevitable bazouki music in the background. Yes, we were back in the Land of the Gods!

We moved on to have dinner at Penguins Restaurant and were greeted by Gary and Mary who owned Penguins. They recognised Helen's accent and volunteered that they were Australian Greeks. Much joviality followed with their young son, Dimitri, joining in. Gary and Mary are still good friends today and they return to Melbourne, almost every year, after closing Penguins, to stay with relatives. There are many Greek people in Melbourne and it is the third biggest population of Greeks, outside the Greek mainland. After some suggestions from Mary about what is good to do, we returned to our boats to repose after another fabulous day.

We woke at about 7 am to a perfect day. I walked down the main street to the start of the road out of town and there were the hire car companies along this part of the road. About 20 minutes later I drove to the dockside and Helen and I were off to Katsiki Beach. This is a truly spectacular beach and was voted the Most Beautiful Beach in the World a few years before. After parking the car, we walked across to a pathway leading down to the beach, about 200 steps. The white pebble beach was there to reflect the turquoise water, with sun beds and umbrellas. We had our water shoes with us as we were used to the smooth stones on some of the beaches in Greece and to get any traction in or out of the water, then water shoes are a must. The water temperature was just right and we went in four or five times that day. Day boats arrived in late morning and disgorged their passengers into the water for a flap around. To be on Katsiki Beach is like being in a shallow depth Greek Theatre with the audience on land and the performers in the water. Ice creams were had during the day and more than once.

After climbing the stairs, we took lunch at one of the tavernas overlooking the beach. We then drove the car a circuitous route back the town to see the valley that was through the town to the north. We looked at the tiered sides of the valley and realised that this work was, as always in Greece, carried out some 200 to 300 years ago and of course, all by hand tool. What a job to undertake!

Katsiki Beach – Voted Europe's Prettiest Beach 1992

On returning to dockside we met up with Aubrey and Richard and the two nephews. I thanked the nephews for their on-deck greeting to us from afar as we approached them at sea. They said that their Uncle Aubrey had made them do it, at the point of a sword! I still don't know if that was true or not? Back to the Penguin that night and a table of eight.

Next day we visited the Wind Surfing Schools around the bay. They are there, of course, because there is wind in this bay whenever there is sunshine and there is sunshine most of the year. During the 2004 Olympics, the Greeks won their first Gold Medal at Wind Surfing right here in this bay. After returning from this long walk, we went to some natural springs near the small beach, around from the marina. The weather was hot and it was a cooling relief to sit in one of the tubs to get our body temperatures back to normal.

There were other places to visit and we bade farewell to our friends the next day. It was about a four-hour sail to Meganisi Island and a beautiful secluded anchorage in Kapali Bay. After laying the anchor in about 10 metres depth and 50 metres of chain, I rowed ashore and put our land line around a tree. Secure at both ends, we rowed ashore to walk over a hill and into a small village called Vathi. There are five or six towns of this name in Greece. It means, deep water. We had dinner in a taverna at dockside and I tried moussaka, the traditional Greek dish. It was delicious and a little different from the same dish that we had whilst living on Samos, some years before. After arriving back to TS, the evening was still hot and we both jumped overboard to cool. Kapali Bay was quite a find of tranquillity after the busy last few days.

We had noticed a small sandy beach on coming into this bay and the next morning we rowed ashore to explore it. There was a small BBQ that someone had put together, back from the beach, so we decided that we would bring some food ashore that night, cook it and then sleep on the beach. Helen went to the shops and I went into the bush to find what little firewood that I could. I came back with enough firewood, but somewhat bloody of skin on arms and legs with the bracken and the spikes accompanying.

That night, we had the company of a small family who had arrived in the afternoon and came stern to the beach with their stern anchor dug into the sand, on the beach. The kids were kept busy returning to their yacht, via the dinghy, as the parents had forgotten quite a few items to satisfy their BBQ needs. They were English and great company with the kids entertaining both parents with Helen and myself. It was about midnight when the fire embers went out and the family returned to their boat and we got to sleep. Another perfect day, really.

It was hard to leave this anchorage the next day. It was 12.20 pm when we left for the very short sail to Tranquil Bay, opposite the town of Nidri on Lefkada island. It only took a little over an hour. On the way, we passed Skorpios Island which was owned by the Onassis family. It was here, on a small beach, that Aristotle Onassis married Jackie Kennedy, wife of the late American President. I always thought that this was a strange marriage as Onassis was a great chauvinist, this character trait being endemic in the Greek persona. It is a beautiful island in the Ionian Sea which is now the most popular of all cruising grounds in the world.

We anchored at Tranquil Bay and I got a land line ashore so that we did not swing, as there were a few yachts there and more coming. After lunch, we motored the dinghy ashore, some 300 metres. We could have gone stern to at the town dock but preferred the peace at being at anchor away from the crowds.

Nidri is a busy place and is a base for two yacht charter companies and near many resorts with diving and sailing schools also close. Helen and I went to Nico's Taverna for lunch. Nico came out and introduced himself and his daughter who was working there as well. We became friends straight away and on my many returns here, in the years to come, I always visited Nico with the customary hug between us. There were a million Nico's in Greece and I only knew 2, and they were both good people.

After returning to TS to store the supermarket stuff, I noticed a yacht which had anchored nearby, flying the Australian flag. The skipper would not have noticed our Australian flag and flying kangaroo flag on the port shrouds, to identify the nationalities of those on board, as there was no wind to show them. So I got into the dinghy and rowed over to say hello. The yacht was a Roberts 44-footer, designed and built in Australia and the Skipper and family had sailed from Australia the year before. We were leaving the next day and I wished them good luck after recommending a visit to Vasiliki and the Penguin, to say hello to Gary and Mary.

The Greek Island of Ithaca was our next sail destination. Ithaca is the home of the Palace of Odysseus, named after the Greek sailor/explorer. It is not a myth as Odysseus did live and built his Palace, before he said goodbye to his wife, to return seven years later. There are some foundations left today, where once the Palace stood. We arrived, on Ithaca, at another town and port, called Vathi and came to the town dock, bows to. After going ashore, Helen went to the shops whilst I bought a Frape, an iced coffee, and wondered across to the park, opposite the dock. It was here, in this park that a rather strange event took place. It went something like this.

There were seven elderly Greek chaps sitting on a half-circle seat in the park on a large concrete slab. There were trees about for shade and I sat down not far from them as the first fellow got up from his seat and went a few metres, turned and addressed his friends. His message was received with agreement by some and scorn by others. The speaker was allowed to say his bit with little interruption and then take his seat on the bench, from whence he came. There was some animated discussion then before the next speaker got up and moved to address the friends. This was repeated for all the seven friends and I realised after the third speaker that I was watching a forum that was something that the Greeks had designed thousands of years ago, BC in fact. It was democracy of course and

I was just in awe of this moment. It is still evident in the country where it was invented! How wonderful.

Next day, we sailed for an hour to enter another beautiful harbour of Kioni, on the same island of Ithaca. We downed sails at the entrance to the bay and motored into the bay. Just beyond the small ferry wharf there was a spot for us, to bows to the dockside. Again we deployed the stern anchor in deep water and let out about 40 metres of chain and rope. After securing the bow lines ashore after a couple of chaps caught these, we laid the plank down from bow to dockside. Kioni is a very popular town to visit and as we looked around we could see why.

Bay of Kioni – Admiral Nelsons holiday home

For boat people it was safe and very pretty. Tavernas lined the inner dock and some resorts were perched in the hills. Another attraction was a house almost opposite us. This was a house where Admiral Nelson would bring his beloved Lady Hamilton for a brief holiday. Lady Hamilton was married to Lord Hamilton who was the British Governor of the two Sicilies, in Italy in the 1790s. Hamilton and Nelson were good friends and this relationship was accepted by Hamilton. I stood in front of the sandstone house and thought…well, if there is a prettier spot for a holiday then I had not seen it.

We strolled about the village and had a great lunch of calamari and a Greek salad, of course. Some of the yachts left that afternoon and others came in and tied up. A flotilla of eight yachts came in as well and they rafted up in the middle of the harbour. House full. There was bound to be a party that night at one of the tavernas, with so many sailors around. We joined them for dinner that night. The flotilla left early the next morning and the bay was almost empty.

It was such an attractive bay that I took my sketch book around to the other side of the bay and sat on a rock and completed a sketch, which then became a watercolour painting. I still have to this day, hanging on a wall.

Next day, we sailed about four hours to Sami, a large town on the island of Cephalonia. We came in bows to again as there were large rocks under the town key. It was a busy place and a little uncomfortable with a harbour swell. This swell did not worry us. However, the yacht next to us and its skipper were having some problems fitting a generator to the motor. The skipper asked me to help him and I went onto his boat and down to the engine compartment. Of course I did not mind doing this, until I went below. The smell of diesel and other odours, with the movement of his boat made both he and I feel sick. We came back on deck and the fresh air. I said that he was better to get a marine mechanic, who is used to these odours, to do the job. We both admitted defeat and had a drink aboard his boat. Best solution.

Later that day, Helen's sister, Jude with her two daughters, Jess and Jane, arrived from the US. Much hugging and merriment, as they came aboard TS. We explained to the young girls that I ran a very tight ship and any misdemeanours by them would result in lashings on deck at mid-day the next day. They believed me for one nanosecond, and for the rest of their time on board, took absolutely no notice of me. I need to improve a serious countenance. It was fun to have some willing extra hands on board and they loved their stay. We visited the Melissani Caves on this island of Cephalonia. They are underground caves inland and we got into a small boat with a guide and explored them. Quite a treat for us all.

We drove to one of the beaches which was used as a location in the film, Captain Corelli's Mandolin. It was a true story of this island's experience during the Second World War. Very brutal punishment was handed out here when the Germans occupied the island, after the Italian Armistice in September 1943. The Italians had been on this island as partners of Germany before the Germans arrived to take over. Hundreds of Italian soldiers and Greek civilians were murdered from late 1943 and onwards, before the war ended in May 1945. The manner of these crimes, by the Germans, is never forgotten on this island.

Fiskardo harbour

With an abundant and willing crew, we then sailed to Fiskardo on the same island. It was a 4.5-hour sail, going north with a north wind, so we tacked a few times and the girls saw how TS does its thing. We motored into the harbour of Fiskardo and a very pretty pastel coloured village. Fiskardo is the only town, on this island, which was not damaged in the 1953 earthquakes which devastated this region of the Greek Islands. We came bows to again and went ashore to have a late lunch in one of the tavernas at dockside. Walking through the town, after lunch, we entered the old Town Hall, which now is a general store and coffee and cake shop. This building is perhaps 300 years old and is as good as the day that it was built.

Johns daily shower aboard Tequila Sunrise

Our visitors bought the regulation souvenirs to take back home for "show and tell" at school. For the mother, it was a gold bracelet with the distinctive Greek design. Our visitors were having a lot of fun and we left the next day to return to Sami, where they were to get a ferry to a bus connection and then to Athens. During our sail to the south, Helen rigged a rope to trail behind us and we slowed down. The girls then jumped in the water and were towed along for some distance. We had done this before for others and it was always great fun. After some tears the next morning in Sami, our visitors left us.

We slipped our lines early the next morning to go into the Gulf of Patras and our first visit to mainland Greece. We were leaving the Ionian islands behind, never to be forgotten. Mesolongion was our first port of call on the north coast of the Gulf of Patras. The run into the marina was sign posted by vertical tree branches stuck in the sea bottom and you needed to stay between them, to port and starboard, to avoid running aground. This was the Greek way of showing channel markers and they had probably been doing it for centuries. I smiled as we made our way to the marina.

We came alongside for our mooring here and this was a pleasant surprise as we had been bows to a few times recently, with the awkward getting on and off routine. This was our first visit to a mainland town. On the first morning, we walked into the town proper. From a street leading from the marina, we stopped at a dungeon taverna where the staff were just setting up for morning coffee and the lunch trade. The dungeon adjective here is the only way that I could describe this most unusual place. On entering, from the street, you walked down stairs to what was like a medieval space with the most basic of amenities for patrons. As the staff were writing on the blackboard menus, we stayed to see what was on offer. It sounded delicious, so we booked a table outside on the pavement, for dinner. It was a chance, but what the heck!

On arriving in the town square, we had coffee and walked around to get this experience of our first time, in a large town, on the mainland. It seemed very un-Greek to us and that feeling stayed with us all day. The poet, Lord Byron's heart is buried here, as this was his last known address. He may have moved from his apartment at the foot of the Spanish Steps in Rome, Italy. He certainly moved around Europe. Dinner that night was just so good. No least, I suppose, because we were expecting a below standard fare, following the first impression. It just shows you, don't judge a book...

After staying another day, for some writing and a visit ashore to sketch we sailed to the delightful town of Navpaktos with its small harbour. This is the oldest medieval harbour in Europe and it had an old castle overlooking the harbour. I motored TS into this small place and went in bows to again, squeezed in between two small fishing boats. Whilst coming in bows to, I had slightly moved the fishing boats on either side, as someone caught the lines to secure TS to the dock. Later that afternoon as Helen and I walked around the harbour, we ascended a set of stairs and at the top of these stairs were a group of fishermen having a few drinks, with a view to their boats. I sensed something by their looks and stopped to say hello. I then mentioned our arrival on TS, which they very well knew, and my apologies for slightly moving a couple of the fishing boats to get into the harbour, instead of anchoring in the gulf. My apologies were given to the owners of these boats if any offence was taken. They all smiled and one of the guys stood and shook my hand. All is okay, he said and thanked me for stopping to say hello. Maybe the Australian hat I had on had something to do with it?

The castle was lit up that night and some music was playing from the foreground. It was another wonderful scene as we whiled away the night. Another day was spent walking the area and realising that the atmosphere here was totally different from our previous port town of Mesolongion. Strange that never did work it out.

Our next short sail was to the small island, in the Gulf of Corinth, called Trizonia. From our Cruising Association Magazine, it was suggested that we visit Lizzie's Yacht Club here, situated half way up a hill overlooking the harbour and marina. On arrival in the harbour of Trizonia, we anchored instead of going into the marina. I took a quick swim and then we went ashore. There were two tavernas on the island and we had lunch in one of them. From here we walked to Lizzie's Yacht Club, past the marina and up the hill to the Club.

The Club was an old, well-built home and we walked onto the balcony at about 3 pm. Sharon came out to greet us and after we ordered some drinks, she sat with us for a chat. We told her of our story and she was envious. She was here, after her mother Lizzie, had returned to England. They were English and her mother was not well. She had worked here for over a year, with staff but had to return soon to England to care for her sick mother. So she was looking for someone to take over the business. Helen was most interested in this as we enjoyed the afternoon and sunset. I returned to TS to change and Helen stayed at the club and waited for me to return to have dinner. We met Matt, an employee, and it was good to speak with some English people about their experiences in Greece.

Matt took us on a circumnavigation of this small island the following morning. It was about a five-mile trip around this island which Aristotle Onassis wanted to purchase from the Greek Government some years before. The Government would not allow this and Onassis eventually purchased Skorpios Island in the Ionian Sea, as mentioned previously. We then moved into the marina for a night and went to the Club again for the dinner and some more questions from Helen about the business of the Club.

Another great sunset and we returned to TS for rest. I spent a further day doing some minor work on TS and chatting to a fellow Skipper who had come in through the night. He also had some work to do on his yacht and stopped as soon as I approached. Isn't it funny how we can stop work for the slightest of reasons and offer some drinks to the visitor and then forget what you were actually doing before the visitor or visitors arrived. I think that this is a common medical complaint. When mentioning it to doctors however, there seems to be no prescription to help with said problem.

As we sailed away the next day, Helen and I briefly discussed the outside possibility of us taking over that business in the new year. That was next year and we still had a long way to go. We would think about that proposition later.

The beautiful harbour of Galaxidi was our next stop and it took about four hours to reach it. This was another delightful town and port as it was flanked by a pine forest and the sound of whistling birds. The birds even had an anchored floating platform, with shelter, in the middle of the harbour. It was a nice touch to a lovely harbour. Helen visited the ruins at Delphi, by bus, from here the next day. Delphi was the mythological centre of the earth for the ancient Greeks and is a hallowed place. I stayed and completed a sketch of the harbour and an old boat tied up at the end of the harbour wall. This old boat was a Motor Cruiser with the year of 1928 on the transom [stern].

It was beautifully restored and in this harbour setting, it was as if those years in age did not exist. I could be standing here looking in 1928 and nothing would be changed. If I ever get a chance to meet the owners of these restored boats, I always thank them for their effort and the undoubted expense. Towards the evening, I strolled over to this old Motor Cruiser again and had a coffee nearby. Some people were gathering on the rear deck and I wondered over. I said hello to a few people on board who were dressed in costumes of the 1930s, the heyday of these boats. Their conversation for this party on deck was of events happening in the 1930s. Someone went to a lot of trouble to make this experience quite real and no doubt very expensive.

Helen returned from Delphi and told of a moving day with the impressions of the site and its significance for the Greek people. We had an early night for a change.

It was the forest here in Galaxidi that made it different from other harbours and ports. The forest was close by and we walked through parts of it. Over lunch we met some Greek locals who were there on a family holiday in a home owned by all the Greeks in the family group. They would take it in turn, with other families, to holiday here, with other families of the larger group. Democracy, you see.

Now it was time to sail towards the Corinth Canal, which virtually splits Greece in half. The canal was built between 1882 and 1893 and is 6.4 kilometres in length. It is a one-way passage and you need to wait to get the okay to go. It took us about eight hours to get to the entrance to the canal after a mixed bag of weather during this passage. We entered the canal at 4.30 pm and exited at 5.10

pm. The high sandstone walls made it a strange fantastic trip, but we sobered up at the other end when we had to bay the toll after coming alongside a long wharf wall. It is the most expensive waterway in the world. But it is either pay this or go around the Peloponnese to the south and out into the Aegean Sea that way.

Soon after we left the canal, I was below having a rest, when Helen called me up to the cockpit. She said, as I moved, that she was not sure how far away this approaching ship was. I arrived on deck and turned to see a large ship bearing down on us. I immediately grabbed the wheel and turned off to port, as the ship made blasts of their horns. I asked Helen "What was that?"

She said that her 3-D vision was not that good and she thought that she would ask me when she needed to turn away to avoid a collision. I was gobsmacked! I soon settled down, and smiled and said, "Well, you might have told me before, but now that I know it's okay."

We anchored in Kalamaki Harbour, on the mainland at 6 pm and motored ashore, in the dinghy, for a well-earned dinner and drinks. It had been a long day as we had been up at 6.30 am to prepare.

I have mentioned before that wherever we went was all new to us and the expectation and apprehension is always there, the uncertainty of what you are going to do to get TS in safely is there and this does take some form of nervous energy from you, apart from the activities of the day. Jolly good fun though.

We weighed anchor in Kalamaki Harbour at 8.15 am and were sailing to Aegina Island, one of the closer islands to Athens, the capital of Greece. It was a clear sunny morning and after a couple of hours of sailing with good speed, we noticed the outline of Athens City off to port. I could see the Acropolis and the Parthenon at the top of this mountain in central Athens. It was another surreal sight as I thought of the gifts given to us by the Greeks.

They have given us Greek Theatre with drama and comedy, rational and basic sciences as shown by Pythagoras and philosophy, in all its meanings and use. But above all, it is democracy that we owe these people a great debt. I felt insignificant and lucky to be around an historical scene, which would have been viewed countless times, as history unfolded around where TS was sailing.

Our passage to Perdika harbour on Aegina Island was busy with all types of shipping including ferries and day boats full of tourists. We had to be alert and follow the rules of the sea as we had learned from our courses back in England. It was a short sail to Perdika and we came into the harbour at 1.40 pm and went in bows to again. The Meltemi wind was just starting to pick up as we went ashore for a lunch at one of the tavernas, along the waterfront.

This harbour was open to the strong prevailing Meltemi wind and all boats in harbour were rocking about. The next day I took my sketch pad to a spot on the western wall of the harbour and completed a sketch. After that I returned to dockside to have a Frape coffee, whilst watching the passing parade of people. It was then that I noticed a small yacht coming into the harbour with the sails mostly down but not tied up. Two people were on board and the yacht was headed, under motor, towards the corner of the harbour walls, just below where I was having coffee. I went down to this spot to catch their bow and stern lines to help.

The girl on this boat threw the bow line, which I caught and put around a bollard and tied off. She then moved to deploy a fender over the side of their charter boat and jammed her hand between the hull and wall. She let out a scream and blood immediately appeared. The chap on the tiller had thrown the stern line to me meanwhile and I dealt with that.

There was plenty of confusion here as their boat had also hit the wall and damaged the topside of the hull. We managed to get the boat alongside and the girl stepped ashore with a towel around her damaged hand. Some people had gathered and showed great concern. It turned out that this English couple were on their honeymoon for a two-week charter. They were not experienced sailors and had spent the night at sea in high winds. They were tired and the girl announced to her husband that she could not get back onto the boat and wanted to go home. She was taken by one of the locals to a doctor whilst the husband went back on board to tidy and pack their bags. It was a bit sad for their honeymoon. At least they will have a story to dine out on for the rest of their lives.

Chapter 13
The Very Emotional Return

We slipped our lines at Perdika the next day at 4.15 pm to sail back "Home". We always had considered Pythagorio, where we had lived for nine months, to be our "Home" whilst we were in Europe. By this stage, our spiritual home was anywhere in the Greek Islands anyway, but the village of Pythagorio, on the coast, was very special. It was to be a three-day, two-night sail and our expectations were almost audible.

I will attempt to describe theses next few days and our emotions for this passage, but superlatives are rather inadequate here as we headed towards "Home".

We could still see the Athens area as we headed east towards the Kea Channel, south of that island and southeast of Athens. Sunset at 7.45 pm was brilliant again and still plenty of boats everywhere. The sailing conditions were excellent and we were making between five and six knots on a flat sea with the Auto Wheel Pilot engaged. We could relax and just look out for any traffic.

Sunrise at 6.45 and we could see Siros Island off to starboard. A little while later we were passing Tinos Island off to port and the very famous Mikonos Island to starboard. Helen and I had talked about going to Mikonos and decided against it for two reasons. The main harbour was open to the north west Meltemi wind which would make the nights a little uncomfortable at anchor. Next was the expense of being there with anything costing two to three times more than elsewhere. In any case, we had lived on the most beautiful island of them all in Pythagorio, Samos Island. So we sailed past Mikonos and kept going east.

We had always intended to return to our "Home" in Pythagorio when we left it. Our thoughts were to fly back or to drive across Europe and get a car ferry to the island. I am sure, when we were living there, that if anybody had told us that we would be returning in this style, on our own sailing yacht, we would have said that it was very fanciful and quite silly. But here we were, in perfect sailing weather, coming up to our second night of sailing where the morning would have us at "Home".

What happened through this night was the start of such an emotional time that it is hard to describe. I'll try. I was behind the wheel sitting with the Auto pilot on at about midnight and Helen had just gone below to have a sleep for about four hours. The sea state was good with just a slight ruffle with the Meltemi wind from the north west. It was Tuesday the 10th September, which is probably the best month to sail in the Mediterranean Sea.

The Greek Island of Ikaria was coming up on our port bow and I could see the outline of the mountains on the south of the island. The moon had risen to be just above the horizon and it was a balmy night. It really does not get any better than this. Or so I thought! At about 1.15 am I looked ahead and saw some shine coming off the sea surface. It was quite a few miles ahead and I thought that it was the moon's light and a haze producing a glassy look. However, the closer that we came to this shining, I realised that it was a glassy sea surface and that we would run out of wind as soon as we reached this area. Glassy sea equals no wind. We would then have to motor.

As we approached this rather beautiful sea state with the moon up and reflection everywhere, I prepared to start the motor as the sails went slack. But then a strange thing happened. We were well into this glassy sea area and the sails on TS were still full and we were still sailing at about four to five knots. I stood up behind the wheel and looked around in amazement. How was this happening. The wind should be ruffling the sea surface and negating the glassy sea. And then I worked it out. The wind was coming over the mountains of Ikaria, to the north and spilling out onto the sea. It was at such a strength that it was coming across TS at deck height and filling the sails, whilst keeping the sea state as a glassy area.

Well, I thought, you cannot buy this! What a phenomenon and I was in the middle of it. I grabbed a can of beer and went to the bow and sat on the pulpit with my back on the forward stay and with my legs over the bow, I sat there to look at this night. The "Wine Dark Sea" as the Greeks call the Aegean Sea, the moon, the sea state and the dark mountain outline to the north produced an aura that is impossible to describe.

And then it happened! A pod of dolphins arrived around the boat. There were about 12 to 14 of them and three of them were babies. The babies were pirouetting out of the water and spinning three or four times before flopping back into the sea. The adults were doing this as well, but could only manage one turn. The babies and the adults were talking all the time. I sat there as they passed along and under the bow, in total wonderment.

I was so excited that I had to wake Helen, for she just could not miss this. I moved to the stern and woke her through the stern deck hatch. She came up on deck rubbing her eyes and saw this extraordinary night. We moved to the bow and I sat on the pulpit again. The dolphins were still talking and I started to reply with a tick-tick sound. Helen thought that I was a little balmy as she laughed at me trying to communicate, as like a marine version of Dr Doolittle.

So, this was what it was like to sail in the best scene possible on the sea, on this planet! Emotions were there to experience and all that I can compare this to, is the birth of my children and any parent will tell you what that is like. Helen did not go back to rest as the night was heading to morning. The pod of dolphins went away and about half an hour later another pod appeared, this time with two babies doing their show of pirouetting. The sea state continued until almost sunrise. It had been a wonderful night, by any measure and just showed nature at its very best. We were very lucky to have seen it.

Sunrise was the usual beautiful time and we were approaching Samos, which was visible off the port bow. Helen had sent a postcard some weeks before to Sandy and Tony Karides, who had the Iliad Tavern on the seafront. She said that we were to arrive there soon and gave Sandy a date range of about a week. In other words, we and Sandy did not know the date of arrival. I did not know how we were going to handle this homecoming, particularly after that night that had just passed.

We saw the entrance to the little harbour of Pythagorio and downed sails and trimmed the boat neatly to enter. It was a fairly wide entrance and I steered TS straight into the harbour and towards the Iliad Tavern. I had the binoculars on the seat next to me and while Helen was preparing the fenders, I looked through the binoculars and saw Sandy, out front of the Iliad Tavern sweeping the outdoor area, ready for the day's trading. She had her back to TS as we motored through the entrance. We were about 250 metres away when Sandy did the strangest thing. She put her hand to the back of her head and turned and pointed to us and waved her arms.

I gave the binoculars to Helen and said that there was no way that she would know that it was us as we were pointing at the tavern and the name of TS was not visible to her. We had dodgers around the cockpit with the name Tequila Sunrise in large white letters on a navy background. She could not, at this time, have seen the dodgers. But she just knew that it was us! Helen was jumping up and down and waving back to Sandy. I was still steering TS and the emotions for us started to arrive. A tear first appeared for us and joy at coming "Home".

I took TS passed the Iliad and Sandy yelled out that we could come stern to, in front of the Iliad as they had rights to two places here. We manoeuvred TS very well and got the bow anchor down and Sandy and another person caught the stern lines and whipped them off. I put the boarding plank down to dockside and Helen skipped down the plank into the arms of Sandy. I turned off the motor, locked the wheel and went ashore. The three of us were crying with so much happiness that some people stopped and asked what had happened. You would have thought that it was the return of Odysseus to Ithaca after his absence of seven years.

Eventually we settled down, thank goodness and had a coffee at the Iliad. Sandy phoned her husband Tony [Adonis, in Greek] and he came down from their home on the hill behind the seafront and it all started again. We had come home. What emotion! I took Tony across to TS and showed him the Greek Flag flying on the starboard shrouds and said that this means that Helen and I salute his country. I then saluted Tony and we hugged each other. Is it any wonder that Australians and Greeks get on so well together?

Helen and I then walked around the village and up a hill to where our home had been. It was a wonderful nostalgic walk and we said Kalimera [hello] to many friends and neighbours. Over the next few days a procession of friends came down to dockside and the Iliad tavern to greet us and celebrate our return. The common questions were, why and how was this odyssey done? We explained as best that we could. Nobody had ever done this before and for our friends, it was a bit quizzical. Most of our friends came on board TS and were given a cook's tour by Helen or myself. We always had a bottle of Tequila on board and each visitor was given a shot glass of this to signify that they had been on board and entertained. The bottle did not last long.

Tony and Sandy's children, Gregory and Marissa, came on board after school one day and it was all that we could do to get Gregory off the boat to go home and do his homework. He was fascinated with all that he could see and when I showed him the Radar screen and how it worked, he looked at me in wonder. He was a budding sailor and he and I knew it.

We hired a rental car from Nico, from whom we had purchased the second-hand Piaggio motor bikes when we arrived in Pythagorio. Visiting some of the beaches and other villages on Samos, where we had been, was a treat. The main port of Samos town was busier that we had remembered and I returned here to sketch the bay the following day. The painting still hangs on my wall today. You see, some of the paintings I just would not sell, after some people offered to buy.

We stayed in Pythagorio for 11 days and then it was time to leave. Naturally it was emotional again but not as it was when we arrived. The farewells lasted two nights and we left the harbour at about 11 am to sail the short distance to the island of Agathonisi. We had first been here when originally arriving in Pythagorio for the two-week charter sail many years before. There were two tavernas here and, as usual, one taverna was open for the flotilla boats, whilst the other stayed closed. That way they both enjoyed patronage and income. We never saw that arrangement on any other island. There had been no changes in the seven years since we were last here. George's Taverna was host for us this night with Greek dancing after dinner and that has been happening here for decades.

Tequila Sunrise Stern to, Gulf of Vathi

The passage the next day was also a short one to another Vathi on the island of Kalymnos. The Gulf of Vathi is long and narrow and we took TS to the end of it and went stern to and were well situated, being the only boat there, at that time of the day. It was just another beautiful place to be. We went ashore and Helen stopped at the shop and I kept going around the end of the foreshore. I came across two fishermen who were knee deep in the water and they were throwing their catch of squid and octopus against the rocks. Of course they did this to tenderise their catch for cooking. They have been doing it this way for thousands of years and we were to have the benefit of it that night.

Tequila Sunrise Stern to, Gulf of Vathi

On returning to TS, we went for a swim in a netted area of the bay, very near to us. The foreshore had been concreted with tiers for lying or sitting. For such a remote spot, this was an unexpected bonus. Later in the afternoon, a small ferry boat arrived and some tourists got off the boat from the nearby island of Kos. We had, as usual, afternoon drinks on board and then at about 7 pm went ashore for dinner at one of the two tavernas.

As we approached the tavernas Helen chose to go to Poppy's Taverna, probably because of the name. A young girl, who was heavily pregnant, came out to greet us and introduced herself as Poppy. Well, this girl was a treat. She guided us to our table, ordered one of the waiters to fetch the mandatory ouzo and carafe of water, and said that our order would be taken a little later. Poppy was the life and soul of this place. Some customers arrived a little later and all of them walked up to her and embraced her. Music was playing in the background and Poppy was singing the song as well as the artist. She had a great voice and we remarked to the next table that she could certainly hold her own in the singing department.

Poppy's demeanour was infectious. Some people can do that and in a manner that makes you want to be alive. One of the waiters came and took our order for dinner. After Helen ordered a house speciality, I of course went for the Calamari and the usual Greek salad. We had to wait a little because it was so busy. Many people, as we later learnt, had driven a long time to get here from around the island. We didn't mind waiting as the atmosphere there was just sparkling. When our food arrived we started to eat and my first taste of the calamari was sensational. I had never had such a flavoursome taste of calamari and at just the perfect softness, thanks to those rocks which we could see from our table. We stayed too late again at dinner and listened to some Bazouki playing, then wondered back along the shore to TS and a good night's rest.

After staying another day in this gulf, we left the next morning for a brief stopover at Kamares on the southern shores of the island of Kos. Time was getting on for the year and we still had to get to Cyprus, our winter place. We arrived at Kamares at about 4 pm and into a safe harbour and to a berth alongside a wharf. This was a bit of a surprise for a Greek island and easier to get in. We slipped our lines the next morning and sailed to Symi. There was plenty of wind up and we only used the headsail to get to the attractive harbour of Symi town. We went stern to and secured TS.

The town capital was busy and the harbour accepted ferries and day boats, all disbursing tourists at all times of the day. Symi was an Italian occupied island during the Second World War. Many Greek islands were occupied by Italian garrisons during this time as they were at war with Greece up until September 1943. In most cases, there was very little to do for the Italians as fighting did not really start until the Germans came after September 1943.

So the Italians did what they do best, and that was to build or renovate existing buildings. They really were not interested in the war, that Mussolini had injected them into via his huge ego that you could not jump over. The evidence of the Italian craftsmanship was there to be seen. If it was not building, then it was rendering in concrete or plaster. They are the best at this as any older Australian will tell you with the Italian immigration and skills that they showed the building industry.

Symi harbour

Symi was also home to fine cotton products and the signs said that they were made by the religious Nuns on the island. The merchandise was everywhere and of good quality. I did ask the Port Captain how many Nuns managed to make all these good quality products and he said there were three Nuns only. They were the busiest nuns on the planet! Isn't marketing great, if a little exaggerated? Symi was also a cosmopolitan town with a variety of tavernas offering all manner of European food. Some of the shopkeepers that I spoke to could speak up to six languages. Natural sponges were also taken from the sea bed around this island and are known to be of good quality, all over the world.

We went swimming at the end of the harbour and watched the passing parade of tourists as they picked up some bargains. After two full days, we left to sail to the port of Kas on the southern coast of Turkey and little did I know then, but mother nature was not finished with us just yet.

The forecast, posted outside the Port Office, looked okay with a chance of increasing wind through the day. We reached the Rhodes Channel, with Turkey off to port, at 1 pm. It was a busy shipping channel and we needed to be alert. About an hour later I looked across to Turkey and a storm of some type was forming over inland Turkey. In hind sight, I should have turned back then to sit this one out in Rhodes Harbour.

Unfortunately, the storm moved to the sea area where we were sailing. Some rain looked to be there, so I got my "oilies" on to stay dry. The sea state was not very rough and with a wind on or about the beam it was reasonable sailing with TS pitching a little. I did not engage the Auto Pilot as in this weather, with the sea state getting a bit rougher, it can overpower the Auto Pilot and damage the motor. You are better off, in any case, with weather about, to steer yourself. Sheets of rain came again at about 4 pm and the wind increased a little. I stayed on the wheel as I knew that by this time that Helen had enough of storms and worried too much when they were about. That was fair enough. We had been in our share of bad weather and Helen was not keen on sailing in it from the get go. But for now we stood on. Too late to turn back.

I was okay on the wheel and suggested to Helen that she go below and try to chill out, in the middle of the saloon, where the pitching of the boat is least felt. She did this and as I looked behind TS I noticed some lightning over the sea. The electrical storm soon caught up with us at about 7.30 pm. It was spectacular at sea. It was bolt lightning and after some of the bolts were hitting the sea near TS and bubbling. It was rather close and I looked across to this happening and suggested to the weather gods that it can stop now! It did not and Helen came on deck briefly and saw some of the lightning and this was an omen that registered with her. She went below.

The lightning continued, but the wind stayed the same and TS was handling the conditions okay. I just had to be as good a helmsman as TS was in handling the storm. A small bird, meanwhile, had landed on the deck at the stern. I turned around to see it shivering near our Life Raft. I called to Helen to come up and take the bird to some shelter. She did this, with great compassion and wrapped it with some towel and placed it under the cockpit hood, mostly out of the wind. The bird was obviously scared and distressed, although Helen said that it did not appear to have broken any bones. The bird now became a "Cause Celebre" and I willed it to stay alive. Helen went down to the saloon after sitting with the bird for a little time.

At this time, steering was getting more difficult, requiring more effort. The lightning was still bolting into the sea near TS, but I took a rather blasé attitude at this, as it had been around now for over an hour. It seems that the storm was moving at about the speed that we were going through the water. Not the best circumstance, but we were handling it okay. Helen came up briefly to check on the bird and it had died! I took the bird from her hands and threw it overboard. This was not good and another bad omen for Helen.

I was getting used to this passage when I looked to starboard to see a small skiff sailing boat with a single sailor at the tiller. I looked back to the cockpit and then to starboard again and the skiff had disappeared. I shook my head and realised that I had hallucinated. There is a first time for everything and this was it. However, some 10 minutes later, whilst looking over to port I saw a chap rowing a small boat the opposite way to our going. I looked back on board and returned to see the boat had gone. I had hallucinated again. This was rather weird, as physically I felt fine. I called to Helen to say that needed about a 20 to 30-minute-rest from the wheel as I had just seen stuff that was not there. I rested by lying on the cockpit seat which was long enough to do this. About 30 minutes later, I sat up and was as clear headed as I could be.

I took the wheel and the conditions were steady, if you can call high wind at sea, steady. Some residual lightning was still about and then Helen came half way up the companionway steps and said to me, "We are going to die and I love you." I told her to pour a scotch for her and myself and try to see that the sea state is okay and the lightning is going away. I think that she did this with some success.

An Imray chart of the Turkish coast was next to me in a plastic sleeve. I grabbed it and saw that there was a bay coming up to port where we should find some shelter out of this weather. I had been at the wheel for about 11 hours and it was prudent for any sailor to get some rest, after this amount of time, no matter how he or she feels. I had chosen Kalkan Bay to enter and said to Helen that we were going into Turkey a little earlier than expected to find some quiet water. She came up on deck and the closer we sailed to the coast, the water flattened out and the wind dropped a little.

Kalkan Bay is reasonably big with Kalcan Marina at the end of it. We could not go into this marina as Kalcan was not an Official Port of Entry to Turkey. The Turks insist that boats must enter to an Official Port where Passports and Ship's Papers are to be presented. So we had to find an anchorage that was safe and where we could rest. We downed sails and it took some time whilst we tied off the sails as the wind was still up. As we motored around the bay with Helen at the wheel, I untied our dinghy, which had been lashed down, on deck, forward of the mast during this stormy passage. We kept on slowly looking around the bay and then stopped at a place where we could drop the anchor and I could then get in the dinghy and get a land line ashore with the chain, at the end of the land line rope, around a rock or tree, so that we would not swing in this weather.

This is not the easiest thing to do in this sort of weather. Again I wrote down what I was going to do and gave it to Helen. The only question mark here was the holding of the anchor on the harbour bed. I did not have a Pilot Guide for this bay, so we would just have to play it by ear. I dropped the dinghy into the bay with a line attached and took it to the stern of TS. After tying the two land lines together, I climbed down the transom ladder and placed them in the dinghy in such a way that the land line would unfurl out of the dinghy as I rowed it ashore. I had already chosen the rocks that I was going to step onto and up to a tree on the foreshore where I would get the chain around the tree and secure our land line. If this sounds a little involved, it's because it certainly is involved and preparation is everything.

Helen went astern and we laid plenty of anchor line out, when Helen stopped TS. We trusted that the anchor was in sufficiently to hold us against the wind, which was blowing down the centre of the boat from bow to stern and I had chosen this spot for that reason. After cleating one end of the landline to TS, I jumped into the dinghy and started to row ashore. Then onto the first, second and third chosen rocks and to the foreshore and up to a tree. On reaching the tree, I put the chain around it but it was about a metre too short to join the chain links. I then called out to Helen and she let out a bit more anchor chain, to bring TS closer to shore and I was then able to secure the landline. I almost skipped down to our dinghy and pulled myself back to TS on the landline. Job done!

This was at 12.30 pm and we had a few beers to celebrate our work to have us out of the storm, which was still happening out to sea, as we could observe. Helen was smiling and all was well again. It was relatively calm here, so Helen cooked a warm meal for lunch. During the afternoon, we had a chance to reflect on the circumstances of the storm and I said that we should have gone to Rhodes to sit it out. This was little comfort for Helen, but she was in good spirits and we only had one more Turkish port to go to before we sailed to Cyprus, our winter spot. We could have sailed to Cyprus from here, but we were glad to go to another Turkish port town and it turned out to be the right decision.

After a good night's rest, we were bright eyed and weighed anchor at 9.15 am for the short sail to Kas, Turkey. About four hours later we arrived at Kas Bay and motored into a busy bay. We had to go stern to here and by now we were pretty good at this awkward manoeuvre and I jumped ashore to secure the stern lines. On looking about the harbour, there were Turkish Gullet boats, which were for tourists for a day sail or extended sailing for up to one week where guests would live aboard. Ferries came and went, fishing boats were there and yachts such as TS were here. The whole gambit of a commercial harbour was encapsulated here. It was great to see and we decided to stay a few days.

I went ashore to the Port Office and presented Passports and Ship's Papers. On returning to TS, a Port Officer was there to collect the mooring fees. He was a young Turkish teenager with a willing smile and pleasant personality. He gave me the receipt without the carbon paper in the receipt book for that receipt. I noticed this because it was so obvious. A little bit of corruption to supplement the income.

Helen and I then went ashore to have a late lunch. We had been to Turkey when we were living in Pythagorio, Samos, as part of the Visa needs but had not really tried traditional Turkish food. Kas is a holiday destination for Turkish people and others. Firstly, though, we needed to get to a bank and acquire some Turkish Lire, the local currency. We looked at the exchange rate for Australian Dollars on the electronic board, outside the bank and there were 72,600 Turkish Lire to the dollar. When I withdrew about $50.00 dollars into Turkish Lire a lot of notes fell out of the machine with lots of noughts on them. It was going to be difficult working out what note to hand over as there were so many noughts printed on them.

In any case, lunch was very good with a lamb dish, which Helen had, being the winner. We walked around the town and it was colourful with the usual bizarre shops that Turkey has, where you can buy non related items from clothing to car parts in the one shop. There was a French restaurant in town and we decided that we would go there for dinner the following day. Some military personnel were present as they always are in this country. Turkey has been under attack for ever and at this time there were always skirmishes on the border areas. The troops, however always had a smile when we would say hello. We decided to return to TS and have drinks as we watched the locals and tourists stroll past us. It was such a beautiful evening and people watching is enjoyable, especially when we could wave to them and get a wave in return. The passing parade, once again, thought that we were millionaires and we were but not of a monetary sense.

The morning had us up on deck for breakfast and a bright day ahead. We said hello to some of our boating neighbours. There were and English couple on a charter boat and a German sailor named George, on his boat, waiting in Kas, for his girlfriend to join him. I did not know it then but I would seek his help in a couple of days' time. It is always impossible not to be cheerful in any marina or popular harbour mooring spot. We had seen and lived in this atmosphere for the last couple of years. It was another reason why it was going to be a bit strange when we returned to Australia to take up work again. Later in the morning, our teenage Port Official was walking past and I invited to come aboard for coffee, which he readily did. I also gave him a cigarette and he pulled three from the pack and put two cigarettes in his pocket. He was a little bold and after the coffee he was off to the Mosque for prayers. This he did three times per day and he said that his brother goes five times per day. Are they that big as sinners?

We went ashore later in in afternoon for drinks at a bar and then to the French restaurant. Not far along dockside, some people were setting up for some kind of function, with tables and chairs and a band. It was all very busy and we continued on. We eventually arrived at the restaurant and were shown into one of a few rooms there. The seats were low to the ground with large pillows everywhere. We sat on some pillows to await the menus. It was a bizarre scene, with some Turkish colours and a French bordello setting. We had some French wine to start and followed by authentic French food. The setting looked over the harbour and we spent a couple of hours there. It was a great experience with French speaking waiters, dressed in Turkish garb.

It was dark by the time that we left the restaurant and we returned to TS. When we arrived at the scene of the function, we saw that it was a wedding reception happening on dockside. The band was playing and the bride was dancing with one of the guests. Along with a lot of other people, we watched as the bridal reception continued. It transpired that the bride had to dance with each of the men present as that was Turkish tradition. I returned to get a drink for Helen and myself and we stayed for about another hour. During this time, the bride was gradually getting tired and she had to sit down a couple of times for a rest. We felt very sorry for her as we left and looked over to the bride, who at this time, had a glazed look in her eyes. Turkish tradition is hard work, especially at a wedding.

The following day was spent resting and buying some provisions for the long sail to Cyprus. In the afternoon, I noticed that some of the anchor lines were deployed by various boats at an angle to the dock and not perpendicular to the dock which would avoid anchor spaghetti as we call it. I judged that some of these anchor lines were lying over our own anchor line.

We were to leave the following morning and my fears were soon realised the next morning. I motored out to where I thought our anchor was and started to winch the anchor up from the bottom. However, it was to no avail. Other lines were over ours. So there we were, in the middle of the harbour and nowhere to go. I put the dinghy in the water and with a pair of goggles had a look below. I could count three anchor lines over ours. We were in about 14 metres of water. I could not dive down that deep as it affected my ears at that depth. It was then that I remembered that our German friend, George, was a scuba diver and maybe he could help. I rowed over to his boat and knocked on the hull of his boat.

George came up eventually on deck and I told him of our problem He offered to help. However, he looked a little dusty and he explained that a late night at a bar was the cause. I felt badly in asking for his help and I told him so. He brushed that comment aside and said that he could probably free dive to fix our problem. I thought that this was a big call, considering his state at the time. In any case, his diving tank was empty and he could not get it filled for some hours. George was a willing helper.

He came into the dinghy with me and we rowed out to TS. He looked over the side into the water and saw what I saw. He went down for the first dive for a good look at what he would have to do and returned to the surface. He had colour back in his face and smiled as he went below again. He did this two more times over about 20 minutes and we were free. I could not thank him enough and gave him a bottle of wine and some money for another night on the town. It was the least that I could do! He thanked me and we motored out of Kas harbour.

It was about 10 am when we left the harbour and we stopped outside the harbour while I got the dinghy on board and secured it to the front deck. We then set sail for Cyprus and our winter home. It was a three-day passage of fine weather and basically heading on a south east direction. The wind was variable, but we were able to set a good point of sail all the way to the southern shores of Cyprus and the town of Larnaca. During the second day, I was having a rest, whilst Helen was on alert and she called that there were small fish cascading onto TS.

I made it to the cockpit to see flying fish flying over the boat and landing on deck and into the cockpit. This was the first time that this had happened and it was crazy. I tried to catch some of these fish, but since I was not a good slips fieldsman in cricket, I never caught one of these small fish. There was a bit to do aboard TS but we left most of the jobs to do when we arrived at Larnaca Marina. There were two recommended marinas on the south coast of Cyprus and we had read a story in our Cruising Association Magazine, sent to us each quarter from London, and decided that Larnaca would be the better option. It turned out to be a good decision.

The passage was a relaxing one, with the Auto Pilot engaged most of the time. We even had a couple of games of Scrabble on the way. I also took the opportunity of going to the stern of TS and just stand and watch as the trade wind blew and TS did her thing with the sail dynamics making the bow spear into the rollers and delve into the sea. It was always a wonder to do this and it would be well over a year before I would be back to do it again. We arrived at Larnaca Marina at 10.30 am on the 16th October 1996. This was good timing as we came alongside the outer dock and secured TS. I went to the Port Office to report our arrival and was advised that an Officer would visit us on board soon. Within 10 minutes, our Officer arrived with an Immigration Officer and after some inspection of TS and Passports and Ship's Papers we were allowed to take TS into the inner harbour. We then came onto a finger wharf and tied off.

We were here, safe and sound, in an attractive marina and very close to the town with its variety of shops and commerce. A beach was located beside the marina and there was the mandatory Marina Bar. It was another affable place to spend some of the northern hemisphere winter before heading back home to resume a normal life, whatever that meant. Naturally it was exciting to be in another country and to see that Cyprus is basically of a Greek population with a lot of other nationalities in the mix.

There was however a large shadow hanging over the island and it involved a lot of Greek families. In 1974, Turkey invaded Cyprus and took the top half of the island by force. These two countries had been arguing for decades and a military invasion by Turkey had them installed in the north of the country. A border was marked out to separate the north from the south. It was called the Green Line with the capital, Nicosia, being south of this line or in the Greek half of the island. Greeks, living and owning homes in the north of the island, were shunted off to the south and never to return. No compensation for their homes at all! The Green Line was patrolled by both the northern Turkish and southern Cypriots.

Whilst it had been over 20 years since this had happened, there was still a lot of feeling in southern Cyprus about the illegal invasion. Throughout our two-month stay here for the start of winter, we met a few families who had been living in the north of Cyprus and who were now in the south. They were still hopeful of some money to come from Turkey for their homes. It has to be remembered that Greece and Turkey have been fighting most of the time, for almost 3000 years. Some of full wars and some skirmishing. So much for the history lesson.

Meanwhile, Helen and I walked the town. This took two days with stops for refreshments. The weather was sunny and T-shirts, the order. Cyprus was a different "feel" to Lagos in Portugal, our last winter spot. The Greek population was a little subdued, but still very welcoming as they always are. I ordered a frappe from one of the cafes near the marina and it came with a dollop of ice cream. This was the Cypriot version of iced coffee and very nice too.

We then set about meeting our neighbours and the best place to do that was at the Marina Bar. There was the usual mix of nationalities. One of the unusual married couples were Anwar, the Vice President of an Arab bank and his French wife Simone. They were restoring and old Motor Cruiser moored here. I briefly went aboard with them to see some of the work to still be done. It was a large boat and I could see that another $300 K needed to be spent to get this boat to seaworthiness. It was like a money box with black money in the box.

An English couple, Harry and Liz had just built a steel yacht and were to take it on an extended sail to the east of Cyprus for a few days. They did this later and were moored in a bay to shelter from an electrical storm when some lightning hit the top of their mast and destroyed their Anemometer, which reads wind speed and direction. I met Harry when he returned and he said that it was quite scary with the mast seeming to light up when the lightning struck. This was just another reason to confirm that a steel boat will attract lightning. Another English couple were Freddy and Julie, who had a yacht in the marina and a home in the town. He was trying to get a licence to run an SP betting business and Julie was the glamorous partner, driving a Jaguar Sovereign and loving life. It was certainly the place to do it.

Helen and I hired a car to go to the capital of Nicosia, which was in the middle of the island. The city was well planned and laid out but the buildings looked a little tired. We drove to the Green Line, separating Turkish northern and Greek southern halves of the island. The troops from both sides could be seen and some smiles were apparent with some of the troops for what would surely be a boring tour of duty. Later in December, we drove to the Troudos Mountains and got out of our car to see some snow on the peaks. It is possible to ski here when the good snow falls come and is as pretty as any area of snow-capped regions that I have seen. During the ski season, it is possible to come to Larnaca and have a swim in the sea as well. Not too many places can boast that.

One of the Greek girls working at the Port Control Office invited us to a student event at the local High School. It was for a dinner in one of the rooms off the library and the Cookery Course students were to cook for us and serve our meals. This was a first for us and we arrived at the library entrance to be greeted by students who were dressed formally and who showed us to our seats. They looked glorious and were so polite and so proper. It was all part of the Cookery Course and each student would gain marks towards a final end of course Diploma, if they passed. The food was superb and the local newspaper was there taking photos of us all. I couldn't fault the evening and Helen and I left and walked back towards the marina and a late-night drink aboard TS.

A group of us went to a local restaurant and bar one evening which had just opened. This place had been derelict for years and when we walked in I had a sense that I had been here before and the feeling of deja vu took over. After drinks were ordered, I turned to Helen and said, "This is Rick's Bar in the film Casablanca." It was the same and one of our friends agreed. This was a throw back in time and was a lot of fun as only first nighters should enjoy. So if there is a film producer out there, who wants to remake the film, Casablanca, then go straight to Larnaca in Cyprus.

Each Sunday, there was a BBQ at the outdoor area as you walked towards the Marina Bar. It was a bring your own meat and drinks and the Marina management would supply the salads and accoutrements. What a good idea and a nice gesture. It was here that we met our American friends, Greg and Monica. They basically loved life. They were a jovial couple who loved travel, food, wine and sailing. It was great talking to them and they could afford to do it after selling some of the family shares worth a lot of money. Good company in these circumstances was easy to find and not one person who was staying in this marina, was less than good to know. Try and say that as you look up and down the street where you live.

One day, Helen and I were walking over to the Marina to have a morning coffee. We walked along the north edge of the marina and I looked down to see a catamaran of about 16 feet. I had a mast, of sorts, and looked to be in poor condition with half a headsail drying in the sun. Both the hulls were marked with all manner of dints and scratches. Al in all, a bloody disgrace, as the British would say! We smiled and kept walking. I got some drinks as Helen sat at a large table with some of our friends. I returned with the drinks and there were two young people there at the table as well, holding court and relating their story to the others who were spellbound.

These two young people had just arrived in our Larnaca Marina from sailing around the world in that disgrace of a catamaran that Helen and I had just looked at. They looked bedraggled, unkempt and generally in a state, the same as their boat. Whilst the others at the table were shaking their heads I caught up with the story.

They had left England some 20 months ago and sailed across the Atlantic to the Panama Canal and entered the Pacific Ocean. They headed to the north to be nearer the Equator, where there is little or no inclement weather, for up to five to eight degrees north or south. They then sailed basically west and dipped to the north or south of the equator for landfall and provisions or to find some wind. They stopped many times for food, rest and some good sleep as sleeping in the hulls of the catamaran was not conducive to a good night's rest. They looked a wreck, but what a story! They continued with their story for a while and then left for the showers.

At the Marina Bar table, we were left in silence. Then one of the Englishmen, I think it was Freddy, the bookmaker, said "well of course they are English and that is understandable". That produced some laughter and we could not agree if these people were mad, brave, silly, inquisitive or just had a death wish. A little bit of everything I suspected. In any case, they were to be applauded and the next day we all chipped in and bought them lunch as they related some more adventures. The things people do!

It should be pointed out though, that there are quite a few people who try this and are never heard from again. After digesting this story, we went into the town to get some provisions and I visited a boat chandlery to get some boat bits. It was at the far side of town and during this walk, I noticed more posters showing Turkish soldiers beating up on Greek adolescent children. The authorities were never going to let the Turkish invasion be forgotten.

Since our arrival here, Helen had expressed her desire to return to the island of Trizonia and take over the lease of the Trizonia Yacht Club. It was a good idea for her. She needed to do something of her own, as I had been calling most of the shots for our four years of this odyssey. It was not a business that could support an income for two people and I needed to return to Australia and work again. Helen would return in the future. Helen had spoken to the English girl who had the current lease and Helen would go there in the new year to stay for a week with some guidance from the English girl and then take over.

We were busy at the marina as Christmas was approaching and all sorts of things had to be done to get ready for the celebrations. We had our secret Santa presents to get and a tree to buy with decorations. It was a great Christmas Day with some of the marina staff joining us later in the day. Boxing day was a bit slow as we all recovered. Helen had started to pack a couple of bags to take with her, early in the new year. The weather was just perfect, as it had been in Portugal in the previous winter, with t-shirts only. Helen left by boat a few days into the new year and I started to prepare TS for wintering here. There was, of course, a travel lift to take us out of the water and onto a cradle on land.

There is a fair bit to do, to prepare a boat for an extended stay on land. Apart from the cleaning, there are motor preparations, galley work and a myriad of minor jobs to do. I made a list and started. By lunch on the first day I retreated to the Marina Bar for a drink and lunch. Marie, our friendly Port Office girl, introduced me to two American girls who were staying in Larnaca on holiday. They had heard, from Marie, that I was a watercolour artist and asked to see my portfolio. Both these American girls were artists as well. I arranged that they would come to TS the following afternoon, at about 4 pm. Marie would show them the way.

In the meantime, after returning to TS, I went to the top of the mast to lock off the Anemometer, at the top of the mast, for the period of inactivity. The jobs were slowly getting done and by 4 pm the following day I was ready for a break. It was getting near to cocktail hour in any case, when the girls arrived. I had tidied the boat and the cockpit table was still up with the bottle of chilled wine there to have. After a cook's tour, for the girls, we settled down for a wine and nibblies.

Some neighbours joined at about 5.30 pm and a party looked like happening. But before more people arrived the American girls wanted to see my paintings. They looked at my Portfolio and chose to purchase one painting each. I had always charged $100 US for the paintings that I sold and the girls were happy to pay that, in today's money of about $300.00 Australian. The party then ramped up a bit and finished well into the night as a couple of the marine staff joined us.

TS had always been a party boat throughout this last four years and this party was its last hoorah.

Chapter 14
Home

I continued with the preparations for the storing of TS on land for what turned be well over a year before I returned. Farewell drinks were had for a day with friends. It was then time to get TS out of the water. My bags were packed and the travel lift took TS to its place on land. I got off the boat after putting the winter cover over TS.

Then I stood back and looked at this wonderful boat that had brought us through our travels and some bad weather on the ocean and the seas. It was a boat of great design and a great sea keeping boat. We had matched that with the skills needed to sail to and from everywhere that we went. I then walked over to TS and gave her a big kiss on her hull and stood back and saluted her. Naturally a tear or two appeared and I walked away to get a taxi to the airport to go to Athens for the flight home.

An overnight stay in Athens had me in a hotel in the Plaka area and a small balcony afforded a great view of the Acropolis and the iconic Parthenon atop. I was a perfect spot to draw a street scene and the Acropolis. I drew this scene as my last reminder of that great city.

I boarded the flight the next day and a transit two hours in Singapore saw me on the last leg to Sydney's Kingsford Smith Airport. I now had time to reflect on our Odyssey. This four-year period saw us leave Australia at the top of our professional lives in the computer industry and go to live on a Greek island. It was then onto England to work again where we were successful. Another fork in the road appeared and we chose a sea change after completing a three-month sailing and navigation course. We met some wonderful people and I guessed that our personalities had engendered the hospitality that we had wherever we went. The adventures were experienced with the romance of the sea always present. Over all this, were the emotions that, at times, were overwhelming.

During these four years, we never met anyone who had done all that we had done. Plenty of people had done all or part of the sailing bit. But nobody had constructed a hemisphere change and then a sea change in quite the fashion and style that we had done. I thought, then and now, that it was unique.

The aircraft was approaching Sydney Airport from the north, along the northern beaches where I grew up. We passed over Palm Beach, then Avalon Beach, then Newport and then Narrabeen Beach where our family home had been. It was very emotional and it was also then that my father's words came to me and kept ringing in my ears. He had said to me many times, specially during my formative years and these words could easily have been the name of this book. He said:

What is life without a risk, son!

Ingram Content Group UK Ltd.
Milton Keynes UK
UKHW022206130723
425090UK00003B/15